THE TROUBLE WITH TRAUMA

MICHAEL SCHEERINGA

THE
TROUBLE
—— WITH ——
TRAUMA

The Search to Discover
How Beliefs Become Facts

CENTRAL RECOVERY PRESS

LAS VEGAS, NV

Central Recovery Press (CRP) is committed to publishing exceptional materials addressing addiction treatment, recovery, and behavioral healthcare topics.

For more information, visit www.centralrecoverypress.com.

Publisher: Central Recovery Press
3321 N. Buffalo Drive
Las Vegas, NV 89129

26 25 24 23 22 21   1 2 3 4 5

Library of Congress Cataloging-in-Publication Data

Names: Scheeringa, Michael S., author.
Title: The trouble with trauma : the search to discover how beliefs become
    facts / Michael Scheeringa.
Identifiers: LCCN 2021022560 (print) | LCCN 2021022561 (ebook) | ISBN
    9781949481563 (paperback) | ISBN 9781949481570 (ebook)
Subjects: LCSH: Psychic trauma--Physiological aspects. | Stress
    (Psychology)--Physiological aspects. | Post-traumatic stress
    disorder--Physiological aspects. | Self-deception. | Evolutionary
    psychology.
Classification: LCC RC552.T7 S38 2021 (print) | LCC RC552.T7 (ebook) |
    DDC 616.85/21--dc23
LC record available at https://lccn.loc.gov/2021022560
LC ebook record available at https://lccn.loc.gov/2021022561

Cover design and interior by Sara Streifel, Think Creative Design.

For Claire,

the only one I could talk
to when the implications
of my ideas worried even me.

CONTENTS

INTRODUCTION

Imagine the situation five hundred thousand years ago of an adolescent prehistoric male walking through the woods when he hears rustling in the grass. What does the sound mean? The gears of his mind unconsciously whirl into action and make a decision. It could mean a poisonous snake or it could be just the wind. If he believes it is a snake, he takes protective measures and survives another day. He will live to pass his genes on to another generation that will share his safety instinct. If, on the other hand, he believes it is just the wind but it turns out to be a poisonous snake, he runs the risk of being bitten, dying, and losing the opportunity to pass his genes on. The odds are thus slightly in favor of genes for believing in danger when danger might not exist being passed on, while genes for ignoring danger signals would die out. One could argue that if the human species is to survive, we *must* believe rustling sounds might be snakes.

The leadership in the White House of the United States witnessed attacks on American soil by foreign terrorists on September 11, 2001, that killed 2,977 people. What did that mean for the future safety of Americans? The leadership had a longer time to react than the prehistoric adolescent, but they too had to make a decision eventually about how to react. If they reacted forcefully and powerfully at the right place and time, they might stave off future terrorist attacks. The American citizens they were required to protect would be safe. If, on the other hand, they reacted too weakly when more attacks were imminent, they ran the risk of being attacked again. The odds for being safe favored reacting forcefully. One could argue they *had to* attack someone or something, but the terrorists did not come from one clear physical location. The story of how the American leadership settled on attacking the country of Iraq, which had nothing to do with the September 11 attacks, and convincing the American public of the need to do so is at the most fundamental level a story of how the human mind believes what it needs to believe for safety and status.

During the twentieth century, doctors, psychologists, and a range of other advocates realized the massive scope of maltreatment and violence that was routinely perpetrated on children and women. What did that realization mean for the safety of our most vulnerable tribe mates? The advocates had an even longer time to react than the leadership in the White House, but, alas, they too had to make decisions about how to react. Through their efforts, laws to prevent or punish acts of victimization against children and women became nationalized, common, and government funded for the first time in history. In 1874, citizens formed the New York Society for the Prevention of Cruelty to Children. In the 1960s, every state enacted mandated-reporter laws, which legally require professions that interact frequently with vulnerable populations to report observed or suspected abuse. In 1974, the United States Congress passed the Child Abuse Prevention and Treatment Act that provided funds for states to develop child protective agencies. In 1994, the US Congress passed the federal Violence Against Women Act. Most states in the United States have specific laws that criminalize domestic violence and additional laws to provide resources for domestic violence victims.

But progress to rid the world of child maltreatment, sexual assault, and domestic violence hit a wall. As of 2012, national survey data indicated a steady decline in physical abuse and sexual abuse in the US over the previous two decades. Sexual abuse had declined by 62 percent since 1990, while physical abuse had declined by 56 percent.[1] But it was also estimated that forty-six out of ten thousand children were still being physically abused each year and thirty-seven per ten thousand were still being sexually abused.[2] Worse yet, when using a broader definition that encompassed violence, crime, and victimization, a national survey published in 2005 estimated that 53 percent of children experienced a physical assault each year in the United States.[3] While many new protections had been put into place and had brought about significant improvements, it looked as though the public health prevention and policy strategies were only ever going to go so far.

Advocates began to realize they did not have a powerful enough message that could get them to the front of the line for all the resources it would take to prevent all these problems. New laws and new programs were needed to support investigative teams, committees, task forces, public awareness campaigns, and prosecutions of offenders to activate everyone in "the village." All of these required funding, and the tap was not open wide enough, and it was never going to be wide enough if something did not change. There was no snake in the grass that could focus everyone's attention and bring them together to do more.

Then something remarkable happened to change all of that. Stakeholders discovered a single problem they could point the finger at that nearly everyone could believe in. They discovered their "Iraq" in the work of Vincent Felitti, MD, and his study on adverse childhood experiences (ACE). They combined this message with other research on posttraumatic stress disorder (PTSD) to create a narrative that psychological trauma permanently damages the human brain. With a clearly defined "enemy"—psychological trauma—that was physically toxic to the human brain, and possibly other important organs, they had the poisonous snake that could, perhaps, finally get everyone's attention.

Since then, the "toxic stress" message has been used to indoctrinate clinicians and researchers to believe that it is real. It has been used to persuade government agencies and professional organizations to endorse and create programming around it. It has been used to dupe state and national legislatures into passing resolutions affirming its existence and to leverage city governments to fund new social programs. It is perhaps the first instance of weaponizing modern neuroscience to try to shape society according to ideological beliefs. While many, if not most, scientists, clinicians, and stakeholders in these fields now believe, or at least believe there is a strong possibility, that stress can permanently damage brains, the problem is that none of it is true. How did this happen?

· · ·

Humans are belief engines.[4] From prehistoric man guessing at the source of rustling in the grass, to leaders in the White House wondering how to protect American citizens, to humanitarian clinicians strategizing how to help disadvantaged populations, we form beliefs and sort out the facts later, if needed, or maybe never.

Beliefs need the possibility of being true to give them authenticity. Much of the foundation for the possibility that psychological trauma can have devastating consequences comes from the historical development of PTSD. The diagnosis of PTSD was formulated in the 1970s, stimulated by the large number of American soldiers returning from Vietnam with psychological disturbances. The Vietnam conflict was the first major war to occur after psychiatry had systematically organized the taxonomy of mental disorders. As veterans returned with emotional and behavioral symptoms, psychiatry finally had the scientific language to describe their troubles, and PTSD was formally recognized in 1980. This was followed by hundreds of research studies and the development of effective treatments, and the concept of PTSD quickly found "stickiness" with the public and the media.

With the popularity of the PTSD diagnosis, the concept of trauma would eventually become a new type of instrument in the world. Trauma would become a rallying cry that had the power to bring together researchers, clinicians, policy makers, journalists, and other types of stakeholders who were concerned about the safety and healing of all types of victims. Understanding the power of the human belief engine helps us appreciate how this message was so psychologically appealing despite being so unsupported by the evidence.

Traumaville is a name I made up. It is a mythical place, a destination one never quite reaches because the attraction of it is more the righteous path than the destination. The path is fighting for victims and social justice. The road to Traumaville is driven by the politics of victimhood and involves the suspension of reason, and if one ever reached Traumaville, with all the goals accomplished, there would no longer be anything to fight for. As Ralph Waldo Emerson said, "Life is a journey, not a destination." The road to Traumaville has become the mission path of a science-based political ideology that is trying to shape medicine, psychology, childcare, schools, courts, and other institutions and public policies all over the world.

I have spent over twenty-eight years conducting research on PTSD in children and adolescents. I have been the principal investigator on five large federal research grants in this field. I have either conducted or supervised the treatment of approximately 200 youths with PTSD, and I have conducted or supervised the assessments of over 700 trauma-exposed youths in both clinical practice and research studies.[5] Much of that work has been with very young children (six years and younger). I might have more direct experience with very young children with trauma exposure and PTSD than any clinician in the world. I have devoted my career to understanding trauma reactions so as to help these unfortunate victims.

The Trouble with Trauma is the story of how the idea of psychological trauma appeals to the human mind. It will explain how beliefs about trauma that are wrong, like other missteps of the human mind, spread easily. It is the age-old story of reason versus belief applied to the relatively new body of research on psychological trauma. It is about the unique dilemma faced by nearly all of psychological research: how our willingness to accept research studies that might be on shaky ground and our need to derive meaning in the world is best thought of as the dominance of belief systems.

It will borrow some concepts from Malcolm Gladwell's book *The Tipping Point*, which explained the spread of social behaviors as contagious epidemics.[6] *The Tipping Point* described how a few influential individuals can be key to adoption of new behaviors in society (the Law of the Few), and how small things can make all the difference to separate the memorable from the forgotten (the Stickiness Factor). But *The Tipping Point* described mostly *behavior*—for example, how individuals started wearing Hush Puppies again after a long hiatus, and how criminals decreased their bigger criminal behavior when police enforced laws about smaller criminal behavior. It did not describe how the human mind is dominated by belief rather than reason when faced with information in the world that it needs to make sense of, or why it must make sense of information in the first place.

. . .

The concept of toxic stress—the notion that experiences of extreme psychological stress can cause permanent damage to the structure and function of the brain—was not fully embraced in the early years of PTSD research. The concept had been speculation for approximately twenty-five years in the early brain-imaging studies of Vietnam War veterans with PTSD, researchers employed it as a hypothesis-generating idea and discussion piece to drive up the excitement level in their journal articles and grant applications. The concept was interesting, but the specific phrase *toxic stress* did not yet exist.

It is an extraordinary notion to claim that one brief experience, or even a number of prolonged experiences, can permanently alter the fundamental sizes of structures in the brain and the network circuitry that evolved over millions of years and has involved much worse stress, trauma, and suffering than in modern times. There are no comparable theories in medicine that stressful life experiences can cause a cascade of internal physiological processes that permanently alter the size or function of the liver, kidneys, lungs, or heart. The only known methods to create those types of changes are from external chemicals or microorganisms, uncontrolled immune reactions that attack the body, or actual physical injuries. Accordingly, prior to 2010, scientists were understandably cautious about fully endorsing this notion of toxic stress.

Then something unexpected happened. Leading scientists started fully embracing this extraordinary notion as fact. At a scientific conference in 2005, I was sitting in the audience listening to a presentation by one of the leading brain-imaging researchers in the world, who stated that based on the brain-imaging research he was absolutely certain that stressful experiences in childhood had caused permanent changes in the brains of the adults whom he studied.[7] His level of certainty shocked me so much that I immediately wrote down what he said so I would not misremember it later.

Scientists are usually cautious people in their public statements. They spend their lives testing hypotheses that *maybe* something is true or *maybe* something is not true. Even when they find evidence in their experiments that something seems to be true, they usually say that something is *probably* true. Unless they have rock-solid, indisputable, replicated experimental results, they shy away from publicly announcing that they are absolutely certain.

I was mystified. I knew the evidence as well as this presenter. Nearly all of the PTSD studies that he referenced were cross-sectional studies. Cross-sectional studies have little to no power to determine what causes what because subjects are examined at only one point in time. In cross-sectional studies, with only one slice of time, you cannot tell whether the chicken or the egg came first. Everybody knows that. The subjects were always examined *after* their trauma experiences, meaning that scientists literally had no idea what their brains looked like or how their brains functioned *prior to* their trauma experiences. It made no sense to me that he would use his respected position in the field to profess certainty about a concept that so obviously lacked rock-solid, indisputable evidence, and about a topic that was so obviously important—alteration of the human brain. He was a lifelong scientist. Wasn't he supposed to be cautious?

Over the next fifteen years, dozens more leading experts would go on the record with their certain conviction that traumatic stress and other types of psychological stress in childhood permanently damaged brain structures, rewired the functioning of neural circuits, and altered fundamental personality construction.

A social movement arose with the endgame of trying to influence law and policy. Advocates would convince several major cities, three states, and both chambers of the US Congress to pass laws or resolutions confirming toxic stress as fact. The media would promote the narrative with almost unquestioning enthusiasm. The social movement hit a jackpot of publicity on March 11, 2018, when *60 Minutes* featured a report by Oprah Winfrey on trauma-informed care that highlighted as its centerpiece the concept of toxic stress that damages brains, which she called "a revolutionary approach that's spreading across the nation." Working on the story was "life changing" for her. During a personal interview on *60 Minutes Overtime*, she elaborated, "I can say that of all the stories I've ever done in my life, and all the experiences I've ever had, and people I've interviewed, this story has had more impact on me than practically anything I've ever done."[8] Strong stuff from someone who has virtually made a career out of finding inspiration in life. This was followed in 2021 by her book with Dr. Bruce Perry, called *What Happened to You?*, which became an instant bestseller.

The problem is that none of it has been proven true. The scientific evidence does not support the concept of toxic stress. There have been many fascinating studies that go a long way toward disproving the extraordinary idea that stress damages the brain, and there have been few, if any, properly designed studies that support the idea.

The attractiveness of the toxic stress narrative is powerful, but it is ultimately not enlightening. Individuals appear to be attracted to this theory when searching for things they can do to help victims. A more enlightening approach is apparent when one is more ready to accept the way to help victims may be to understand them better as having inherent vulnerabilities that they were born with. After all, the Latin root of the word for doctor—*docere*—means to teach, not to heal.

So, how did this happen? Those first researchers who conducted brain-imaging studies in Vietnam veterans with PTSD in the 1990s were not trying to start a social movement. Chapter Two will explain how a plausible scientific hypothesis related to Vietnam War veterans with PTSD remained unproven but exploded into a mainstream social-policy movement.

• • •

The official recognition of PTSD as a psychiatric disorder in 1980 has generally been regarded as one of the great accomplishments of psychiatry. Prior to the recognition of PTSD there had not been a psychiatric diagnosis that described the distinct symptoms of the post-trauma syndrome. The creation of the PTSD diagnosis provided formal recognition to a syndrome that plagues approximately 10 percent of the population at some point in their lifetime. It gave credibility to the psychological suffering of combat veterans instead of them being viewed with suspicion as defective soldiers. It spawned an enormous area of research into neurobiology, cognition, and memory. It enabled the development of trauma-specific psychotherapies.

But that was not enough for many clinicians. In 1992, psychiatrist Judith Herman, MD, at Harvard University published a paper that invented a new disorder she called complex PTSD.[9] Complex PTSD, according to Herman, applied only to victims who suffered prolonged and repeated trauma, such as in concentration camps, prisons, coerced prostitution, and chronic childhood abuse. She said that regular PTSD, or, as she called it, simple PTSD, was only for victims of briefer forms of trauma such as war, automobile accidents, natural disasters, time-limited child abuse, horrific injuries, one-time rapes, and so on. She wrote that "the diagnostic concepts of the existing psychiatric canon, including simple PTSD, are not designed for survivors of prolonged, repeated trauma, and do not fit them well."

In the early 1990s, the fourth edition of the *Diagnostic and Statistical Manual of Mental Disorders* (*DSM-IV*) was being assembled, which is the official taxonomy of psychiatric disorders used in the United States and many other countries.[10] Herman and some supporters lobbied the *DSM* committee to formally recognize complex PTSD. The effort was rejected for lack of evidence. About fifteen years passed, and as the fifth edition of the *DSM* was being assembled,[11] supporters repackaged complex PTSD as a childhood disorder. This effort was also rejected for lack of evidence.

But then something remarkable occurred. Years of promotion by supporters seemed to have given complex PTSD greater acceptance despite the rejections by the *DSM*. Those rejections may actually have spurred on the supporters because the *DSM* was official orthodoxy, and they could view themselves as revolutionary outsiders fighting for their disadvantaged patients. Despite the lack of scientific validity, complex PTSD has now become one of the most influential notions in the field to the extent that the majority of practicing clinicians now believe that complex PTSD is a real disorder. Herman and her followers are viewed as heroes to many people in the field. Even with the lack of scientific evidence, complex PTSD is recognized by nearly every relevant national organization as either complex PTSD or complex trauma.

It is easy to see why individuals who are not researchers tend to believe in the narrative of complex PTSD. They believe that complex PTSD stands for something that resonates with their view of the world, which is relatively more important than details like evidence. Clinicians will tell you that complex PTSD just makes sense to them, and that is enough for them. But none of that explains why researchers and national organizations have embraced it. Chapter Three will explain how a proposed disorder that has none of the traditional medical evidence needed to recognize it as a real syndrome has come to be believed by so many experts in the trauma field.

• • •

The full embrace of the toxic stress model and complex PTSD is similar to other episodes where science crashed into other motivations of human nature. The cosmological and ideological motivations of beliefs versus evidence have perhaps never been more apparent than in the belief that the Earth is at the center of the universe. This belief was initially quite understandable, as the sun does appear to move across the sky, as opposed to the Earth moving around the sun, and our ancestors had no technology to peer into space and observe other solar systems. Nicolaus Copernicus published a treatise in 1543 with detailed astronomical observations to support his theory that the sun, not the Earth, was the center of the solar system. In 1633, Galileo Galilei was convicted of heresy by the Roman Catholic Church for his refusal to denounce Copernicus and was confined to house arrest for the remainder of his life. It was not until more than one hundred years after the publication of Copernicus's work, following the work of Isaac Newton, that the heliocentric view was finally widely accepted.

In the famous Piltdown Man hoax of 1912, Charles Dawson claimed he had found the missing fossil link between ape and man when he "discovered" a set of bones in a gravel pit in Sussex, England. The set of bones consisted of an orangutan mandible with filed-down teeth deliberately combined with the skull of a small, modern human. The bones possessed just enough intriguing yet inconclusive scientific features to create controversy for over forty years until they were decisively exposed in 1953 as a forgery.

In 1989, the University of Utah held a news conference during which two electrochemists, Martin Fleischmann and Stanley Pons, claimed they had discovered cold fusion. The essence of their claim was that hydrolysis of heavy water on the surface of a palladium electrode caused marked elevations of temperature within their apparatus. Because hot fission is used in nuclear power plants to generate electricity, cold fusion could theoretically do the same with much greater ease. The research methods and the theory had just enough possible authenticity to receive serious attention. However, as flaws in their research were exposed and other researchers failed to replicate their experiment, cold fusion was declared dead within five weeks of their news conference. Nevertheless, their research had generated numerous attempts by other scientists to replicate it, had garnered millions of dollars of funding, had gotten Fleischmann and Pons invited to a meeting with White House advisors, and still has adherents today. Because they claimed that cold fusion could lead to an inexhaustible source of clean energy and solve the world's energy crisis, the claim received worldwide attention.

In 1998, *The Lancet* medical journal published a study by British physician Andrew Wakefield that claimed to show that the MMR (measles, mumps, rubella) vaccine caused autism in children. Wakefield's paper included histological evidence of inflammation in the colon, suggesting a novel form of enterocolitis-induced autism. The paper contained just enough interesting evidence about a disorder with no known etiology to be believable. The paper was instantly controversial and was eventually retracted by *The Lancet* due to evidence of fraud. But the research touched a nerve among those who had already been against vaccinations. It was followed by substantial drops in vaccination rates in multiple countries and continued belief in the research by many people to this day.

In 2003, nineteen-year-old Elizabeth Holmes dropped out of college and founded the company Theranos. The company claimed to possess breakthrough technology that could perform dozens of tests on a single drop of blood in less than an hour in a self-contained automated device the size of a desktop printer. After an investigative report in 2015 questioned Theranos's technology, the company faced a series of challenges from government regulators, state's attorneys, and investors. In 2018, Holmes and the former president of the company were charged with fraud by the Securities and Exchange Commission. Holmes and Theranos settled the claim without either admitting or denying the charges. Later in 2018, a US attorney in California filed criminal charges against Holmes, with the trial scheduled to begin in August 2021.

By September 2018, the company had ceased operations. The science behind the breakthrough was never articulated. Holmes never published research, and there seems to be evidence that her pitch to investors never revealed the nitty-gritty details, either.[12] The pitch seems to have been that they had worked out several technologies (amount of blood, speed of testing, automation inside the machine, and reduction in size of the machine). The pitch seems to have worked because there was just enough plausibility for all of those technologies for investors to think that somebody had just come along and made existing processes smaller and faster. The pitch resonated with investors, perhaps because there were obvious benefits for things like testing newborns, patients with cancer, and people in poor countries. Before its dramatic fall, Theranos was able to raise over $700 million over twelve years from venture capitalists and private investors and had secured testing contracts with Safeway and Walgreens.

One would think that the line between truth and belief would become clearer over time with the rise of scientific professions and methods to disseminate information. The opposite seems to be happening. As scientists have mastered the low-hanging fruit, we are left to grapple with more and more complex issues. These cases involve a mixture of motivations for believing things that are not true. On the surface, the motivations appear sometimes to be purely for monetary profit. Other times they appear to defend a cosmology that is fundamental to a larger belief system. In each case, the motivations for people to believe in them are different in the particulars, but they all have in common dreams of wealth, status, or protection from danger that the belief would bring.

· · ·

The purpose of this book is not to tell you there is harm in beliefs, unless perhaps your job involves control of public policy. The purpose is not to try to convince you that humans are not the most powerfully rational animal on the planet, because we are. The purpose is to make the shaky foundations of beliefs visible. What you do with this is up to you.

The goal of this book is to answer one question: why do experts in psychological trauma believe ideas that are not true and feel so strongly compelled to sell them as scientific facts? The answer may tell us something about our interest in and skill at deciding whether anything is true as the scientific questions around us become more complicated.

The answer to this question may improve the lives of the victims of trauma and give better objectives for which stakeholders can fight. All those involved can make sounder decisions about interventions because they can ignore the insufficient guidance of incorrect theory. More appropriate psychotherapy can be selected. Instead of psychotherapy that focuses on trauma and promises unrealistic changes, psychotherapy that provides insight, acceptance of one's limitations, and problem-solving strategies for real solutions may be better. For example, isn't the fundamental principle of addiction recovery based on accepting one's limitations?

That's the kind of wisdom I'm promoting in this book. I'll explain how the principles discussed in this book are adaptive and when they are maladaptive. We are confronted in modern society by many complex problems to understand and manage. The human mind provides us with sophisticated cognitive tools that were not designed for modern social groups, but there are other tools for resisting misjudgments and slowing down the mind to make more constructive assessments. These adaptive tools are more essential than ever as neuroscience uncovers ever-more complex knowledge, and the internet and social media can more rapidly and widely create fear and misinformation around complex problems than ever before.

I'll show how to reframe automatic beliefs in the context of the human need to garner cooperation in groups and acquire status in our relationships. Above all, I want to show that automatic beliefs that originate to make thinkers feel comfortable with themselves in the world can be changed so that better decisions, based on truth, can prevail to help individuals with their problems. It requires more energy for truth and reason to prevail over automatic beliefs, and the answers often reveal that quick fixes are not feasible, but you will see the world more realistically and, ultimately, engage in more adaptive solutions.

On this road, I'm going to take you to scientific conferences, to a cadre of trauma experts around the world, and inside psychology experiments about the inner workings of our minds. I'll explore the notions of toxic stress, complex PTSD, and, the oldest shill in child psychiatry, mother blaming. I will explain how, when desperate attempts to improve the plight of disadvantaged youth, address violence, and prevent domestic violence hit a wall, researchers found a way to get attention for their causes.

The Trouble with Trauma is a behind-the-headlines explanation of the science that helps us make sense of the world around a big question. The big question is not why some people are disadvantaged and some are not. The big question is why some people believe they know the reasons for people being disadvantaged when, in fact, they do not. The explanation is the best way to think about the emergence of beliefs that psychological trauma is the cause of brain damage, early death from physical disease, homelessness, incarceration, and personality deformation is to think of them as heuristics for survival, safety, and status.

"Heuristics" is a term cognitive psychologists use to describe the process of how human minds use mental images or shortcuts to efficiently understand complex data with minimal effort. A heuristic is like an aid for the mind to quickly tag and categorize incoming information. "Heuristic" can be both a noun to describe the shortcut and an adjective to describe the type of shortcut.

The process that weaponized neuroscience to try to explain how disadvantaged populations became disadvantaged is analogous to our need to believe in poisonous snakes and a terrorist organization in Iraq. In the human brain, mysterious beliefs in things that are not true can be thought of as heuristics for survival or to achieve status.

The rise of beliefs in toxic stress and complex PTSD when the scientific evidence has been so clearly lacking are classic examples of believing the enemy is there when it is not. Both beliefs share several things in common. One is that they share the notion that there is a lethal enemy, namely, trauma. A second thing is that they share a similar background of being built on shaky evidence that is suggestive only, but not definitive. The so-called evidence has just enough detail and fancy-sounding mechanisms to sound plausible but is not quite verifiable. Third, the popularity of the beliefs depends on a cadre of respected scientists to stoke the fires enough to scare others into believing.

A small army of psychology researchers has been uncovering secrets of the human mind during the past century and doing so with increasing rigor and speed in the past forty years. Cognitive psychologists have discovered secrets of how we repeatedly make the wrong decisions. Social psychologists have made amazing discoveries about how the actions of those around us influence our decisions because of our concern about status. Evolutionary psychologists have shown that there are good reasons for why we see what we want to see. Despite these fascinating advances, there has also come the realization, as science writer and professor Philip Tetlock has pointed out, that much of psychology is politicized psychology, and research is often driven by ideological agendas of which the psychologists often seem to be only partly conscious.[13]

I will tap into all these fields to flesh out a rounded understanding of why we need to believe in the first place and how it gets us into trouble when we are confronted with complex and threatening situations. We all believe we are rational, and that we have greater control over our capacity for reason than we really do. But as more than one psychology researcher has observed, the paradox is that it is so much more important to have certain beliefs than to be right, and therefore the more wrong you are, the more strongly you believe you are correct. The road to Traumaville is where we get sold something we are eager to believe, and we pick and choose which facts we double down on that we want to believe.

The problem with the idea of Traumaville, and at the same time its main attraction, is that some of the main models that are currently believed are not true. The story of how smart people believe these things despite the absence of evidence is the story of this book. This is the road to Traumaville.

Chapter One

THE THREE RULES OF HOW BELIEF BECOMES FACT

Humans are belief engines. The human mind seems designed to impart meaning to sounds, sights, and smells automatically, and use logic later, if ever, to confirm or deny. This process works well in everyday life because it is rapid and seems to err on the side of detecting danger. This process seems reliable because it is based on our enormous memory capacities for past events. This process keeps us safe and makes life consistent and somewhat predictable, while also allowing us to learn if we so choose.

In simple, everyday events, this process works efficiently. We hear a rustling in the grass, believe it is a snake or believe it is the wind, take a few more steps to obtain more data and get a quick confirmation, and then move on down the road. Beliefs made on the spot can be filed away in memory and need no further consideration. There do not need to be debates with one's family and friends about whether the belief is right or not. The process is akin to trying on a new shirt. You may like the shirt, or you may not. If you like it, wear it again. If you do not like it, do not wear it again. No big deal. No more thought and energy need be expended on the issue. The process is rapid, temporary, and energy efficient.

When problems are complicated, however, and there is no simple answer, as with most modern problems, this creates vacuums, and beliefs inevitably move into the vacuums. The problems with this process begin when we are exposed to situations beyond everyday life, when the stimuli become more novel and more complex—when we are confronted with complicated situations that demand extensive, expensive, and long-term responses. In these situations, we can no longer make rapid interpretations of meaning, shrug it off if we are wrong, and walk on to the next thing.

For these knotty situations of modern life, we must make decisions that we have to stick with for the long haul. We cannot get more data with just a few more steps, and we may never achieve clear confirmation. If there is to be any moving on down the road, individuals must make best-guess estimates of which course of action is right, and then embark on long-term, multistep, and expensive projects that are capable of making, at best, incremental progress in further understanding.

In the more complicated situations of modern life, the interpretations of meaning cannot simply be tossed aside like a shirt you do not want to wear again. Those in charge must pick a metaphorical shirt to wear and keep wearing it for a long time. This brings us into foreign territory where the beliefs have to be evaluated and wrestled with. The human mind must call into play the forces of logic to determine which "facts" are truly true and which "facts" are truly false. Beliefs cannot remain as conjectures. Beliefs must evolve into facts.

In dictionaries, "fact" means something that has been proven true; "fact" and "true" are synonymous. In this book, I use "fact" a bit differently to mean anything that individuals have convinced themselves is true. In their minds, it is proven true, and has the perception of truth to them. A "true fact" is proven objectively true and is the same as the dictionary definition of fact. A "false fact" is not objectively true, or at least has not yet been proven true, but in the mind of believers, it is believed true. It is acknowledged that "false fact" is an oxymoron, but it serves a useful purpose in this book.

Humans are very bad at determining which beliefs must evolve into facts and which beliefs must remain uncertain conjectures if we are to judge by how frequently we get it wrong. Our minds *can* be excellent at that task, but it takes enormous hard work and persistence. Our minds simply do not work that way. One *can* slowly roll a round ball up a hill, but it takes enormous hard work and persistence. Take one's eyes off the ball for a moment and it will roll downhill, and it will always roll downhill, just as the mind will always automatically form beliefs.

To say that human minds are bad at determining which beliefs are true is not the same as saying that our minds are flawed. Our minds are not flawed in this respect. Our minds are designed to be bad at these kinds of judgments. When our minds are bad at that process, they are functioning well and doing exactly what they were designed to do. The problem, if there is one, is that our minds are imperfect instruments for dealing with modern, complicated problems.

There is no natural law of the universe that says what brains are supposed to be good at it. Brains do what they do, end of story. Our minds are designed to create beliefs. We then collect the "facts" that support our beliefs. In this sense, beliefs always evolve into facts. *The goal is not that we arrive at true facts. The goal is that we arrive at the most useful beliefs.* We are belief engines.

The three rules of how belief becomes fact

On September 11, 2011, terrorists hijacked four airplanes in the eastern United States and planned to fly the planes into heavily populated, iconic American buildings. Three of the planes hit their targets. This provoked a concentrated effort by the US government to combat terror. The terrorists of the 9/11 attack were part of a group called al-Qaeda. The leadership of al-Qaeda had planned the attack while stationed in Afghanistan under the protection of Taliban rulers.

However, within one year after the attack, US President George Bush and his inner circle of advisors had settled on a plan to invade a totally different country. Iraq had no involvement with the terrorist attack and all the US intelligence experts knew that. While Iraq was no friend to the US, it posed no credible terrorist threat of any sort to the US. Yet, the Bush team had managed to convince a clear majority of the members of Congress and most of the American public that Iraq had supported al-Qaeda and posed an imminent terrorist threat to the US. This support allowed them to launch the Iraq War on March 20, 2003, topple the government of Saddam Hussein, and occupy Iraq for nearly eight years. What caused members of Congress and most of the American public to believe that Iraq had supported al-Qaeda and needed to be invaded to protect the US from another terrorist attack?

The first rule of how belief becomes fact is called a Set of Small False Facts.

According to most of the members of Congress who voted for the war, the case against Iraq was supported by a set of small pieces of information. Each piece of information alone was not convincing enough, but when all were considered together, they created a convincing impression.

The set of small pieces of information, which were all widely known by intelligence experts at the time to be questionable, and sometimes false, included the following: A terrorist training camp instructor who had been captured allegedly confessed that al-Qaeda operatives received chemical weapons training from Iraq. One of the 9/11 hijackers, Mohamed Atta, purportedly met with an Iraqi spy in Prague. Iraq had supposedly made efforts to purchase uranium yellowcake from Africa in the hope of making nuclear bombs. Iraq had purchased aluminum tubes that could allegedly be used in centrifuges to enrich uranium for nuclear bombs. An Iraqi defector in German custody, nicknamed Curveball by US intelligence personnel, had asserted that Iraq had mobile weapons labs capable of making anthrax and other biological weapons. Iraq had supposedly developed flying drones that could attack the US with chemical or biological weapons. These small false facts were widely known because they had been disseminated repeatedly by the media in dribs and drabs for months.

Then something happened to make the set of small false facts seem even more believable for members of Congress. In late summer 2002, the Senate Intelligence Committee held a closed-door meeting with Central Intelligence Agency (CIA) Director George Tenet to review the Iraq situation. Senator Robert Graham asked Tenet what the National Intelligence Estimate (NIE) said about the situation. Tenet said there was no National Intelligence Estimate.

A National Intelligence Estimate is like a review paper. It pulls together all the information from the approximately seventeen government intelligence agencies to summarize what is known on a topic. It is essentially the written embodiment of the same process the human brain goes through to determine whether a belief ought to become a fact when the brain is slowed down and being rational. NIEs are produced by the National Intelligence Council.

NIEs are not automatically produced for every topic. As one can imagine, it takes an enormous amount of time and energy to produce a consensus-driven report from seventeen agencies. They are often produced only because Congress asked for them. CIA Director Tenet said frankly that he was reluctant to create one because personnel were stretched thin during the crisis, but ultimately he could not turn down the Senate's request for one.

NIEs are classified documents for government officials, so the full version of the estimate was not available to the public at the time. Based on interviews with individuals who had access to the NIE, its principal flaw was that the small false facts were reported as though they were true facts corroborated by multiple and valid sources. As Melvin Goodman of the CIA told the PBS documentary series *Frontline* years later about the NIE, its writers produced the argument that the administration wanted. "This was comparable to sort of judge shopping in the courthouse: If you want a certain verdict on a decision, you usually know which judge you can go to."[1] Goodman stated that the full NIE should be released so that it could be analyzed as part of the understanding of how the country went to war.

One of the more amazing aspects of the NIE is there was an earlier version that was longer and more detailed than the classified version that was sent to Congress. This longer version of the NIE included qualifications about the validity of the information. It described specifically how the sources of information were unreliable and uncorroborated. The revised, final version of the NIE that was sent to Congress did not contain many of these qualifications, and thus created a false appearance of authenticity.

Interestingly, many members of Congress who voted for the war have admitted they never read the NIE. It is an interesting psychological question as to whether members of Congress did not read the NIE because they already believed what they wanted to believe and did not want to risk reading anything that would contradict their belief.

Nevertheless, all the members of Congress knew of the existence of the NIE, and they knew roughly what was contained in it from all the other briefings and chatter. They knew the NIE did not outright contradict the set of small false facts that had been circulated in the media. Having the small false facts in writing in an official document only added to the belief that they must have been true.

All of these pieces of information were known at the time by the intelligence community to be based on unreliable sources. The White House administration knew the information was unreliable. The NIE clearly stated it contained asserted facts that were not corroborated. But the administration officials promoted this information openly in the media with the certainty that they were either true facts or probable facts. The Bush administration understood that each small false fact by itself was not enough to persuade Congress and the public that Iraq had weapons of mass destruction, but all of the little facts together were both confusing enough and convincing enough. Rule 1 accomplished.

The second rule of how belief becomes fact is called Stokers.

The set of false facts by itself has little impact if no one is talking about it. The NIE is a neat embodiment of the set of false facts in one document, but the American public had no knowledge of the NIE at the time. The set of false facts, however, did exist in the public's mind, as there was a constant drumbeat of news stories that were repeated so often that everyone who was paying any attention to the news media knew about these stories. There was a coordinated effort by influential individuals to promote it, or, in other words, stoke the fire. Key individuals who were highly respected by Congress and the public lent their public support to the case against Iraq.

Vice President Dick Cheney repeatedly went on news programs to say that Iraq harbored terrorists and that hijacker Mohamed Atta had met with an Iraqi spy in Prague. President Bush delivered speeches on national television that placed Iraq in an "axis of evil" with Iran and North Korea to support terrorists and build weapons of mass destruction. Defense Secretary Donald Rumsfeld publicly stated that there were undeniable links between Iraq and al-Qaeda and that Iraq had stockpiled large quantities of chemical weapons. National Security Adviser Condoleezza Rice wrote an editorial for the *New York Times* repeating the claim that Iraq tried to buy uranium. Both Bush and Rice stated publicly that despite the inevitable uncertainty about intelligence reports, they did not want the final proof to be a mushroom cloud; in other words, we all should fear that Iraq already had a nuclear bomb.

The most memorable of the stokers was perhaps the most reluctant among them. Secretary of State Colin Powell's speech at the United Nations in February 2003, just one month before the invasion started, has been considered a pivotal moment. Other people in the Bush administration could have given that speech, but Powell was reportedly chosen because of his impeccable reputation for integrity. In a dramatic one-hour-and-sixteen-minute speech, live on national television, complete with a slide show, audio recordings of phone conversations, and props, Powell summarized many of the false facts including the claims about mobile biological weapons labs, the aluminum tubes for centrifuges to enrich uranium, and Iraqi support of al-Qaeda training camps. Powell said, "My colleagues, every statement I make today is backed up by sources, solid sources. These are not assertions."[2] And he repeated this a few minutes later as though he were a barker at a circus: "Ladies and gentlemen, these are not assertions. These are facts, corroborated by many sources, some of them sources of the intelligence services of other countries."

For some of us who witnessed the speech in real time, our most vivid memory was Colin Powell theatrically holding up a small vial of white powder to demonstrate the purported danger of anthrax attacks from Iraq. It did not matter that the anthrax attacks that had occurred in the US in 2001 were not from Iraq. And to further authenticate Powell's speech, CIA Director George Tenet sat behind Powell, as if in a posed tableau for the cameras to convey figuratively, "I am the head of the CIA and I am on board with all of this."

It is acknowledged that "stoker" may be perceived as an inflammatory way to describe these individuals. I do not mean it to be derogatory because I believe these individuals were not acting maliciously or unprofessionally. I believe they were humans doing the best they could in tough situations. Other words that could describe them, such as *maven* or *supporter*, would seem to me to describe them as blithely enthusiastic, whereas I think *stoker* best conveys that there was intent to achieve a specific end.

Powell's speech was powerful because it came from a man in the Bush administration whom many people highly trusted. I believe the effect for many listeners was: "If Colin Powell believes Iraq has weapons of mass destruction, then it must be true." Powell, to his credit, admitted years later his disappointment in himself for giving in to pressure to deliver that speech, admitting it was a "blot" on his record. At the time, however, the administration wanted to go to war, Congress wanted to go to war, and the American public wanted to go to war. They just needed a country to attack. Powell and the other stokers served up Iraq on a silver platter. Rule 2 fulfilled.

The third rule of how belief becomes fact is called the Power of the Clan.

This explains the psychological behavior of individuals getting sucked into the vortex of social relationships in stressful situations. The Power of the Clan means that modern individuals are a product of our ancestry. Before there were countries, before there were cities, before there were organized infrastructures for living that we would call civilized societies, our ancestors lived in small hunter-gatherer clans. Clans were small bands of approximately ten to forty individuals who depended on each other for everything needed for their survival. The fossil record indicates that our *Homo sapiens* ancestors lived in clans for approximately 300,000 years, and our more distant ancestors of other species lived this way for nearly four million years. That represents a long time for psychological traits to become embedded in a species.

Two features of clans seem most important. The first feature is that *the primary goal of every clan is survival*. Clans had to provide food, shelter, and opportunities for reproduction. The second feature is that *clans are social*. Nearly every function performed by the clan for the survival of its members depended on social cooperation. Survival and social interaction—the most basic functions of human life. The clan had to exist to facilitate survival and social interaction.

There needed to be rules for what social function each clan member performed: rules to govern how hunts were conducted, how food was shared, when they moved camps, who was in charge of healing, who was in charge of cooking, who was in charge of making tools, and who was allowed to mate with whom. For social rules to be enforced there had to be a hierarchy with a leader and subordinates. Clan members not only needed to cooperate in these social interactions for survival that evolved as clan culture, but clan members who wished to maximize their own status for their personal gain naturally learned how to take full advantage of the culture.

Following 9/11, the US population came together as one clan as it had few other times in history, and Bush and his advisors felt it. As Tyler Drumheller, chief of the CIA's European division at the time, told *Frontline*, "I do think there was just incredible momentum, just a huge force, an irresistible force, for the war coming in."[3] Gary Schroen, a CIA operative in Afghanistan, said, "Personally, this whole Iraq thing, it just sucked us into this vortex. We're in a giant whirlpool which you can hardly get out of."[4] That vortex was the Power of the Clan.

Much has been said and written in retrospect about how Bush, Cheney, Rumsfeld, and their colleagues felt an immense urgency to protect the country. The Power of the Clan suggests that they not only felt an urgency toward protecting the country, but they felt a force within their inner circle to follow their leader and to maximize their own status within the inner circle. Rule 3 was fulfilled, as they were operating not just on a need to unearth facts, but on the far more powerful need to maintain the roles of social interaction within their small clan inside the White House while feeling the weight of an entire country.

There are almost an infinite number of stories throughout human history of how belief becomes fact. Not all of them depended heavily on all three rules—a Set of False Facts, Stokers, and the Power of the Clan. The story of 9/11 and the 2003 Iraq War, however, is simply one of the best-documented and best-publicized stories where all three rules came together. Each of these rules by itself was powerful and might have been enough to persuade Congress and the public to believe the case against Iraq. Each of them tapped into a different deeply embedded function of the human brain to believe first and reason later. None of the small false facts alone were knockout proof or cold, hard evidence. Antipathy for Iraq had been around for years, but the set of small false facts in the NIE report gave people a reason to believe Iraq was something else. None of the outside forces that touched on this saga were enough to be a smoking gun, but the involvement of respected individuals stoking the fire gave people a sense of independent proof. Nor could Powell or Tenet dramatically change their relationships with leaders or benefit from promotions or personal wealth by their shows of support. Their almost subtle acts of loyalty to the administration simply kept them in good graces in the inner circles, and by circular reasoning, kept them entrenched as leaders in the minds of the American people. They believed they were protecting their country and their people, and thereby maintaining the social bonds of the clan.

With this outline in mind, let's examine the three rules in more detail. We will use examples of nontrauma to flesh out the rules in this chapter. In Chapters Two, Three, and Four, we will apply the rules to trauma.

1. A Set of Small False Facts

The observation that a set of false facts can amount to a believable certainty for many people does not mean that just any false facts will do. The false facts have to be close enough to what could be believable that people will accept them. Take the example of whether vaccines can cause autism.

Autism and the vaccine scare

Concerns about dangerous adverse effects from vaccines had been around since the very first publication of vaccine experiments for smallpox in the 1790s. By the 1970s, the concerns about vaccines had started taking a consistently darker aspect. Perhaps people became complacent because the magnificent benefits of vaccines were no longer apparent, since vaccines had been so successful at eradicating the diseases from view. Perhaps attorneys had become better at filing lawsuits. One of the first signs of a major shift of negative feelings toward vaccines appears in a paper published in 1974 that described three dozen children who appeared to develop neurological problems following DPT (diphtheria, pertussis, tetanus) vaccination.[5] This story seemed to catch hold in the United Kingdom. The Association of Parents of Vaccine Damaged Children was formed in 1973 by two mothers who blamed their children's brain damage on the poliomyelitis vaccine. Rates of vaccination fell, and cases of whooping cough increased.

In 1982, a local news channel in Washington, DC, WRC-TV, produced a documentary called *DPT: Vaccine Roulette*, which claimed the pertussis part of the vaccine caused permanent neurological damage and mental retardation.[6] The one-hour special aired three times locally and was excerpted on NBC national programming. The investigative reporter, Lea Thompson, won an Emmy for the show. Almost immediately, there were reports of pediatricians and health officials being flooded with calls from frightened parents.[7] The American Academy of Pediatrics quickly responded to point out the distortions in Thompson's documentary and warned that it would cause parents to panic, lower immunization rates, and do harm to children who would not be protected.

In 1992 the British government ordered the withdrawal of the two most widely used brands of MMR vaccine because the mumps component was believed to cause a mild form of meningitis as a rare adverse effect.[8] Then in 1994, UK public health officials noticed an increasing number of cases of measles in children. The officials warned that there would soon be an epidemic of measles in the UK unless massive numbers of children were vaccinated. The government announced a plan to vaccinate seven million schoolchildren by the fall. This action by the government triggered a rise in parent groups opposed to vaccination.

Simultaneously, scientific reports showed that cases of autism appeared to be on the rise. For example, a study conducted in one Swedish city showed that rates of autism had nearly tripled from 4.0 per 100,000 children in 1980 to 11.6 per 100,000 in 1988.[9] This was most likely due to greater awareness and better detection by health professionals, but to the public it could easily look like an actual rise in cases of autism.

At the same time, lawsuits targeting a variety of different vaccines were rising in the 1980s. By one account, tort claims increased from twenty-four in 1980 to 150 in 1985. The amount awarded to plaintiffs was more than $3.5 billion.[10]

Parents started organizing and formed numerous advocacy groups. The Association of Parents of Vaccine Damaged Children had been around since 1973, but their focus was originally driven by parents who believed their children were brain damaged by the poliomyelitis vaccine. In 1994, the National Alliance for Autism Research was founded by parents who were frustrated by the lack of resources for their children with autism. In 1995, Defeat Autism Now! was formed to advocate for alternative treatments. In 1995, Cure Autism Now was founded by another set of parents frustrated with the pace of research and interventions for autism.

Then Dr. Andrew Wakefield happened, and he created a powerful set of small false facts. While the media stoked the fire about the dangers of vaccines with a regular diet of hyped headlines, and parent groups stoked the fire with publicity campaigns and lawsuits, Wakefield was putting together a set of small false facts with shoddy and sometimes fraudulent scientific research papers that would supercharge the controversy.

Wakefield was a gastroenterologist on staff of the Royal Free Hospital School of Medicine in London. In 1993, he and his coauthors published a paper in *The Journal of Medical Virology* claiming that the measles virus caused infection in the intestine and could also cause Crohn's disease.[11] They examined tissue from the bowel under the microscope in a small group of individuals with Crohn's disease and claimed to have found remnants of measles virus in all cases. The claim seemed so controversial that Britain's Medical Research Council convened an investigation and found significant problems with Wakefield's methods.[12]

The negative attention seemed only to embolden Wakefield. In 1994, he was a coauthor of a study that counted the number of adults who had been born in four counties in Sweden from 1945 to 1954 and developed Crohn's disease before the age of thirty. Five measles epidemics had affected those four counties during that time period. They found fifty-seven individuals with Crohn's disease and concluded that this was higher than the thirty-nine that would be expected normally. They concluded that "our results strengthen the hypothesis that measles is related to Crohn's disease." The paper was published in the highly respected medical journal, *The Lancet*.[13]

Then in 1995, Wakefield and coauthors followed this up with another paper published in *The Lancet* using epidemiologic evidence from thousands of individuals.[14] They claimed to have found a higher incidence of Crohn's disease and ulcerative colitis in adults who had received the measles vaccine as children in the 1960s. This paper was so controversial that *The Lancet* asked two experts to write a commentary about the methods used by Wakefield's group in the same issue. These two experts described several fundamental flaws that called Wakefield's results into question.[15] Further, one month after publication of the study, *The Lancet* published six letters to the editor pointing out numerous additional flaws.

By 1998, Wakefield had built up enough small false facts that he was ready to publish the infamous paper that would fuel a firestorm of controversy and eventually end his medical career. This paper, published once again in *The Lancet*, suggested that the MMR vaccine caused autism.[16] The paper reported on twelve children who were seen as patients by Wakefield for gastrointestinal symptoms including diarrhea, abdominal pain, bloating, and food intolerance. Ten of the twelve children were diagnosed with autism by coauthors of the study. The other two cases were diagnosed as "post-vaccinial encephalitis" and "post-viral encephalitis." In eight of the children, parents reported new-onset behavior problems one to two weeks following the MMR vaccination. Doctors performed ileocolonoscopies on the children and took biopsies of tissue from the ileum, colon, and rectum, and found microscopic indications of inflammation of the tissue in all twelve children. Wakefield claimed they had found a new subtype of autism that was caused by enterocolitis following MMR vaccination.

The publication was the fuel for the firestorm, but it was actually a news conference held by the Royal Free Hospital School of Medicine that lit the fire. The Royal Free knew the paper was going to be controversial and apparently decided to take the publicity head-on. Shortly before the paper was published in *The Lancet*, the Royal Free held a press conference with Wakefield and four other experts and also distributed a twenty-minute video. Free from the constraints of peer review, Wakefield speculated that the MMR vaccine created an immune reaction in the intestine that caused a "leaky gut." This allowed opioid products produced during digestion to leak out to the brain, as claimed by the old but never-proven "opioid excess" theory.

The public attention to the press conference, and then the publication, was instant and explosive. No one had ever found an etiology of any sort for autism. Now Wakefield appeared to have found the smoking gun, the snake in the grass, the Iraq that everybody could point to. Soon, vaccination rates plummeted and, predictably, cases of measles rose.

It turned out later that there were many things wrong with Wakefield's methods and his motives. First, the twelve patients in his paper had not shown up randomly in his clinic. Some of the patients had been referred to him by a law firm that was already preparing a lawsuit against manufacturers of the MMR vaccine. The lawyers knew these families because the parents already believed that the vaccine had caused their children's autism. In fact, Wakefield had been paid by the law firm to collect data for the lawsuit.[17] This makes Wakefield unethical for not disclosing it, and places the parents' historical reports about their children's autism symptoms under some suspicion.

Second, the so-called signs of inflammation reported for many of the cases, known as lymphoid nodular hyperplasia, are normal in childhood.[18] Wakefield was not a pediatric expert and he did not appear to know this fact, or if he did, he did not seem to care.

Third, nine months before publishing his paper, Wakefield had filed a patent for a modification of the MMR vaccine without the measles component.[19] Wakefield had a financial incentive to disparage the MMR vaccine, which casts a long shadow on his motives. This again makes Wakefield unethical for not disclosing his business interests in the paper.

Fourth, Wakefield and his hospital held their press conference, complete with twenty-minute video, prior to publication of the article. Such a stunt had all the earmarks of publicity seeking that was guaranteed to scare the public and cause controversy that would quickly overrun the slower pace of scientific review and replication of results. It is not amazing in retrospect that a man like Wakefield would engage in such a stunt, but it is amazing that he was able to convince a panel of more sober colleagues and hospital administrators to participate in the stunt.

After other investigators could not replicate Wakefield's data, and people started asking questions about Wakefield's methods, it later turned out that he had fabricated his results. Investigative journalist Brian Deer uncovered many of these facts. The United Kingdom revoked Wakefield's medical license. *The Lancet* retracted the paper, (which now ranks second on the all-time list for the number of times others have cited a retracted paper).[20]

But until it was found out to be a hoax, many people were willing to believe it because the small false facts were just close enough to other things that were true to be believable. The MMR vaccine worked by generating an immune response, so it was believable that it could stimulate an infectious process in the body. The vaccine was given early in life and autism developed early in life, so it was believable that the two could be connected. A previous study had made a connection between actual measles disease and Crohn's disease, and another previous study had made a connection between the measles vaccine and inflammatory bowel disease, so it was believable that the measles vaccine, bowel inflammation, and autism could also all be connected.[21] Wakefield had mastered Rule 1—a Set of Small False Facts. Every piece of Wakefield's narrative was just close enough to other plausible things to be believable.

2. Stokers

The set of false facts in the vaccine-and-autism story would not have had their impact if they were not widely known. In almost every case of how belief becomes fact, there is the added element of individuals who stoke the fire to get the story in front of the public. In the autism case, Wakefield was perhaps his own best stoker, but he had plenty of assistance. Somehow he got his employer to hold the infamous press conference. *The Lancet*'s editor in chief, Richard Horton, must also be under suspicion as a stoker. The journal's editors knew when they published the paper the controversy it would generate and the potential damage it would cause if it persuaded parents to not vaccinate their children. The editors should have used extra caution to verify Wakefield's methods. Richard Horton had been the youngest editor of *The Lancet* ever at thirty-three and had already been accused of taking a mass-market approach to headline-seeking.[22] The law firm Dawbars referred clients to Wakefield's study and Wakefield knew they were future litigants.[23] Parents formed groups, including Defeat Autism Now!, Cure Autism Now, Mercury Moms, and SafeMinds. Indiana congressman Dan Burton convened hearings on thimerosal, a preservative added to some vaccines, in 2000 because his grandson was autistic.[24] The *Vaccine Roulette* report in 1982 and many news outlets all contributed frightening news stories. Mark Geier, a physician who would eventually have his medical license revoked because of concerns about his autism practices and misrepresentation of his credentials, testified against vaccines in approximately 100 vaccine-related lawsuits.[25] Class-action lawyers filed an increasing number of lawsuits.

Elizabeth Holmes and Theranos

One of the more fantastical stories of the influence of stokers played out recently in the rise of Elizabeth Holmes and her company Theranos. Holmes's nearly impossible story is one of legend. She was a nineteen-year-old student at Stanford when she dreamed up the idea of starting her own company. She dropped out as a sophomore in the fall of 2003, started the company in a small office near Silicon Valley, and immediately had incredible success at recruiting people to work on her vision. After three years, she had a company of sixteen employees, including many Silicon Valley veterans, and an impressive board of directors; had raised $47 million in venture capital; and had the first promise of a deal with a major pharmaceutical company. Her product, however—a portable, desktop printer-sized machine that she claimed could process over 100 blood tests with smaller amounts of blood and more rapidly than a whole laboratory of machines—was completely fraudulent. The growth of Theranos would be even greater in the next nine years. How did a nineteen-year-old college dropout with absolutely no experience or credentials and a completely fraudulent product that never worked do that?

The answer is in large part the story of Stokers. Elizabeth Holmes's greatest power, perhaps, was persuading others of her vision. When she trained her big blue eyes on you and spoke in her baritone voice, which some claim was faked, you believed her, or at least you believed her enough to want to be around her in case she was right. John Carreyrou chronicled the power of Holmes and the rise and fall of Theranos in his book *Bad Blood: Secrets and Lies in a Silicon Valley Startup*.[26] The book begins with a prologue about the stokers who made the launch of Theranos possible. In just the first two pages of his book, Carreyrou painted a clear picture of the power of stokers.

Henry Mosley joined Theranos in March 2006 as the chief financial officer. Mosley was a longtime veteran of Silicon Valley who had started out at Intel and then ran the finance departments of four other tech companies. Mosley had been drawn to Theranos in large part because of the supporting cast of all-stars that Elizabeth Holmes had attracted. The management team included Tim Kemp, who had spent thirty years at IBM; Diane Parks, who had twenty-five years of experience at biotechnology and pharmaceutical companies; and John Howard, who had overseen Panasonic's chip-making subsidiary. The board of directors included Channing Robertson, the dean of Stanford's School of Engineering. The chairman of the board was Donald L. Lucas, who had worked with billionaire Larry Ellison and helped Ellison take Oracle public in the mid-1980s as one of the earliest tech success stories. The famous Larry Ellison himself was one of the early financial backers. Another early financial backer was Tim Draper, a well-known Silicon Valley venture capitalist who had invested in many successful startups. It was a dream team of high-profile players.

In the next few years, even more all-stars would join the company. Right before the company was exposed as a fraud, or twelve years after the company had been dreamed up in Holmes's childhood bedroom, the company had raised over $700 million in venture capital and had launched multimillion-dollar contracts with Walgreens and Safeway, largely on the faith investors put in the all-star cast. If these experienced, smart, and/or rich individuals believed in Holmes and Theranos, why shouldn't investors and CEOs?

The all-star stokers, the venture capital investors, and the CEO leaders of Walgreens and Safeway believed in large part because of Rule 1—the set of small false facts Holmes used to pitch it to them. The pitch deck of slides Holmes allegedly used in 2006 when meeting with venture capitalists was posted on the internet.[27] The pitch deck is a brilliantly concise package of a set of small false facts. The pitch proposed no new breakthrough technology and not a single patented new laboratory method. It proposed using a few drops of blood from a finger prick instead of several vials of blood from a venous blood draw. Processing for over a hundred different tests would take place inside a small machine that could sit on a desk instead of several large machines because she claimed to have miniaturized the process. The tests could be conducted anywhere because the machine was portable. The tests would take less than thirty minutes instead of days. Their reaction-on-a-chip chemiluminescence technology would be more sensitive than traditional lab machines. The results could be sent wirelessly from the machine for rapid dissemination.

The pitch deck contained no scientific studies to support Holmes's claims. There were no details on how the laboratory assays and physical equipment had been miniaturized.

Nothing she proposed was wildly outlandish. Everything she proposed was just plausible enough to be believable. Everything in the world was being miniaturized, and many lab reactions were processed on tiny chips coated with microscopic particles, so it made sense that blood processing might be accomplished with smaller and smaller components. Technology was always making things faster, so it made intuitive sense that blood processing could be speeded up, too.

All of these lies were wrapped around a heart-tugging narrative that this breakthrough technology would save lives. For example, they claimed they could conduct near-continuous monitoring of blood levels of chemotherapy drugs to avoid spikes of toxic levels that would cause adverse events. Like the NIE and Wakefield's paper, the pitch deck laced together all the small lies into a slick written narrative that sounded authentic while it tapped into our fears of survival and investors' dreams of wealth and status.

The problem, or perhaps more accurately, the fraud, was that almost none of it was true. Theranos had never been able to produce hundreds of different test results with a working model of the machine. They could not even get reliable results on a few tests from such small quantities of blood. Theranos certainly had never monitored the blood levels of any medication in real time to detect therapeutic or toxic levels. It seems that hardly anyone asked for evidence first.

Around 2006, some employees were already starting to figure out that Holmes's vision was more science fiction than science fact and achieving her vision was impossible. The small amount of blood that Holmes demanded they work with was too small for all the tests she wanted. The microfluid assay approach did not work. All of the tests she promised required different lab procedures with different reagents and different equipment, and all of those simply could not fit in a small box. The chemistry that was needed on this small scale was unreliable from the start.

Holmes tried to cover up these flaws. John Carreyrou documented in his book how Theranos fooled potential investors who came to the lab for demonstrations. A technician would take a few drops of blood from an investor and place it in the machine. In a matter of minutes, investors were wowed as a lab printout appeared on a computer screen with the results—except that it was not the investor's lab results. Theranos had such difficulty getting the machine to produce reliable results that they faked them by showing the same computer-screen printout of results at every demonstration, but they did not tell the investors that it was someone else's printout. If Holmes left a machine with an investor group for show-and-tell hype, she made sure the box was sealed with tape, and admonished the group that breaking the tape to look inside would amount to intellectual property theft. Employees who brought concerns to Holmes were fired. Fake revenue projections were created. During the company's short-lived collaboration with Walgreens, blood tests were transported from Walgreens to a lab Theranos was running secretly to conduct the tests on traditional machines, not the Theranos machine. When conducting reliability tests on the Theranos machine, employees were told many times not to report inconsistent values, calling them outliers, in order to create false reliability metrics. When employees who raised concerns would not quietly drop them, Holmes and Theranos tried to strong-arm and intimidate them.

While the cover-ups fooled many people, it is worth noting that not everyone was fooled by Holmes. Many employees tried to honestly address the technical problems with Holmes, but they were fired for their efforts or they quietly quit. At least one venture capital firm, Medventure, was not fooled. When Medventure officials asked Holmes too many questions at a pitch meeting, she allegedly walked out in a huff.

But many, many people were fooled. Investors kept pouring money into Theranos. Walgreens and Safeway signed multimillion-dollar contracts. Safeway even spent $350 million remodeling their stores for the Theranos testing stations. The military wanted to make a deal because of the attractiveness of portable testing stations on the battlefield, but was thwarted by one of its own experts who smelled a rat during the due diligence process. Employees kept pouring in, too. Despite unusually high turnover of employees who either were forced out or had the good sense to jump ship, Theranos kept growing. How were they all fooled?

They were fooled because they desperately wanted to believe in a tech company that promised to save lives. As Holmes repeated many times, her mission was to change the healthcare system and the world, "a world in which no one ever has to say goodbye too soon." When she said that with her big blue, innocent, unblinking doll's eyes, she was a figure people wanted to believe in.

Mostly, they were fooled because of the stokers. In the heyday of Theranos, the board of directors included Avie Tevanian, who was former head of software engineering at Apple under Steve Jobs; George Shultz, who was one of only two people to hold four different cabinet posts; Henry Kissinger, who was a former US secretary of state; James Mattis, who was a former US secretary of defense; William Perry, who was another former US secretary of defense; Sam Nunn, who was former chairman of the Senate Armed Services Committee; and Gary Roughead, who was a former navy admiral. New venture capitalists kept pouring in funds, no doubt because they saw this board and they saw the list of their fellow venture capitalists who had already invested.

The media, as always, were another one of the stokers. In 2014, *Fortune* magazine ran a feature story about Holmes and put a picture of her on the cover. The *Fortune* cover helped to create a sensation around Holmes as the new whiz kid on the block. In 2015, *Forbes* also put Holmes on the cover with a close-up shot of her face as she held up a tiny vial of blood. The photographer for the *Forbes* cover was to say years later that he realized what it was about Holmes that lured investors: "The facade of quiet wisdom. Eye contact from huge blue eyes that made you feel you were hearing the unvarnished truth."[28] She made *Time* magazine's 2015 list of the 100 most influential people, with a blurb about her written by Henry Kissinger. Soon, cover photos and videos of Holmes were nearly everywhere, touting her as the next Steve Jobs and Theranos as the next big thing in tech. Even though no one outside of Theranos knew the machine didn't work, stokers had mastered Rule 2 and made people believe.

3. The Power of the Clan

Why do we believe false facts so easily? Why are we influenced by stokers so easily? False facts are believed because we want to believe them, even though a part of us knows they are probably not true. But going along with the belief is incredibly easy for humans because we are designed for it.

Scholars from a variety of different fields have explored this intriguing aspect of humans, and many of them have converged on the curious idea that humans are designed to deceive their own minds. This is not a flaw of human minds. It conveys an advantage in human relations to not always understand your own motivations.

Science writer Judith Rich Harris proposed a theory to explain how the human mind works to prepare us for the social interaction that has contributed to our success as a species during our long evolution. In her book *No Two Alike*, Harris proposed that the human mind contains three systems for social interaction.[29] The systems are designed to process and store information about people. One collects data on individuals, another does the same for groups or social categories, and a third system puts the first two together to help individuals understand their place within groups.

One system in Harris's theory is the Relationship System. "Its function is to furnish answers to evolutionarily important questions like these: Will this person help me if I am in need? Does this person repay favors? Can this person be relied upon to be a fair partner in trade? Is this person a close relative? Would this person have sex with me? Would this person be a good long-term mate? Can this person beat me up? Will this person take my side if someone else tries to beat me up? Does this person like me?"[30] Harris saw that the need to manage relationships is Job 1 for human infants, and they are designed to "begin assembling a lexicon of people" soon after birth.[31]

A second system in Harris's theory is the Socialization System. Human life depends on being a member of a group. "The baby's Job 2, therefore, is to learn how to behave in a way that is acceptable to the other members of his or her society. This is the process that developmentalists call 'socialization.' It consists of acquiring the social behaviors, customs, language, accent, attitudes, and morals deemed appropriate in a particular society." [32] The motive is "to go where my group goes, to do what my group does." [33] "The first step for the child is to figure out the social categories that exist in his or her society."[34]

Harris's third system is the Status System. She thinks this system is responsible for human individuality. The child's Job 3 is to compete successfully within one's group, to strive for status, and "to be better than one's groupmates."[35] Humans "collect information on how they compare with the others who will be their rivals."[36] The motive is to maximize the amount of good things you can acquire in terms of mates, security, and resources.

Thousands of years ago, human minds were trying to explain relatively simple things: Can this person be trusted? What is my job in the clan? Where do I fit in the power rankings of about ten other people in the clan? They also expanded beyond the clan to try to understand the world around them: How does fire jump from flint? What causes bad weather? Where do infections come from? In modern times, however, the low-hanging fruit of things to explain has all been explained. We are left with trying to explain increasingly complex problems. It is not clear that our mental systems that evolved for the original problems are well suited for these more complex problems.

How does this help us understand complex situations like Bush's White House figuring out how to respond to 9/11? It helps to understand both the big and small contexts of how the individuals in that administration functioned within their clans. The administration had already committed to responding to 9/11 with vigor and attacks against the external threats. They had already invaded Afghanistan, but that was unsatisfactory for a variety of reasons. The decision had been made at the highest level by President Bush and Vice President Cheney to attack Iraq next. Given the hierarchical function of any clan, everyone below Bush and Cheney had to figure out their roles.

The Relationship System was triggered in subordinates to appear as loyal individuals. The US was in a fight, and each subordinate would naturally want to be thought of as someone who could be relied on in a fight. The Socialization System was triggered to adapt to the new culture of the group. In order "to go where my group goes, to do what my group does," the group members had to be on board with the notion of attacking Iraq.

Last, the Status System was triggered "to be better than one's groupmates." For these highly ambitious men and women, it was not enough to simply go along with the group; they were the type who were capable of leadership and persuasion. At the core level, they were not just performing their jobs for the sake of the country, they were trying to excel at their jobs to be impressive in their own eyes and in the eyes of those in their inner circle. As Tyler Drumheller explained to *Frontline*, Washington, DC, is full of bureaucracies that are full of individuals striving for status. "People want to get ahead, and the way to get ahead was to move ahead on Iraq."[37]

Bush, Cheney, Rumsfeld, Rice, Powell, and Tenet all felt an immense urgency to protect the larger clan—the American people. They also felt an urgency within the smaller clan—the inner circle of the Bush administration. They all recognized that if they spoke against a plan to invade Iraq, they were likely to be left out of the inner circle and all that that would entail.

This phenomenon describes a much older concept called "groupthink," a term coined in 1952. Groupthink has been applied most clearly to another White House inner circle debacle—the 1961 Bay of Pigs invasion to attempt to overthrow the Cuban government. Groupthink is certainly applicable to the decision process that led to the 2003 Iraq War, but groupthink describes the behaviors of individuals with only slight theoretical understanding of why groupthink exists in the first place. The Power of the Clan takes groupthink further to explain why individuals are prone to engage in groupthink in the first place and explains the origin of groupthink.

Perhaps the most telling point of the whole run-up to the 2003 Iraq War was Colin Powell's speech at the United Nations. This speech was given February 5, 2003, just six weeks before US forces would invade Iraq. The speech was quite literally the theatrical embodiment of the entire case put together by the administration to go to war. Powell could have declined to give the speech, and in fact, expressed his reservations at the time and then more strongly admitted his poor judgment years later. George Tenet could have declined to sit behind Powell in full view of the cameras, and he too expressed his reservations about this show of support years later.

Both Powell and Tenet made those public shows of support because they wanted to be team players. Powell reluctantly agreed because Bush "selected me, and I think he thought I had credibility to deliver a speech, and it would be believable. . . . The reason I went to the UN is because we needed now to put the case before the entire international community in a powerful way, and that's what I did that day."[38]

Tenet sat behind Powell because he was a gregarious personality who had been eager to be included in the Bush inner circle. Tenet had already made his infamous remark to Bush to help secure his place in the inner circle by saying the strength of the evidence against Iraq was a "slam dunk." His number of personal visits to the White House and his level of friendliness to the White House administration were in marked contrast to many of his predecessors, who had kept themselves more distant to preserve the impartiality of the CIA.

Tyler Drumheller described Tenet to *Frontline* this way: "I think he was just caught up in it. . . . It's intoxicating to be around the president, to be in power."[39] As the drumbeat kept building toward war almost as a sort of revenge for what happened to the clan on 9/11, Drumheller noted that people did things they would not normally have done. Drumheller described it as "incredible momentum, just a huge force, an irresistible force," and Gary Schroen described it as "a giant whirlpool which you can hardly get out of."[40] They were describing the Power of the Clan.

The Power of the Clan was not limited to the decision makers. In a Harris poll, 50 percent of Americans believed Iraq had WMDs, up from 36 percent the year before.[41] This poll was taken in 2006, nearly three years after David Kay's Iraq Survey Group of inspectors had free access to Iraq following the war and concluded that Iraq neither had WMDs nor was trying to make them. The American public was also concerned about safety and status.

The largest Ponzi scheme of all time

The Power of the Clan was also on display in the largest financial fraud in US history. On December 11, 2008, FBI agents arrested Bernie Madoff at his New York City apartment. Madoff was a stockbroker and money manager who had been running the largest Ponzi scheme in history. For approximately twenty years, he had been taking investors' money and telling them he was investing it in stocks when he was really using it to pay fake returns to previous investors and to enrich himself and his associates. Madoff confessed to the fraud during which he bilked investors out of nearly $65 billion and wiped out the personal savings of 4,800 of them.

Madoff not only got away with the Ponzi scheme for nearly twenty years, he got away with it while many people inside the business knew he was most likely a fraud and with the watchdog Securities and Exchange Commission being fooled by him. The SEC had investigated him in 2005 because of whistle-blower tips, three years before he was arrested, and they failed to uncover his fraud. The only reason Madoff was caught was because changes in the economy broke in the wrong direction for him, the finances of the scheme were finally falling apart, and he confessed to his sons, who turned him in to the FBI. The question is: How was Madoff able to bamboozle so many smart people for so long?

Financial journalist Diana Henriques spent a couple of years unraveling the story of the Madoff fraud and described it in her book *The Wizard of Lies*.[42] She once described him as being like the fictional Wizard of Oz behind the curtain. Madoff was able to build his scheme "only because such an extraordinary number of people decided to *believe* him."[43] As she was someone who perhaps understood the history of Madoff's scheme better than anyone, it is instructive how Henriques described it in the end as a function of human belief systems. The scheme did not work because the lies were undetected. The scheme did not work because it was some fancy and new mysterious technology that no one else understood, and they were just slow to catch up to it. The scheme worked because humans were easy, almost willing, to be fooled. "Time and again, people caught Madoff in an obvious lie and gave him the benefit of the doubt."[44] Where did Madoff get this power?

The power of Madoff's method came from the Power of the Clan. Madoff's scheme touched on key aspects of Judith Rich Harris's mental system that operate in human clans. He met all the requirements of Harris's Relationship System. Can this person be relied upon? Is this person trustworthy? Madoff had been a trusted name even before he started the Ponzi scheme. He was a founding member and former chairman of the NASDAQ in 1990, 1991, and 1993. Unlike other con artists, he was never showy. "Instead, without saying a word, he seemed to create a quiet but intense magnetic field that drew people to him, as if he were true north, or the calm eye of the storm. One associate called it 'an aura.'"[45]

Perhaps most importantly, Madoff's scheme relied heavily on Harris's Status System. The Status System compels humans to compete within one's group and strive for status. Humans are constantly collecting information about how they rank next to others. One of the principal ways to achieve higher rank is, of course, through money. Another way to achieve status is to be connected. Madoff never publicly sought investors. Everyone knew that it was difficult to join Madoff's fund, and if you were lucky enough to get in, you were part of the highest-status group. As Henriques described it, Madoff had near-magical intuition about the market that no one else possessed—"he had the decoder ring."

As a result, Madoff attracted some of the richest and most famous who wanted in to benefit from the Wizard's aura and magical decoder ring. These included well-known and powerful investors such as garment industry legend Carl Shapiro; real estate giant and philanthropist Norman F. Levy; investor and philanthropist Jeffrey M. Picower; Nobel laureate Elie Wiesel; owner of the New York Mets Fred Wilpon; former owner of the Philadelphia Eagles Norman Braman; baseball Hall of Famer Sandy Koufax; real estate tycoon and owner of the New York *Daily News* Mort Zuckerman; Hollywood actors Kyra Sedgwick, Kevin Bacon, and John Malkovich; screenwriter Eric Roth; an ex-wife of actor Michael Douglas; the heirs of singer John Denver; a foundation set up by Jeffrey Katzenberg, cofounder of Dreamworks; and one of film director Steven Spielberg's charitable foundations. This was one of the most exclusive investment clans in the world. Madoff had mastered Rule 3 and sucked in the investors with the Power of the Clan.

Why we believe what we believe

Evolutionary biologist Robert Trivers spent a considerable amount of time studying other cultures, including animals. He concluded that the underlying principle driving self-deception is the need for self-inflation. "Self-inflation is the rule in life," Trivers wrote in his book *The Folly of Fools*.[46] He noted that individuals say and do things to inflate their status in order to appear beneficial and effective to others. This seems obvious because we are social animals who depend so much on each other. Humans are essentially engaged in a constant game of impressing others, and this can easily stretch beyond truth and merge into small untruths and minor deceptions. The thing that is not obvious, however, is that we do not realize most of the time that in order to be better at deceiving others, we have to believe these things about ourselves. Trivers has become known for his conclusion that we fool ourselves so as better to fool others.

Stokers promote false narratives without ever wanting to question the details too much because when they believe the narrative they will be more effective at persuading others to believe the narrative. We believe the stokers when they describe the set of small false facts because when we believe the false facts we gain something from the transaction. Maybe the false facts coincide with what we already believe. Maybe the false facts are what those who are closest to us believe. But those explanations still do not quite explain why we need to believe what others believe.

The underlying force to believe what those close to us believe comes from our ancestors. The Power of the Clan is the notion that this underlying need to believe certain things is not a flaw or a bias of our big brains. Our brains are designed to turn beliefs into facts. *The goal is not that we arrive at true facts. The goal is that we arrive at the most useful beliefs.* Achievement of this goal represents an accurately functioning component of the human mind doing exactly what it was designed to do in ways that were extremely useful for our ancestors but a sneaky trap for us in modern society.

It makes sense that humans would have this capacity built into their DNA. In survival, many things are unknown and threatening: bad weather, bad luck, disease, and animal attacks can appear to have no rhyme or reason. Other things are simply unknown without being threatening. For example, when the early human ancestors struck a piece of flint stone with a rock, they noticed a spark jump from the stone. They figured out that they could use this to start fires much more easily than the old-fashioned ways. How could fire jump from stones? Stones don't contain fire.

Humans needed to explain these things, and our human ancestors made explanations as best they could. Their minds were designed to formulate beliefs to explain the world around them because making meaning out of life appears to convey a huge survival advantage. Beliefs provide comfort. Beliefs allay anxiety. For the unknown to stay unknown can be frightening.

Currently, the world is faced with the frightening mountain of facts that many humans are victims or disadvantaged. Despite a past century of reform efforts to curb domestic violence, prevent child abuse, eliminate poverty, and stop violence in our streets, reform efforts have hit a wall. Activists, politicians, and politicized psychologists and psychiatrists have found that the thing they can all believe in is the impact of trauma. The impact of trauma has become a key narrative for individuals who are on the righteous road to Traumaville for the purpose of influencing policies to help victims and achieve social justice. Trauma is their Iraq that they can all point to. Trauma is the MMR vaccine that is finally the smoking gun. Trauma is the Theranos that will explain it all, without asking too many questions, with magical, groundbreaking neuroscience. The following chapters describe that the trouble with trauma is how trauma and neuroscience have been taken over by well-intentioned humanitarians and weaponized to attempt to scale the wall of human nature.

The cornerstone of how beliefs become fact is our willingness, nay, our inherent drive, to believe things that do not have to be true. Robert Trivers observed a force of human nature in many cultures that we deceive ourselves so as better to deceive others. Diana Henriques saw exactly the same force play out in the Madoff scandal. Henriques ended her book on Madoff with her explanation of it all as a social game. I am not sure whether she was aware of it, but after spending years of her time researching the Madoff story and untangling how it all happened, and after 360 pages of explanation, her final sentence ended the book with exactly the same conclusion as Trivers's about human nature: "That is the most enduring lesson of the Madoff scandal: in a world full of lies, the most dangerous ones are those we tell ourselves."[47]

Chapter Two

A SET OF SMALL FALSE FACTS AND THE RISE OF TOXIC STRESS

The book titled *The Body Keeps the Score* is perhaps the most widely read book about a psychiatric topic of all time. It was published in 2014 by psychiatrist Bessel van der Kolk.[1] It became an instant best seller. At the time I am writing this, it is ranked number seven among all books sold on Amazon, and it has been ranked the number-one book in the psychiatry category for seven consecutive years.

What is so compelling about *The Body Keeps the Score*? From the start, van der Kolk portrays himself as a guru with special powers to listen and discover knowledge that his colleagues cannot see. As the book opens, he is a younger man in his new office, hanging his favorite Pieter Bruegel painting, when a loud and distraught patient is led into his office. This marks the beginning of van de Kolk's journey throughout his career to uncover that this man, and all distraught patients like him, are victims. They are victims of their experiences. The experiences they have suffered have assaulted their minds and bodies.

One of the central premises of his book, as one might surmise from the title, is that traumatic and stressful experiences permanently alter the body in many different ways. Not only do victims develop psychological symptoms; their brains are altered. Brain structures are shrunken. Neural networks are rewired. These anatomical and physiological changes can alter the fundamental self of a person. Their character is forever changed, and along with that, their very fortunes and successes in all spheres of life are altered. The trouble is that none of it is true.

The neurobiology of trauma and posttraumatic stress disorder

Trauma came into its own as a cause of psychiatric problems in 1980. That is the year posttraumatic stress disorder (PTSD) was officially listed in the taxonomy of psychiatric disorders. The creation of the PTSD diagnosis, its subsequent validation, and the development of specific treatments for PTSD are among the great achievements of psychiatry and psychology. Those achievements are not in dispute by serious clinicians and scholars. For the first time in history, the world had reliable ways to recognize and help victims who suffered horrendous, life-threatening experiences.

But from the year 2000 onward, the trouble with trauma began to accelerate. A fierce struggle would be waged to determine the true nature of PTSD and all trauma- and stress-related problems. If there was an underlying neurobiology that existed within humans before trauma exposure, it meant we are resilient beings. On the contrary, if trauma exposure caused extraordinary alterations of our neurobiology, it meant we are fragile beings. How a committed group of activists with a social agenda are promoting a set of false facts to claim that we are fragile beings in the service of trying to improve the world is the story of this chapter.

Almost immediately following the creation of the PTSD diagnosis, researchers began exploring the underlying neurobiology of trauma. I call this the First Wave of research on the association of neurobiology with PTSD in humans because the study designs were unsophisticated and cross-sectional. The First Wave of research was conducted between 1986 and 2005. Pioneering studies began with measurement of cortisol and heart rate in 1986, and then added brain imaging in 1995.

The majority of the First Wave research was conducted on Vietnam War veterans. The period following the Vietnam War was the first time in American history when war veterans had returned home and a sophisticated class of research psychiatrists and psychologists was waiting to embrace and understand their psychological problems. By coincidence, it was at the same time that advanced techniques were being invented to study neurobiology. Computed tomography scans, also known as CT scans (originally known as CAT scans), have been available since the 1970s. Magnetic resonance imaging scans, also known as MRI scans, have been available since the 1980s. The functional activity of different areas of the brain can be studied with functional MRI, also known as fMRI, which measures the amount of blood flowing to different areas of the brain; fMRI scanners have been available since the 1990s.

The downstream actions in the body that are controlled by the brain can be measured in multiple ways. The major stress hormone cortisol, which is produced by the adrenal glands situated near the kidneys, is triggered by signals from the hypothalamus and pituitary gland in the brain. Cortisol levels can be easily measured from either blood or saliva.

Heart rate and blood pressure are controlled by nerve fibers with direct connections to the brain. Heart rate is easily measured with three electrodes placed on the torso. Blood pressure is easily obtained with a blood pressure cuff. The amount of sweat produced under stress can be studied easily with small electrodes placed on two fingers. There are other types of tests, but these are the main ones that have been used.

The years during this First Wave of research on the neurobiology of trauma and PTSD were an exciting time. By the early 2000s, the field of PTSD research had accumulated an impressive set of facts to show that there was an underlying neurobiology in victims of psychological trauma who developed PTSD.

Based on this First Wave of research, evidence indicated that individuals with PTSD were different on a number of neurobiological factors compared to individuals who did not have PTSD, including size of brain structures, activation of brain structures, condition of the peripheral autonomic nervous system, and hypothalamic-pituitary-adrenal (HPA) axis function for both resting and reactivity.

The facts uncovered by the First Wave of research seem to be generally true. The non-exhaustive list of neurobiological differences that have been found in individuals with PTSD includes faster resting heart rate, larger increases in heart rate when exposed to trauma-related stimuli, smaller hippocampus, smaller amygdala, overactive amygdala, underactive cingulate cortex, and underactive prefrontal cortex. The picture with the major stress hormone cortisol is more confusing. While meta-analyses conclude there is no simple association between trauma or PTSD and cortisol, many scholars remain convinced there is a more complicated association because of the hundreds of studies that have found differences in regulation of cortisol in individuals with PTSD. The unsophisticated nature of cross-sectional studies, however, cannot determine whether the neurobiological differences existed prior to trauma or developed following trauma.

The key question surrounding this set of facts about the neurobiology of trauma and PTSD is not about whether the neurobiological differences exist. The key question is how those neurobiological differences originated. *Did those neurobiological factors exist before trauma exposure and serve as vulnerability factors? Or did those neurobiological factors develop as a consequence of trauma exposure?*

Diathesis stress or toxic stress?

The two main theories that could potentially explain the origin of these neurobiological factors associated with PTSD are the diathesis stress theory (DST) and the neurotoxic stress theory (NST). The DST attempts to explain psychopathology as the consequence of a predispositional vulnerability (diathesis) and stressful life experiences. DST has always been the dominant model for explaining psychiatric disorders. The DST, first attributed to Paul Meehl's application of the model to schizophrenia in the 1960s, has been applied to depression, anxiety, bipolar disorder, and other disorders.[2] The DST suggests there are individual differences in predisposing factors, usually genetic and biological, for disorders. In the context of a stressor, those with the diathesis are at higher risk of developing the disorder. Applied to PTSD, the DST would suggest that individuals with a preexisting neurobiological vulnerability are at higher risk for the development of PTSD symptoms following the psychological distress resulting from trauma.

The NST, on the other hand, states that the organisms' brains were both anatomically and functionally normal prior to insult, and then the introduction of toxic agents either temporarily or permanently damaged one or more functional capacities.[3] Applied to PTSD, the NST would suggest that the psychological distress resulting from trauma causes neurobiological damage, which then leads to the development of PTSD symptoms. Toxic-agent theories historically have been more useful for explaining medical diseases due to living pathogens (e.g., bacterial infections), ingested chemicals (e.g., lead or alcohol), or airborne particles (e.g., asbestos fibers). The NST is unique in positing psychological distress as the instigating toxic agent that triggers an endogenous chemical that rises to toxic levels. Variations of the NST theory are also known as toxic stress,[4] biological embedding,[5] or how experience "gets under the skin."[6]

If the DST is true, it is unlikely that the NST can also be true, and vice versa. If the DST is true, then the truth about the set of facts is that the neurobiological differences existed prior to trauma exposure and are probably caused by genetic differences. If the NST is true, then the truth about the set of facts is that neurobiological differences emerge following trauma exposure, and trauma can alter the brain.

Which theory is right may have profound implications for our society. The winner of the face-off between the DST and the NST will likely determine many aspects of public policy such as childcare, child education, public health screening, welfare, crime, justice, and other social welfare programs. The differences between the DST and the NST have profoundly different implications for understanding the nature of psychopathology in humans and what we as a society are willing and able to do about it.

The face-off between DST and NST so far has been a lopsided victory for NST. The supporters of NST have routed their opposition. A good analogy is the famous incident of Paul Revere's ride during the American Revolutionary War. In 1775, revolutionaries in Boston discovered a plot by British troops to march on the town of Lexington, which lay thirteen miles to the northwest. The British planned to arrest leaders of the American Revolution. The revolutionaries set in a motion a plan to send two riders from Boston through the north and west at night to warn the countryside militias to assemble. The two riders were Paul Revere and William Dawes. As Malcolm Gladwell explained in his book *The Tipping Point*, both Revere and Dawes set out on the same evening to warn people in the countryside that the British were coming. But their rides had enormously different results.

Revere's ride was wildly successful, while Dawes's ride was a failure. Revere rode north from Boston and then turned west, and was able to rouse the countryside militias who then put up a stout defense against the British in the morning. Dawes rode west and then turned north but had little luck in rousing the militias.

The difference was that Revere and Dawes were very different people with very different skills. Revere was apparently an extrovert who was well connected to his neighboring townsfolk. He knew the local leaders and he knew which doors to knock on to get the word out. Dawes was not as well-known or as well connected and was not effective at getting the word out as he passed through towns. Paul Revere knew these people. He was well liked and popular. Dawes was an unknown. That is an apt analogy for the contrast in the belief in the DST versus the NST. The NST is like Paul Revere. People like the NST and they like what it stands for. In contrast, the DST is unexciting and has little use for social policy change. The NST has trounced the DST not because of the facts of science, but because people like it. Because the world believes the set of false facts about the NST, government agencies, city officials, and state legislators are using it to justify spending millions of taxpayer dollars on social programs and public health campaigns to address violence and inequality.

The alleged power of toxic stress

So, what exactly is the NST theory of toxic stress in humans? Toxic stress is the theory that extreme stress triggers the release of a naturally occurring substance in excessively high levels so that it causes permanent damage to brain cells and brain circuits. By far, the most commonly cited potentially toxic substance is cortisol. Cortisol is part of the class of steroid hormones. It is the major hormone released during stress. Cortisol is produced in the two adrenal glands, which perch atop the two kidneys. The adrenal glands are stimulated to produce cortisol during times of stress by a chemical messenger that is produced by the pituitary gland in the limbic system of the brain.

In normal daily life, cortisol is useful, even lifesaving, in many different functions. Cortisol stimulates the production of glucose, inhibits immune reactions, increases kidney filtration, increases mental focus, and enhances short-term memory. In short, cortisol causes a general sense of well-being and fitness. When patients are having trouble fighting off infections, doctors give them shots of cortisol, which often produces immediate and profound improvements. When President Trump was infected with COVID-19, one of the first things his doctors did was give him a shot of a steroid hormone that is very similar to cortisol.

Cortisol production is increased during many types of normal, everyday psychological stress reactions. In these normal situations, cortisol both facilitates responses needed to be ready to fight or run and acts to inhibit other stress reactions from running rampant.

However, when cortisol levels are too high, it can be very damaging to the body. For example, in a disease called Cushing's syndrome, in which there are excessive levels of cortisol in the body, individuals have high blood pressure, abdominal obesity, reddish stretch marks, round red faces, weak muscles, weak bones, acne, skin that heals poorly, changes in mood, headaches, and general fatigue.

In more extreme psychological stress reactions, according to the toxic stress theory, cortisol is somehow produced at excessively high levels due simply to the experience of stress. The excessive levels of cortisol supposedly act as toxins to neurons in the brain and either weaken or kill neurons. The theory that cortisol can kill neurons in the brain has been bolstered by animal research with rats and chimpanzees.

There are at least two other versions of toxic stress that invoke different chemical processes. These were articulated after the cortisol-as-toxin theory and have received relatively less attention so far. They are the immune system and epigenetic programming by methylation of DNA. The details are different, but the underlying theory is the same.

The problem is that the theory of toxic stress has not been proven true for any endogenous toxin, even by the most basic standards of scientific causal proof. Not only has it not been proven true, but there has been a systematic, deliberate, and well-documented campaign to market the term *toxic stress* to try to persuade people that toxic stress is real. It is perhaps the first example of leveraging neuroscience to promote the remaking of society in line with a political ideology by well-meaning but misguided scientists and clinicians.

Much like the Bush administration's notion that Iraq might be involved with al-Qaeda terrorists, or the premise of Theranos that hundreds of blood tests could be obtained from a drop of blood in a small portable machine, the term *toxic stress* appeared out of thin air around 2000. It was created from a set of small false facts by a highly motivated and committed group of stokers. Next, I will review the research that shows that toxic stress is almost certainly not true.

The evidence

To convince people that a set of small false facts should be believed, it helps to have a sticky name for it like *toxic stress*. But more importantly, the false facts have to be close enough to the truth to be believable. I showed that earlier in the cases of Iraq, autism, and Theranos. Now I show it for trauma.

Showing that the small false facts are close to the truth has been incredibly easy for the toxic stress supporters because the false facts all come from published research. The problem with the research is that the First Wave of research was all cross-sectional designs, views taken as single snapshots in time, which cannot take advantage of the temporal sequence of events and therefore have essentially no ability to clarify causal relationships. Cross-sectional studies have no ability to determine whether neurobiological differences existed prior to the trauma experiences and perhaps served as vulnerability factors, or the differences developed as consequences of trauma and were indices of permanent damage to the brain. Correlation is not causation.

First Wave of evidence: PTSD neurobiology and ACE research, 1986–2005

The question of whether human brains can be permanently damaged by psychological trauma is really a simple question to test scientifically. The way to test it is with more sophisticated, prospective studies. Examine human brains before they are ever exposed to psychological trauma, wait for psychological trauma to occur, and then reexamine the same brains to see whether any changes have occurred. It is not complicated.

The real difficulty, if there is one, in testing whether brains can be permanently altered by psychological trauma is recruiting the individuals for the study. It would be unethical for researchers to recruit individuals into a research study and expose them to life-threatening, traumatic experiences on purpose. However, there is a fairly simple solution to that: recruit individuals who are highly likely to experience trauma due to their professions, such as police officers, firefighters, and soldiers, and wait for trauma to happen in the natural course of their jobs.

Another strategy would be, if one had enough money, to simply recruit a very large group of children when they are young and before they have experienced any trauma, and wait for trauma to happen in the natural course of their lives. However, science does not work that way. Scientists do not start tackling a question by conducting the perfectly designed, large, and expensive study. Scientists have to start with smaller, less expensive, and more rapid studies that can tell them whether they are on the right track. Science has to work that way because researchers have to work out the kinks about recruitment and measurement tools. Science also has to work that way because of funding. Funders of research, chiefly the federal government, will simply not give out large sums of money for huge, complicated studies until there is preliminary evidence that it is worthwhile. All of that makes sense.

By the end of the First Wave of research, that is, the purely cross-sectional phase, there was an impressive set of facts. Individuals with PTSD appeared to have faster resting heart rates, larger increases in heart rates when exposed to trauma-related stimuli, smaller hippocampus, smaller amygdala, overactive amygdala, underactive cingulate cortex, underactive prefrontal cortex, and a complex-but-not-completely-understood dysregulation of cortisol.

Second Wave of evidence: 2005 to the present

By 2005, some enterprising researchers had managed to pull off the new type of sophisticated, prospective study that was needed: they ran the first prospective studies that measured neurobiological factors in individuals before they were exposed to trauma. These are the only type of study that can truly test the toxic stress theory. The Second Wave included studies that examined subjects on at least two occasions, including measurement of neurobiological variables prior to trauma exposures and PTSD symptoms following exposures. These types of pretrauma prospective studies have the power, absent from cross-sectional studies, of testing temporal, and perhaps causal, relationships between neurobiology and PTSD. Although pretrauma prospective studies have more power than cross-sectional studies for understanding causal relationships, such prospective studies are extremely difficult to conduct with humans for ethical and logistical reasons.

To illustrate, the first pretrauma prospective study of neurobiology, conducted by Rachel Guthrie and Richard Bryant and published in 2005, examined skin conductance during a startle-response paradigm in eighty-seven firefighter recruits prior to their first year of active duty. The researchers assessed the firefighters again after they were exposed to life-threatening events on active duty. By knowing the firefighters' skin conductance responses prior to exposures, and then measuring changes in their PTSD symptoms, the researchers could test the DST.

In addition, by measuring the skin conductance responses a second time following exposures, they could also test the NST.[7]

In 2020, I published a qualitative review of all the pretrauma prospective research studies.[8] After sifting through 22,175 papers, I found that a total of twenty-five studies met the inclusion criteria. The twenty-five studies involved a total of 5,675 participants. Sample sizes ranged from fifteen to 2,160. Twenty-one studies involved young adults in the military, police, and firefighting. One study involved college students, two involved adolescents, and one involved children.

Six studies involved brain imaging. Seven studies measured cortisol or other indices of the hormonal stress-response systems. Eight studies measured autonomic stress responses such as heart rate and skin conductance. Four studies measured other types of molecular variables.

Overall, of the twenty-five studies capable of testing DST, nineteen were positive and six were negative. This is pretty convincing evidence that the diathesis stress theory is true.

Of the ten studies that tested the NST, three were positive and seven were negative. This is pretty consistent evidence that the toxic stress theory is false or, at the least, unproven.

My literature review was the second one to examine Second Wave pretrauma prospective research studies. Seven years earlier, Julia DiGangi and colleagues published a similar literature review of neurobiology in these types of studies but also examined cognitive abilities, coping styles, personality factors, psychiatric disorders, and family variables.[9] Their conclusion was the same: "Many of these categories, long considered aspects of posttrauma psychopathology, were actually present before the index trauma."

The central premise of the NST—that psychological stress damages the brain, alters anatomical brain structures, and permanently disrupts hardwired neurocircuitry that has evolved through centuries of human development—is an extraordinary claim. As astronomer Carl Sagan said, "Extraordinary claims require extraordinary evidence."[10] Extraordinary evidence in humans to support the NST premise appears lacking, at least in terms of prospective studies in humans.

This Second Wave of prospective research showed that the theory that trauma and stress can be toxic and alter the brain is false. To be clear, it does seem to be true that individuals with PTSD often have faster resting heart rates, larger increases in heart rates when exposed to trauma-related stimuli, smaller hippocampus, smaller amygdala, overactive amygdala, underactive cingulate cortex, underactive prefrontal cortex, and a complex-but-not-completely-understood dysregulation of cortisol, but the claim that these were caused by trauma exposure is false. The truth is that they were caused by genetics.

Belief in toxic stress is widespread

Despite the strong evidence that toxic stress is not true, belief in it is widespread, growing, and already being used to influence social policy. The notion of toxic stress has been adopted by many institutions as a powerful weapon for trying to improve American society. The endgame of trying to improve society is happening across multiple domains in terms of how we address disadvantaged individuals, particularly urban, violence-exposed children.

The widespread belief and influence of the toxic stress theory has extended far beyond scientific publications. Nearly every national government agency concerned with the well-being of children and/ or trauma has issued permanent public statements that endorse the theory that trauma damages the brain. The set of small false facts including small amygdala, underreactive prefrontal cortex, excessive cortisol production, elevated blood pressure, and so on, has become widely believed across nearly all institutions.

The Substance Abuse and Mental Health Services Administration (SAMHSA) has an entire web page titled "Reducing Toxic Stress in Childhood," which states unequivocally that when children are exposed to prolonged stress, "the body and the brain are bathed in cortisol" which "can cause permanent changes in the brain and gene expression."[11] SAMHSA also published their "Concept of Trauma and Guidance for a Trauma-Informed Approach" in July 2014.[12] SAMHSA went further and created a National Center for Trauma-Informed Care, which declared, "Trauma-informed care represents a significant culture change towards peer-driven, gender-responsive, recovery-oriented, healing partnerships. With NCTIC's help, trauma-informed care has been adopted as a fundamental framework for behavioral health systems across the country."[13]

The Centers for Disease Control published an eighteen-page document on its website titled "The Effects of Childhood Stress on Health Across the Lifespan," which used toxic stress as the bedrock of underlying science, used the phrase *toxic stress* fourteen times, and stated unequivocally that toxic stress "can lead to permanent changes in the development of the brain."[14]

The National Institute of Mental Health (NIMH) has a web page titled "5 Things You Should Know About Stress," which states that severe stress can change the way your body functions and "may contribute to serious health problems, such as heart disease, high blood pressure, diabetes, and other illnesses, including mental disorders."[15] The NIMH has even put out funding announcements asking investigators to submit research studies that study the impact of "toxic exposure" on psychiatric disorders.[16]

The US government maintains a website under the domain name of youth.gov that curates information about violence prevention along with other important topics for children and adolescents. According to this website, the primary underlying cause of crime by teenagers is exposure to trauma. The website states, "Prevention, intervention, and treatment strategies that are trauma-informed are key." Trauma is key because, simply stated, "repeated exposure to traumatic events increases the risk of youth violence."[17]

Nearly every nongovernmental professional organization concerned with the well-being of children and/or trauma also has a public statement that endorses the set of small false facts underlying the theory that trauma damages the brain. The Zero to Three organization published an eight-page policy brief on its website titled "Early Experiences Matter Policy Guide," which states in bold font, "Toxic stress damages developing brain architecture, which can lead to life-long problems in learning, behavior, and physical and mental health."[18]

The American Academy of Pediatrics has a web page titled "The Resilience Project: We Can Stop Toxic Stress," which states that traditional attempts to treat emotional and behavioral problems were misguided because there was an "underlying issue that has been missed."[19] That mysterious underlying issue was, of course, toxic stress, and the contention is that emotional and behavioral problems are really the result of maladapted neural connections in the brain that are "disrupted and damaged during periods of extreme and repetitive stress—'toxic stress.'"

The American Academy of Child and Adolescent Psychiatry has one of the more restrained positions but nevertheless gives authenticity to the toxic stress theory by stating on its website that "toxic stress in childhood is defined as severe, prolonged, or repeated adversity."[20]

One might expect that organizations of trauma specialists would take a more measured position and reflect the evidence more evenhandedly. Instead, these organizations have been the biggest stokers of the toxic stress theory. The International Society for Traumatic Stress Studies, or ISTSS, by far the largest and most influential professional society of trauma researchers and clinicians, unflinchingly promotes toxic stress. ISTSS posts a white paper in the Public Resources section of their website that states, "Disruptions in cognitive development are further observable in long-term structural and functional changes in brain regions."[21] ISTSS provides a training program that can be purchased online teaching about how trauma and stress in childhood permanently alter the brain.[22]

The National Child Traumatic Stress Network, or NCTSN, is a government-funded network of trauma-specialty sites across the United States. The very first page of the NCTSN website, titled "About Child Trauma," states that "repeated childhood exposure to traumatic events can affect the brain and nervous system and increase health-risk behaviors (e.g., smoking, eating disorders, substance use, and high-risk activities). Research shows that child trauma survivors can be more likely to have long-term health problems (e.g., diabetes and heart disease) or to die at an earlier age."[23] NCTSN makes freely available a webinar called "Understanding the Impact of Childhood

Trauma, Adversity & Toxic Stress on the Body & Mind," which relays the accepted belief that "trauma damages the brain's foundation" in young children.[24]

The main consumer organization that is concerned with mental health is the National Alliance on Mental Illness (NAMI). NAMI hosts a blog titled *What You Should Know About Toxic Stress,* which states, "Toxic stress can actually change the structures of the brain. When a child experiences toxic stress, the brain responds by flooding the body with stress-related chemicals."[25] The blog claims that toxic stress is not only a problem for individuals, it is a major societal problem because it "costs our country billions of dollars" and is apparently responsible for most of the crime in the country because "8 in 10 incarcerated women have a history with physical and/or sexual abuse." Toxic stress is also apparently responsible for much of the country's substance abuse problem because "a child that had experienced at least four toxically stressful events was . . . 4 times more likely to become an alcoholic or intravenous drug user."

Another main consumer organization, Mental Health America, published a 2014 white paper on its website with the alarming title "Toxic Stress, Behavioral Health, and the Next Major Era in Public Health." This white paper, written by three psychologists, stated as its central thesis, "We argue that behavioral health is the linchpin for the next era in public health. The argument is based, in part, on our increasing understanding of the role of toxic stress and trauma."[26] According to this white paper, exposure to toxic stress can result in the chronic release of stress hormones, which causes "structural remodeling of the brain," permanently impairs memory and the ability to learn, causes problems with impulse and emotional control, causes criminal behavior, and causes other chronic physical illnesses (specifically asthma, obesity, and cardiovascular disease), and all of these are permanent and extend into older adult years. In short, the disruptions caused by toxic stress "provide the foundation for the behavioral health and general health problems that underlie our current public health crises." In other words, toxic stress is the smoking gun we have been searching for to explain nearly all of our public health problems.

To more fully weaponize the toxic stress theory, the Mental Health America white paper implied that the discovery of toxic stress was equivalent to one of the most outstanding achievements in the history of science. According to the paper, toxic stress is just as profoundly important as the late nineteenth-century discovery of the germ theory, which states there are microorganisms in the world that can infect us and make us physically sick.[27]

How did toxic stress become so wildly popular and so potently weaponized?

Despite the toxic stress theory being false by any good scientific standard, how did its influence spread so widely, so rapidly, and with such unquestioned believability? A large part of the answer comes from the story of where the term *toxic stress* came from.

As I noted in the Introduction, it had become increasingly apparent during the twentieth century that violence against women and children was proving too difficult to eradicate. Study after study had made clear the massive scope of maltreatment and violence that was routinely perpetrated on children and women. Much progress has been made in preventing maltreatment and violence, but efforts hit a wall.

Activists realized they were never going to break through the wall unless they got a bigger megaphone. They did not have a powerful enough message that could get them to the front of the line for all the money they believed it would take to prevent all these problems. New laws and new programs were needed to support investigative teams, committees, task forces, public-awareness campaigns, and prosecutions of offenders to activate everyone in "the village."

Here is how some others have described hitting the wall. In 2005, the journal *Psychiatric Annals* commissioned a special issue on the topic of child abuse and victimization. Jan Fawcett, MD, the editor of *Psychiatric Annals* who organized the special issue, wrote an introduction to the issue titled—get ready for it—"What Happened to the American Dream?"[28] He wrote, "I believe that everyone who wants to reduce the suffering of mankind" should pay attention to this issue. He was sickened by the direction society had taken as of 2005.

Dr. Fawcett noted that experts talk about providing treatment, but the number of people who need treatment just seems to keep growing. He wrote, "It seems to me that something much bigger than what we can treat is going wrong. Instead of evolving as a peaceful, spiritual meritocracy, we are devolving to a society of seeming post-apocalyptic survivalists, polluting society with perpetuated abuse for our own gratification." Clearly, he thought a big, new direction was needed.

David Finkelhor, PhD, was able to provide the numbers for what hitting the wall looks like. Dr. Finkelhor is a sociologist and one of the foremost researchers on the epidemiology trends of child abuse and victimization of children in the US. He published a study that compared national surveys from 2008 and 2011 to look for any improvements in the protection of children. He found there were promising downward trends in some small categories, but there were no significant changes for the big categories of physical assault, physical abuse, sexual assault, sexual abuse, witnessing of domestic violence, or witnessing of community violence. Overall, 58 percent of youth in the 2011 survey had experienced violence exposure, and 48 percent had experienced more than one type.[29] Finkelhor wrote, "The high rate of exposure in children and youth and the complexity and interrelationships among the types of exposure are arguments for much more systematic, frequent, and intensive efforts to monitor the epidemiology of these problems."

All of these prescriptions for a more peaceful society and for more monitoring surveys require funding, and the tap was not open wide enough, and it was never going to be wide enough if something did not change. What the advocates needed to shout about more loudly was the continuing problems of child maltreatment, sexual assault, domestic violence, and other forms of trauma exposure. Where the shouting needed to get them to go was to governments to get more funding. The term *toxic stress* would be their Iraq with weapons of mass destruction that everybody could agree was evil.

Toxic stress is not a scientific term. It was invented by Jack Shonkoff, a pediatrician at Harvard University. Shonkoff found the way to shout louder and get past the wall. In 2000, he authored a major policy review for the National Academy of Sciences titled *From Neurons to Neighborhoods*, in which he coined the concept of "stressors that are toxic."[30] Where did Dr. Shonkoff find the term suggesting that psychological stressors are toxic? He invented it.

In 2003, Shonkoff spearheaded the creation of the National Scientific Council on the Developing Child, which despite its name is not a government agency. The council is a private group of scientists and stakeholders in early childhood with an administrative home at Harvard University and a stated mission to close the "gap between science and policy"[31] This was the group of activists that was formed to change American policies and then the world. A public report from the council gives the clear history of where the term *toxic stress* came from. The members of the council agreed to create and disseminate the phrase *toxic stress* to convey their message to the public because, by their own admission, "just saying 'stress' more loudly wasn't going to get them where they needed to go."[32]

To highlight the danger of toxic stress, they created two other types of stress: positive stress and tolerable stress. These designations were not based on validation from science. The choice of *toxic stress* was brilliant. It played on the human desire for narrative and storytelling, it indicated danger, and it played on people's emotions rather than statistics.

Shonkoff and his private council based their dissemination strategy on the growing neuroscience research. This research came partly from the First Wave of PTSD research. They also based their underlying science on a parallel development of the Adverse Childhood Experiences studies. In 1998, an internal medicine doctor, Vincent Felitti, published the first of what would become a long series of similar studies. In this first Adverse Childhood Experiences (ACE) study, Dr. Felitti and his colleagues conducted a cross-sectional study of 17,000 adults.[33] They asked these adults to recall different types of adverse events from their childhood. They also collected information on the physical health problems of the current adults. They found a positive correlation between the number of adverse life events in childhood and poor health outcomes as adults. Despite this original study and 100 percent of the ACE studies that followed being cross-sectional surveys of adult populations, Felitti and his colleagues believed they had found a causal connection between childhood stressful events and poor adult physical health outcomes. Advocates claimed that calculating one's ACE score of adverse events from childhood predicts one's risk for the poor health outcomes that are caused by this purported permanent neurobiological damage.

This appeared to be a stunning and wide-ranging connection of the long-term impact of childhood on major adult diseases. Never before had there appeared to be a connection between childhood psychological experiences and life-threatening physical diseases in adulthood. Physical diseases in childhood could of course persist into adulthood, and psychological experiences in childhood could of course remain as powerful memories into adulthood. But never had the two domains been crossed to claim that psychological experiences cause lasting physical ailments and even early death.

This 1998 study was followed by approximately twenty studies by the same research group over the next ten years with a consistent conclusion that childhood adverse events *caused* a wide range of mental and physical ailments, which gave scientific backing for a generalizability of the NST concept beyond psychiatry. Shonkoff's private council gathered up Felitti's ACE research and produced a report in 2005 that coined the phrase *toxic stress*, and since then they have pursued a wide-ranging public communication and legislative agenda.[34]

As noted earlier, the private council is an initiative of the Center on the Developing Child, which Shonkoff runs at Harvard University. A visit to the center's website reveals the breadth and depth of their outreach activities. Their resource library includes 107 briefs, infographics, multimedia presentations, lectures, reports, and guides. The ten-year anniversary report on the council describes the "viral impact" of how they disseminated their materials to legislators and other stakeholders in all fifty states, a list of their policy and legislative accomplishments all over the country, their reach into other countries, their training of council members to speak with the media, and a list of 108 legislators, state government administrators, and community leaders who attended their 2008 national symposium.[35]

In 2009, Shonkoff wrote an article in a journal called *Issues in Science and Technology*, which neatly laid out the toxic stress playbook that would be used across the country for the next ten years.[36] First, he described hitting the wall, and the massive medical problems in American children that just will not go away with current efforts. Second, he made the claim that stress damages the brain and the body. Third, he claimed the term *toxic stress* was proposed by the National Scientific Council on the Developing Child. He failed to mention that he was the founder of the council, he still runs the council, and the council is not a government agency. Fourth, all of his science arguments are used as leverage to demand massive prevention and intervention programs in the realm of public health.

Shonkoff published another article in 2009, this time in the prestigious *Journal of the American Medical Association* (JAMA), in which he reiterated the toxic stress playbook steps and wrote that "the design and implementation of new approaches to both the prevention and treatment of toxic stress and its consequences, beginning in the early childhood years, must be" a key priority.[37] He noted that state expenditures totaled $4.5 billion in 2008 on prekindergarten programs for disadvantaged children. He concluded, "Advances in neuroscience and the biology of stress provide a compelling rationale for considering the inclusion of health promotion and disease prevention as a fully integrated part" of the practice of spending billions more of taxpayer money. The main purpose of the article was to promote a narrative that trauma and stress experiences in childhood represent the "roots of social class disparities in health," and to bolster a policy agenda that we need to attack trauma to save our children.

The selling of toxic stress

Psychologist Steven Sloman has thought a lot about how humans draw conclusions from the evidence in their environments. Sloman wrote a book with his mentor, Philip Fernbach, to summarize their years of research. The book, *The Knowledge Illusion*, had a goal of trying to explain one phenomenon of the human mind: why do we think we know more than we actually do? The reason the knowledge illusion exists, and why we think we know more than we actually do, in my much-simplified summary of their book, is that the human mind is designed to believe that "what's inside your head and what's outside of it must be seamless."[38] Thus, the brain is constantly evaluating the degree of agreement between what it believes inside and what it perceives in the world. The mind grasps and holds on to whatever it can find in the external world that agrees with what it believes in order to maintain that feeling of seamlessness. But it must involve a great deal of self-deception to maintain this seamlessness when the inside and outside do not agree. As a result, we ignore a lot of factual information in the external world, and "so we frequently don't know what we don't know."[39]

Prior to 2000, the term *toxic stress* had been used in the scientific literature only to describe animals, particularly fish and shrimp, poisoned by man-made pollutants. The stress on fish and shrimp was not psychological stress. The stress was pollutants that were physically harmful coming from humans. In relation to human mental health, there had been no scientific publications that used the term *toxic stress* to reference psychological stress as a cause of neural alterations of the brain or body.

The *idea* that psychological stress could be toxic to humans, however, was highly attractive and fit seamlessly with what many people already believed. Fueled by Shonkoff and his private council, a remarkable and rapid shift occurred in the scientific and clinical worlds. Between 2000 and 2010 the notion of toxic stress causing mental impairment in humans became accepted on a massive scale. Because of the persuasion campaign by Shonkoff's private council, it is now commonplace and the theory is well accepted as fact by the majority of scientists, clinicians, and stakeholders in the world of psychology and psychiatry.

It has been amazing how, in a relatively short span of ten years, the extraordinary notion of toxic stress became accepted by the scientific and clinical communities. Prior to 2009 the phrase *toxic stress* had never been used in a peer-reviewed science journal to describe a cause of human psychological problems except for Shonkoff's two articles in 2009. From 2010 through 2018, *toxic stress* or an equivalent term suddenly appeared in the titles or abstracts of peer-reviewed science journals eighty-eight times.

In 2005, SAMHSA created the National Center for Trauma-Informed Care. An internal white paper that described the history of that program declared that national acceptance of the concept of trauma-informed care, and the underlying science bedrock of toxic stress, had arrived. "It appears that trauma-informed care has reached a 'tipping point.' While interest in trauma-informed care grew steadily from 2005 to 2010, the past 18 months have seen an unprecedented explosion of interest."[40] This explosion of interest was about to begin paying off in social engineering.

All of this marketing of toxic stress in science journals and professional organizations was just the warm-up act. As the examples that follow demonstrate, the real endgame was to influence governments and legislative bodies. That is where the supporters of toxic stress have sought access to taxpayers' pocketbooks to expand programs designed to address a variety of social disparities by targeting trauma as the cause. Around 2010, the so-called science of toxic stress had been sufficiently weaponized and the culture among many trauma experts had sufficiently changed that they felt comfortable branching into legislative change.

Philadelphia

Philadelphia appears to have been the first government to adopt the Set of Small False Facts under the guise of toxic stress at an institutional level. The adoption of toxic stress grew out of Philadelphia's long-standing commitment to modernize their behavioral health agencies.[41] In 2005, the Philadelphia Department of Behavioral Health and Intellectual Disability Services initiated a transformation of the city's mental health services in order to address high unemployment and murder rates. The keystone of this transformation was the creation of a trauma-informed system based on the premise that exposure to trauma and violence was causing these problems with unemployment and murder. The transformation included efforts to train clinicians in evidence-based psychotherapy for PTSD, and to bring together a large number of community human-service organizations to train their staff according to the Adverse Childhood Experiences studies.[42]

One of the contributors to the Philadelphia transformation, Sandra Bloom, MD, explained the grand ambitions in a 2016 webcast in Philadelphia's *Working Toward a Trauma-Informed City* series of YouTube videos.[43] Dr. Bloom methodically marched through her slide deck of Shonkoff's toxic stress playbook by explaining that (a) Philadelphia is plagued with problems of high rates of poverty, poor academic performance, crime, murder, domestic violence, and multigenerational racism; (b) urban youth are exposed to high rates of trauma and violence; (c) all of the problems are caused by violence and trauma exposure because (d) these trauma experiences cause damage to brains in the form of emotional illness, learning problems, physical illness, crime, homelessness, addiction, impaired parenting, child abuse, and impaired work performance; and (e) the solution is to train everybody in trauma-informed principles, which means educate them on the truth of ACE and toxic stress. Essentially, the webcast stated that trauma and exposure to violence are the largest public health issues we face in modern times that are literally altering human brains and organ systems, and we need massive funding for social programs to attack trauma on the order of the Manhattan Project in the 1940s that created the first nuclear bomb. Dr. Bloom literally compared their campaign to the Manhattan Project, which in today's dollars would cost over $25 billion.

A Trauma-Informed State

In 2013, Wisconsin was the first state to officially adopt the toxic stress playbook when the state senate passed a resolution that proudly proclaimed Wisconsin to be the first trauma-informed state. The resolution formally endorsed this narrative, and resolved that all of the state's relevant future legislation should take this into account. This is the first known instance of a governmental body passing a legislative resolution declaring that stress and trauma exposure permanently damage children's brains. Citing no scientific data, the resolution stated that adverse psychological events literally "shape the physical architecture of a child's developing brain and establish either a sturdy or a fragile foundation for all the learning, health, and behavior that follows."[44] The resolution stated as fact that poverty, repeated abuse, neglect, severe maternal depression, and parental substance were all toxic to a child's developing brain and caused poor physical health outcomes into adulthood. The resolution coincided with, and was probably supported by, a statewide, privately funded, trauma-informed initiative that had started in 2011 called Fostering Futures.

Trauma-Informed Cities

Tarpon Springs, Florida, seems like an odd place for a national trend centering on perceptions of violence to begin. But in 2014, Tarpon Springs was the first city in the nation to declare itself a trauma-informed city. The city adopted a trauma-informed program called Peace4Tarpon, which relied on the Set of Small False Facts as the underlying science.[45] Tarpon Springs is a city of about 25,000 people on the western coast of Florida. It is best known as a tourist destination and for its sponge industry. Tarpon Springs may have been the first city to declare itself trauma-informed simply because a particularly forward-thinking woman named Robin Saenger lived there. She seemed to be the driving force behind the city resolution. She is a glass artist who moved to Tarpon Springs in 1982. In 2005, she was elected to the Tarpon Springs City Commission and then moved up to the position of vice mayor.

When asked what a trauma-informed community would look like, Saenger said, "A trauma-informed community would be a place where folks understand initially that there is reasons [sic] behind behaviors, things do not happen at random, and that they understand that most of the issues, if not all of the issues that we face as a community and in our lives, are directly related to trauma."[46] Really? All of the issues that we face as a community are due to trauma?

Yes, apparently. She provided a comforting narrative that violent acts do not happen at random; instead, trauma is the cause of violence in our world. Once the community is educated about the alleged impact of trauma, then somehow the community will start to react and respond differently to these situations, and, one assumes, in some unspecified way, make the problems disappear. The community just needs "to recognize the true cause, the root cause of what we're looking at and not address symptoms, but address the problem," which is, of course, trauma.[47]

The same year Tarpon Springs declared itself a trauma-informed city, Bessel van der Kolk published his book *The Body Keeps the Score*. The power of van der Kolk's book seems due to its being an almost spiritual call to action. He fully embraced the false facts of the toxic stress narrative, writing that the vast riches of new neuroscience research "[have] revealed that trauma produces actual physiological changes, including a recalibration of the brain's alarm system, an increase in stress hormone activity, and alterations in the system that filters relevant information from irrelevant." Trauma has compromised the part of the brain "that communicates the physical, embodied feeling of being alive. . . . We now know that their behaviors are not the results of moral failings or signs of lack of willpower or bad character—they are caused by actual changes in the brain."[48] This is how the body keeps the score following stress and trauma.

But there was much more. The entirety of how we experience existence has been altered. Van der Kolk wrote, "We have also begun to understand how overwhelming experiences affect our innermost sensations and our relationship to our physical reality—the core of who we are."[49] Trauma leaves an "imprint" on mind, brain, and body that has profound consequences for survivors. Trauma "changes not only how we think and what we think about, but also our very capacity to think."[50]

In other words, the very core of one's existence has been altered by trauma. It almost sounds like a religious dogma, doesn't it? If it is not a religious dogma, it is at least a political dogma. Van der Kolk made an honest admission in the epilogue that he simply cannot contain his ideological fervor. "When I give presentations on trauma and trauma treatment, participants sometimes ask me to leave out the politics and confine myself to talking about neuroscience and therapy. I wish I could separate trauma from politics, but as long as we continue to live in denial and treat only trauma while ignoring its origins, we are bound to fail."[51] The toxic stress playbook has been mastered. The endgame is, he admits, after all, political.

It is of note that van der Kolk did address the possibility that he is wrong and the competing diathesis stress theory might be true. It did not appear until Chapter 10, but at least he discussed it, which is more than Felitti's group has done. In less than one page, in a section titled "Bad Genes?,"[52] van der Kolk bluntly dismissed the diathesis stress theory that genetic differences could have produced any of these neurobiological differences.

Baltimore

Then, in 2015, supporters of toxic stress stumbled upon a new, and perhaps even more potent, strategy. They discovered that when racial tension struck a city or unmitigated violence could not be solved in a city, they could move in with their message of toxic stress as the malevolent root cause that all sides could agree on.

On April 12, 2015, Freddie Gray, a twenty-five-year-old African American man, died in police custody in Baltimore. Public protests followed immediately, partly because of similar incidents involving African American males including the July 2014 death of Eric Garner in New York City and the August 2014 police shooting of Michael Brown in Ferguson, Missouri. Almost immediately, the public response in Baltimore involved large protests that eventually turned violent. Protesters were arrested, police were injured, buildings were burned or looted, and businesses and schools in the city had to be shut down. The governor of Maryland declared a state of emergency, activated the National Guard, and brought state troopers in to assist the Baltimore police.

Within days, the Baltimore City Health Department created a Mental Health/Trauma Recovery Plan.[53] Initially the plan focused on providing 24/7 crisis help to individuals who were stressed from the riots or had trouble getting their medicines due to the burning of more than a dozen pharmacies.[54] However, the plan quickly evolved into a "three-prong, trauma-informed series of transformations." The first prong was the creation of a team of professionals to tackle acute psychiatric, medical, and social service needs, sort of like a crisis response team. Second, the health department demanded more funding to create more social programs for "treatment, housing assistance, or other needs with a 24-hour treatment center" to fight drug abuse and mental illness. Third, they demanded more funding for public health programs to deliver school-based care and home-based care, and "to implement trauma-informed care for every front-line employee in the city."

The Baltimore City Council drafted a resolution in July that was aimed at addressing the underlying causes of all the civil unrest. The answer that all might agree on was, of course, trauma. Dr. Leana Wen, commissioner of the Baltimore City Health Department, submitted a memo in support of the resolution, which noted there were root causes of the recent civil unrest, and the root cause they wanted to fix was unaddressed mental health needs. The only mental health need identified in the resolution, however, was trauma. "The majority of our residents have suffered from trauma, not only from the unrest but from the decades of poverty, neglect, racism, and rampant disparities."[55] Dr. Wen included poverty, neglect, racism, and disparities as types of trauma even though they are not true, life-threatening traumas.

In order to address trauma-related problems, Dr. Wen's memo highlighted three things. First, she was seeking funding for telemedicine in the schools. Second, her department was conducting trainings with all front-line city workers on something called "trauma-informed care." Third, she was seeking funding for a 24/7 treatment center for mental illness and addiction.

On July 20, 2015, the Baltimore City Council adopted the resolution, which called on the mayor and the school system to provide trauma counseling for all children who had been "affected by the recent violence." The resolution included the same embrace of the false facts and the same type of toxic stress language that was in the Wisconsin State Senate resolution, stating in the third paragraph, "Children impacted by violence have been shown to be more prone to developmental and emotional issues and more likely to act violently themselves. This is a vicious cycle that must be stopped before it can mar the lives of another generation."[56]

In September 2015, the Baltimore City Health Department doubled down after their success in passing the resolution and developed a sixty-page plan called "B'more for Youth! Collaborative."[57] The plan, if fully funded and adopted, would eventually prevent violence by youth and reduce overall crime. The plan would shift the old "cradle-to-prison pipeline" and transform it into a new "cradle-to-career pipeline." How would the amazing plan do that? The plan acknowledged that it would not be easy. The very first sentence of the plan acknowledged that while progress had been made in the past decades, it seemed to have hit a wall. The plan stated that "while the City of Baltimore, community and faith-based organizations, and individuals have made progress in reducing violent crime, the levels of violence affecting young people remains [sic] a significant problem."[58]

The plan proposed a variety of new projects, from addressing psychological needs of physical trauma victims in emergency departments, to launching a communication campaign about teen dating violence, to pulling together community groups to create new plans to address violence in hot spot neighborhoods. Why all the focus on trauma and violence? Because of the supposed "decades of research" that has shown, as the sixty-page-plan stated, "experiencing and witnessing violence can result in a 're-wiring' of a child's brain such that survival skills are preferentially developed at the expense of learning and other social skills."[59] Baltimore had mastered Shonkoff's toxic stress playbook to pull the city out of civil riots.

The implications cannot be understated. Trauma was the snake in the grass that we just had not seen before. By identifying trauma as the danger that we could all agree was evil, Baltimore asserted, *brains could literally be saved*. If Baltimore could prevent trauma, the plan proclaimed, "structural and functional changes in the brain that would otherwise compromise a child's success and self-sufficiency can be avoided or reversed." Toxic stress always had an overtone of helping disadvantaged and minority populations, but now it became a more finely tuned message of how to heal the massive and complicated problem of racial disparity.

Federal

In July 2017, a Republican congressional representative from Wisconsin, Mike Gallagher, sponsored a resolution to embed the toxic stress theory at the federal government level.[60] The resolution used the term *toxic stress* and repeated the usual claims that it can "affect brain development and can cause a lifetime of physical, mental, and social challenges." The resolution (1) recognized the importance of toxic stress, (2) encouraged the use of practices to counter it throughout the federal government, and (3) supported the creation of National Trauma Awareness Month and National Trauma-Informed Awareness Day. In December 2017, the US Senate passed an almost identical resolution sponsored by Gallagher's colleague from Wisconsin, Senator Ron Johnson, a Republican.[61] Both resolutions were passed without controversy. Neither resolution called for any specific follow-up activities and seemed to serve the largely symbolic function of many resolutions. Shonkoff's toxic stress playbook now had a foothold at the federal government level.

Florida Courts

Also around 2017, Florida's family court system appears to have become the first major court system to systematically adopt a trauma-informed playbook. Florida has a Family Court Tool Kit with the usual toxic stress–playbook language. The tool kit described the playbook for government agencies well. First, there is the "Problem"—mental problems, health problems, violence, social problems, disability, and crime. There is the "Science Behind the Problem," which is always ACE and trauma. Then there is the "Solution"—a trauma-informed approach. The solution is ten steps for judges to follow. It is also for "judges, magistrates, and hearing officers who preside over family court cases, as well as court partners, including but not limited to mediators, attorneys, parenting coordinators, case managers, juvenile probation officers, and clerks who handle family court cases."[62]

Judge Lynn Tepper, the main proponent of Florida's court transformation, characterized the transformation as the end of a long, bewildering journey that had finally found the Holy Grail. It seems the courts had been doing it wrong all these years, but things would be different now that they understood the impact of toxic stress. Judge Tepper explained, "Boy did we blow it all these years."[63] Just as Shonkoff and the private council had intended, the courts had found their snake in the grass.

New Orleans

In 2017, a group in New Orleans executed a new strategy to leverage toxic stress in a much more specific, and perhaps deceptive, way for social reform. The local newspaper, the *Times-Picayune*, decided to write a series of articles about a football team of nine- and ten-year-old boys. The twenty-four boys, all African American, lived in a predominantly African American neighborhood called Central City, which historically had experienced high rates of violence.

I was interviewed by one of the reporters for the series. Richard Webster came to my office at Tulane University School of Medicine, accompanied by Tulane's public relations liaison. I had been interviewed by reporters many times before, and something about this was different. Reporters usually just call on the phone for a quote. This reporter wanted to meet in person and for some reason was being accompanied by Tulane's PR man. The article was clearly going to be a big deal.

After Webster introduced himself and turned on his tape recorder, he asked me if I had any questions before we started. Because of the obvious importance being placed on this effort, I asked, "Why are you doing this?" I said newspaper stories about young inner-city children exposed to violence had been done many times before.

Webster acted ignorant. He asked, "Who else has published stories on this?" I told him his own newspaper had published a story on it before he joined them, and newspapers in every major city in America had published stories about this for over twenty years. He seemed uninterested. It struck me that his level of disinterest was hiding something else, and it made me even more suspicious about his strategy.

I pressed him. What was the purpose, I asked, of one more story on this topic? Are you reporting on this in some new way? Taking a new angle? What are you trying to accomplish? Is this connected to some bigger agenda? Webster made vague comments about hoping to educate and influence people. At the time I thought to myself that Webster was either really out of his depth and was forced by his editor to do a story on something he knew nothing about, or he was really naïve about how to influence people with power, or he was really deceptive.

Webster was only interested in talking about the availability of mental health treatment. His information had been that mental health treatment was not easily available to poor children in the city. Webster was crafting a narrative that the government was not doing their job of providing free care for these children through Medicaid.

I disagreed with him. I told him clearly that accessibility to care is not ideal, but accessibility is really not the problem. Every city is a bit different, but I know the availability of treatment in New Orleans very well. I created and maintain a website of all providers, their specialties, and the forms of payment they accept. I have also trained clinicians in treatment of PTSD more than anyone else. Good-quality mental treatment is available for poor children, and it is nearly all government funded.

I do not remember whether Webster asked me specifically about toxic stress, but I gave him my opinion about it whether he had asked or not. At that time, I knew about the government resolutions in Wisconsin and the implementation of the toxic stress playbook in Philadelphia and Baltimore. In fact, very recently I had written two blog posts that were critical of toxic stress. I told him it was likely that others he was bound to interview would tell him the narrative of the toxic stress theory. I told him it was my belief that it was not true and there was research to back me up. Webster was polite but showed barely any interest in the topic.

When the series was published, the aim of the journalists became clearer. The aim of the series, called *The Children of Central City*, according to the writers, was "an examination into an often-overlooked public health crisis: chronic exposure to violence and its devastating effects on children."[64]

The central, eye-catching thesis of the entire series was laid out clearly in the first article. As soon as the premise of chronicling a boys' football team in a violent and poor neighborhood was introduced, the very first piece of information we were told, and the only piece of information we were ever told, about any risk factors that put these boys at risk for failure in life, was that toxic stress was the underlying cause of all of these problems. The journalists wrote, "*The Children of Central City* details how repeated exposure to violence alters a child's brain development and other systems in the body."[65] Toxic stress would be the underlying drumbeat of the entire series. Through anecdotes of how many of the boys witnessed, experienced, or heard about trauma and violence in their young lives, and were not offered the mental health care they maybe should have received, the series contended that the boys' brains were, literally, physically altered, and they now lived in an utterly predictable downward path of crime, joblessness, and homelessness because their brains had been permanently damaged by trauma. Webster never used my competing information in the story. My information did not fit his narrative.

The article also clearly laid out a second theme: the government was to blame for neglect of funding. If these boys had been offered mental health treatment for their trauma experiences, they would have been saved. But they were not offered mental health treatment because of government funding cuts. The series was ultimately a call for more government funding for more social programs. The authors never presented any balancing viewpoint that maybe toxic stress was not true. Webster never used my information that mental health treatment is, in fact, available. Instead, he cited me in the story as an expert who says cognitive behavioral therapy works for PTSD.

The series was heavily promoted to make a big splash—nine articles published in one week, three of them on the front page with huge photos of the children. The online version was accompanied by sixteen videos plus an eighteen-minute documentary. They obtained funding for some of these productions from the Dennis A. Hunt Fund for Health Journalism at the University of Southern California. The series was cross-publicized with stories on the daily newscast of their television partner.

The series of articles had followed the toxic stress playbook precisely, and for the first time had packaged it as a public health crisis supposedly uncovered by investigative journalism. They mixed heart-tugging, up-close-and-personal anecdotes about inner-city children with their handpicked set of small false facts. Never mind they had no evidence that the brains of any of the boys in the series had been altered or that any of the boys were actually on a course to juvenile delinquency or joblessness. The series expertly played on the fears of the public that violence, joblessness, and homelessness are not only rampant but are getting worse. They leveraged the theory of toxic stress as salvation through neuroscience that has miraculously discovered the underlying reason that all the experts agree on as the root cause. The answer to the problem was to demand government funding that has been denied these unfortunate victims to provide more and more social programs. The message: trauma and violence are the enemy we all need to agree on, and we need funding for a full-scale Manhattan Project-style social war to eradicate it.

Then in August 2018, it suddenly became clear what the journalists were really doing and why the series had been such a big deal. A resolution was introduced in the New Orleans City Council that specifically cited the *Children of Central City* series in the preamble, and stated that this investigative journalism series had described the problem that children grow up with exposure to violence, and that "researchers have found that frequent exposure to violence causes children to be in a constant state of alarm, which can result in physical changes in their brains."[66] The resolution was remarkably precise in its description of this alleged research, and stated that "these effects can be toxic to the brain, particularly in the regions responsible for memory, emotions, stress responses and complex thinking, resulting in difficulties with anger management, impulse control and the processing and retention of information." Furthermore, the resolution reiterated the ACE mythology that exposure to violence caused some of the most common and severe physical problems of adults, including cardiovascular disease, obesity, diabetes, and a compromised immune system. The social impact of all of these mental and physical problems consisted of all the problems that had plagued young African American males in major urban areas for decades, including failure in school and juvenile crime.

The resolution explicitly called for more government funding for more social programs. The resolution blamed the lack of mental health treatment on "a lack of local, state, and federal funding to support and expand upon existing high-quality programs." The resolution called for the city's Children and Youth Planning Board to provide recommendations for a master plan to prevent trauma and treat the aftereffects of trauma. They wanted a comprehensive, citywide plan to fund public health measures, provide clinical treatment, create collaboration between multiple systems, and transform early education, schools, and justice systems to operate "with a trauma-informed lens." The resolution called for specific "strategies to supplement services that are unfunded or underfunded by Medicaid or other federal programs; strategies to increase funding, including the reallocation of resources and/or the creation of new revenue streams."

The resolution was passed unanimously. The Children and Youth Planning Board rapidly went to work, and in 2019 published a 209-page report that put the size of Baltimore's sixty-page report to shame. Included in the report was an entire chapter titled "New Orleans Children and Toxic Stress."[67] Among the dozens of solutions the board proposed was a call for the city to create a permanent Children's Budget to fund all of these efforts. The report is a blueprint for creating new government positions and processes to review the policies and practices of all relevant government agencies, landscape vacant properties, remediate abandoned buildings, fund a nearly endless stream of education and marketing programs, create new regulations and oversight processes to mandate certain types of trauma treatment, and create more positions to oversee and manage how all of these projects are progressing. The report did not estimate how much all of this would cost the taxpayers.

The Appendix to the report included a sample Trauma Policy template that the council wanted every agency, organization, and perhaps business to sign like a contract. The Trauma Policy included the usual toxic stress claim that trauma causes permanent physical and emotional problems. Every organization that adopts the Trauma Policy would be committing to adopting a new trauma-informed culture, screening their staff for trauma exposure and related symptoms, and joining with other community organizations to promote the so-called trauma-informed community.

Between 2014 and 2018, more cities and counties joined the trauma-informed trend. Gainesville, Florida, adopted a Peace4Gainesville program modeled on the Peace4Tarpon program. Other cities included Topeka, Kansas; Traverse City, Michigan; Meadville, Pennsylvania; Kansas City, Missouri; San Francisco, California; Walla Walla, Washington; and Worcester, Massachusetts.

Schools

School systems were also getting into the action. Trauma-informed approaches were adopted in the school districts of Los Angeles, San Diego, and Philadelphia.[68] In 2015, some enterprising activists, supposedly acting on behalf of five high school students in the Compton Unified School District, filed a federal class-action lawsuit against the district arguing that it wasn't addressing the needs of students exposed to violence and poverty. In 2016, Missouri passed a law requiring that trauma training be provided to any district that asked for it. In 2019, the Kansas City public school system received a $2.59 million grant from the federal government to provide trauma-specific support and resources to students to expand the trauma-informed school system model.

National Policy

In 2019, toxic stress took center stage on another national platform during the congressional hearings about the forced separation of children from illegal immigrant parents. Jack Shonkoff testified before a congressional subcommittee and recited the well-worn toxic stress playbook with the twist this time that being temporarily separated from parents in an immigrant holding camp is toxic enough to permanently damage children's brains for the remainder of their lifetimes.

The president of the American Psychiatric Association (APA), Dr. Altha Stewart, also testified before a House Appropriations subcommittee, and dutifully invoked the full toxic stress playbook. On February 27, 2019, Dr. Stewart testified as the official voice of the APA. She stated unequivocally that the APA's position against separating minors from parents who enter the country illegally is based on the alleged damage from toxic stress. She said, "The reasons for the APA position on this are grounded in an understanding of the brain science that frames the 'toxic stress' caused by separation of children from their families. All children who were abruptly separated from familiar caregivers at the border experienced overwhelming stress. Some will survive without significant problems, but many will be seriously impaired for the rest of their lives."[69] She added ominously, "Toxic stress is like a ticking clock—and prolonged separation inflicts increasingly greater harm as each week goes by." Dr. Stewart used her position of national prominence, and recited the toxic stress playbook perfectly in a political context.

In addition, the American Academy of Child and Adolescent Psychiatry, the nation's largest organization of child psychiatrists, issued a statement against separating children from their parents.[70] The official journal of this organization published a list of all articles they had published over the years on toxic stress, as if this were the weaponized arsenal underlying the science of their position.[71]

California

Finally, in 2019, the toxic stress playbook was implemented with strong financial support. California created a new position called the

Surgeon General of California. The first person appointed to that position was pediatrician Nadine Burke Harris. On December 4, 2019, Dr. Harris issued a press release announcing the ACEs Aware initiative. Using funds from California Proposition 56, (which was passed in 2016 to raise the tax on a pack of cigarettes from 87 cents to $2.87, and funds many different projects), the state allocated $40.8 million to promote screening of children for ACE risk factors. The program offers training to pediatricians on how to screen for toxic stress and provides reimbursement to doctors each time they conduct a screening. Reimbursement for screenings began on January 1, 2020.

Maryland

On April 28, 2021, Maryland became the third state, after Wisconsin and California, to officially recognize toxic stress and the second state, after California, to allocate funding for a trauma-informed approach. The Maryland General Assembly passed House Bill 548 and Senate Bill 299 which establishes the Commission on Trauma-Informed Care to coordinate a statewide initiative modeled on California's ACEs Aware initiative. Funding of $362,200 was allocated over five years to support the commission's planning efforts.

The right set of small false facts can go a long way

By any measurement, the coordinated efforts of Shonkoff and his private council have been highly effective. They crafted a message and enacted dissemination efforts that leveraged neuroscience for a policy agenda to try to improve society. For decades before Shonkoff, advocates had made efforts to shout loudly and get the attention of policy makers so they might act against violence and trauma in our communities. They realized they needed a louder message to obtain funding for their goals.

It undoubtedly enhanced the stickiness of the false facts that they were about danger. Like any animal, humans are primarily concerned about survival. The prospect of Iraqi weapons of mass destruction had traction because we were afraid of terrorist attacks. The premature claim of cold fusion energy got people's attention because of the energy crisis and the public anxiety over nuclear reactor meltdowns. Elizabeth Holmes's pitch for Theranos worked because she played mercilessly on fears that we would lose loved ones too soon because we could not monitor their blood easily enough.

False facts can also have more stickiness if they are complicated and difficult to prove wrong. The toxic stress theory is relatively sheltered from criticism because it is so difficult to measure processes inside a brain, and because trauma exposure occurs so frequently along with other genetic and environmental risk factors that it is complicated to untangle them. It can be much easier to believe a simple, linear narrative that trauma is bad and ruins brains.

Scientists embraced the false facts

Shonkoff's plan seems to have been aimed at policy makers and government officials. But amazingly, belief in toxic stress has thoroughly captured the science world, too. For a phrase and concept that barely existed ten years ago, toxic stress is now everywhere.

There are hundreds of thousands of scientific papers that use *toxic stress* as a supporting rationale or a basis of discussion for their studies. For example, I searched the text of every article published in the journal *Development and Psychopathology* for an entire year. I picked *Development and Psychopathology* because it is representative of general psychology journals that might be interested in the origins of psychological problems. I downloaded all 129 articles published during the year 2018.

I searched every article for words that might be used to describe the toxic stress theory. The different words that are used to invoke the concept of toxic stress are another metric of how popular toxic stress has become. Whenever a concept has achieved some level of acceptance and popularity, psychologists often make up new names for the concept in order to stake their own claim to the concept or to put their personalized spin on it. You know a concept has arrived when copycats come up with other sticky names for it. The concept of toxic stress has taken hold so well that it is also referred to as "biological embedding," "how stress gets under the skin," "weathering," and "the differential susceptibility model of the orchid and the dandelion." When those sticky names are not used in publications, the concept is invoked with a bit more formality in a variety of other ways, for example, "stress-induced alterations of brain function,"[72] or "substantial impact on brain development,"[73] or "early adversity [having] an enduring influence" on physiology,[74] or "stress-related disruptions to neuroendocrine development."[75]

When I searched the articles for the terms *toxic, embed, skin, weather,* and *susceptibility,* at least one of these terms was used to reference toxic stress in thirty-eight articles, or 29.5 percent of all articles published in *Development and Psychopathology* during the year 2018. Within those thirty-eight articles, toxic stress was referenced a total of 133 times.

There are 2,281 psychology-related journals that are indexed in PsycINFO, which is the primary database of psychology journals. I estimated that approximately 800 of these have a similar scope of interest as *Development and Psychopathology.* Some would be relatively more focused on trauma than *Development and Psychopathology,* and some would be relatively less focused on trauma. If we take my estimate from *Development and Psychopathology* and apply it to 800 psychology journals, it can be estimated that toxic stress would be referenced in over 30,000 journal articles in the year 2018. Within those 30,000 articles, belief in the toxic stress theory would be invoked over 106,000 times.

If we multiply that estimate by the ten years that compose the decade from 2010 to 2019, and grant that toxic stress was probably invoked relatively less in earlier years of the decade, we arrive at a probably conservative estimate that belief in toxic stress would have been invoked nearly 794,000 times in over 226,000 articles. This is likely an underestimate because I did not include the newest iteration of the toxic stress theory that has appeared in the literature on epigenetics and so-called fetal programming in utero.

These are not qualified or conditioned statements of scientists tentatively suggesting toxic stress as a possible theory. These are nearly all clear, bold claims that toxic stress is fact. These are Colin Powell at the United Nations holding up a vial of anthrax, with George Tenet sitting behind him saying, in effect, "Ladies and gentlemen, these are not assertions. These are facts, corroborated by many sources."

Psychiatrist Charles Nemeroff is one of the most productive and esteemed researchers in the history of psychiatry. He has been an author on more than 1,000 publications, many of them involving brain-imaging studies of victims of trauma. During a special presentation at the 2019 American Psychiatric Association annual meeting, he invoked the set of false facts and toxic stress and told attendees, "Early life adversity is the single biggest determinant of psychiatric illness, greater even than genetics."[76] Really? Trauma is even more important than genetics? Nemeroff has actually been saying things like that since at least 1999. His reputation in the field is nearly equivalent to being a Colin Powell-like figure who is enormously respected. His PowerPoint slides of brain images are his vial of anthrax. His massive number of publications on brain imaging are his George Tenet sitting behind him.

Neuroscience and football

We have seen a similar and more recent way to weaponize neuroscience in the controversy about chronic traumatic encephalopathy, or CTE, in professional American football players. In 2005, forensic pathologist Bennet Omalu published a paper that reported the autopsy results of the brain of former football star Mike Webster. The story was sensational because Webster died at the early age of fifty after suffering years of emotional and cognitive dysfunction. He had battled problems with depression, memory deficits, and Parkinsonian symptoms. Webster had been an iron man, playing in the offensive line trenches for seventeen seasons, including one stretch of 177 consecutive games.

Dr. Omalu found excessive amounts of amyloid plaques and neurofibrillary tangles in Webster's brain and concluded that these caused his emotional and cognitive problems. This triggered an enormous amount of publicity in the US. In 2008, Boston University created the Center for the Study of Traumatic Encephalopathy and started a brain bank to conduct autopsies of athletes, military veterans, and civilians. The issue became wildly popular in the press. Hollywood made a movie about Dr. Omalu's crusade and a conspiracy involving the NFL to intimidate and silence him. People all over the country called for drastic changes to the way football was played and a total ban on youth football.

Subsequent research, however, has found weaknesses in the early neuroscience, which are detailed in former NFL player Merrill Hoge's book *Brainwashed*.[77] No one is saying chronic traumatic encephalopathy does not exist. Instead, it has become apparent that it is not as common as initially thought, it is not as easy to get as initially thought, and there has been a lot of bias in the samples that have been studied. Dr. Omalu has come under much criticism for making exaggerated and confusing claims, while using his reputation to make large sums of money for testifying in court cases. The case of CTE is cited as another example of how easy it has become for activists to weaponize neuroscience to achieve social change they could not otherwise effect.

The endgame is public policy

Despite all the faults of the activists, one might ask, what is the problem with raising the alarm about something even if that something is not completely proven? Don't we want innovative thinkers creating plausible theories? Science doesn't know everything. Why can't scientists float theories to test? The problem is that activists and many scientists have gone beyond floating theories and acted with intent to achieve specific social outcomes. The activists have deliberately closed their eyes to evidence that does not support their theory, they have refused to listen to alternative arguments, and they have stayed silent on any competing theories. They have actively promoted unproven theories as proven facts as the means to accomplish ideological social-policy changes. When that line is crossed, they lack scientific integrity.

By 2019, toxic stress had infiltrated the science journals, had become the lodestar for public policy in the US, had become the centerpiece for the playbook used by cities to respond to violence and racial crises, had become the key to unlocking $40 million from California's state budget, and had become the hammer for debating national policy at congressional hearings about children that involved stress or trauma.

Arguments for the NST

Could I be wrong? Could the NST be true and I just misinterpreted the evidence or looked at the wrong evidence? Let's look at the different arguments for the NST. An argument may be made that the effect of trauma may be different in situations of prolonged, repeated, severe, and/or interpersonal trauma, such as in cases of sexual abuse, torture, and domestic violence, and those types of experiences have not yet been examined using a pretrauma prospective study design. Until pretrauma prospective studies are conducted with populations that experienced those types of severe trauma, it is impossible to address that argument with evidence. The absence of such studies, however, makes the point that such data with those populations do not exist either for or against the NST.

An argument may be made that the studies in my literature review examined the wrong developmental period by claiming that neurobiological differences that appear to be an inherent diathesis were actually caused by stress in the womb, consistent with the NST. Indeed, there is already another group of researchers making this case. Yet, the latest review on this subject made clear how little evidence exists in humans to support this speculation. In 2017, Kieran O'Donnell and Michael Meaney published a literature review to assess whether maternal stress during pregnancy was associated with excessive levels of cortisol in the womb, which in turn might cause developmental or health problems in children. They found "little or no association between maternal cortisol levels and measures of maternal stress, anxiety, or depression."[78] They found "even less evidence to suggest that maternal glucocorticoid levels mediate the effects of maternal adversity on neurodevelopment."[79]

A further argument may be that ACE research is not generalizable to PTSD research because the ACE theory posits that chronic stress (i.e., non-life-threatening experiences such as living with a mentally ill parent) may be an additional experience that is toxic, as opposed to only life-threatening traumas. There are, however, no known prospective studies that have measured neurobiology prior to non-life-threatening chronic stress in childhood to address that issue.

How did well-meaning people get it so wrong?

While it may be considered prudent to err on the side of safety and do everything possible to protect individuals from psychological trauma, this promotion of the NST raises two concerns. The first concern is that many activists appear to have a misunderstanding of the extant evidence base. Researchers, journalists, and politicians who assert unequivocally that trauma damages the brain either do not know about the Second Wave studies or do not understand the greater importance of Second Wave studies relative to First Wave studies in regard to proving causality. It does not appear to be widely recognized that the body of ACE literature, which is frequently cited by proponents of NST, and has been one of the primary catalysts for popularizing the NST, comes 100 percent from cross-sectional, retrospective studies.

How to explain the findings from the First Wave of research?

The second concern, as I explained in my 2020 review paper on the neurobiological studies, is that it is possible that mistaken support for the NST comes from a failure to recognize that a flaw of cross-sectional trauma studies is that they violate the property of exchangeability.[80] Cross-sectional studies are case-control studies in which individuals with the outcome of PTSD/high posttraumatic stress symptoms (PTSS) are the cases, and individuals with no PTSD/low PTSS are the controls. The principle of exchangeability states that the groups of cases and controls need to be equal on all salient variables prior to their exposure to the variable of interest. Prior to exposure experiences, if a member of one group is swapped into the other group, it would have no effect on group means of the other variables at the beginning of the study. In other words, prior to naturalistic exposures, members are exchangeable between groups. As Kenneth Rothman and Sander Greenland's basic text on epidemiology noted, "Controls should be selected from the same population—the source population or study base—that gives rise to the cases."[81]

Studies have illustrated how the property of exchangeability can be violated in trauma research. A large study of adolescents in Sweden showed that cumulative traumatic experiences were strongly positively correlated with adverse family circumstances such as divorce, a parent who spent time in jail, or a parent with problems of alcohol or other drugs.[82] A large study of very young children showed that those who experienced repeated trauma had higher rates of oppositional defiant disorder *prior to* their first traumas compared to children who experienced single-event trauma.[83] A large study of adults who had been followed from birth showed that children who would eventually be victimized had impaired general intelligence, executive function, processing speed, memory, perceptual reasoning, and verbal comprehension before they were ever victimized.[84] The children who would be victims of trauma were not exchangeable with children who would not be victims of trauma prior to any experiences of trauma.

This violation of exchangeability may lead researchers to mistakenly infer that differences in neurobiology postdated trauma exposure when they actually predated trauma exposure. These studies show that trauma does not happen at random. Trauma occurs more frequently to children in families with other adverse family circumstances, children with oppositional defiant disorder, and/or children with cognitive impairments.

The principle of exchangeability is also vitally important to all of the Adverse Childhood Experiences studies, although none of the activists have ever noted it. One hundred percent of the ACE studies that have been cited by activists in every single legislative resolution and government program are cross-sectional studies. Since Dr. Felitti's initial 1998 study, his group has published more than thirty similar studies, and they all had the same cross-sectional study design. It is guaranteed that these studies violated the principle of exchangeability, but the authors never raise that as a limitation.

All of these facts point to the conclusion that belief in the NST model is premature. This review indicates that a consensus supporting the NST was initially drawn during the First Wave of research when the only studies that existed in humans were unsophisticated cross-sectional studies, and the power of cross-sectional studies to determine causality is low. The NST has no precedent as a model of dysfunction in the rest of medicine, and its popularity appears almost entirely due to the efforts of activists.

The process of self-deception

How can one group of smart people look at the evidence and believe toxic stress is real and another group of people look at the same evidence and understand that toxic stress is not real? The field of social psychology may be particularly well suited to answering this type of question. The unique strength of social psychology is that it focuses on trying to understand the social factors that influence human behavior. Social psychologists Less Ross and Richard Nisbett wrote a book that summarized the field of social psychology.[85] One of the takeaway messages of their book was that situational influences can have great power over how individuals behave. Another takeaway message was that there is a tremendously subjective nature to these situational influences. One individual can perceive a situational influence with one meaning but another individual can perceive the same situational influence completely differently.

Shonkoff and his like-minded activists saw the set of small false facts about trauma and neurobiology and decided the end justified the means. So what if it is not really true? I am not saying toxic stress researchers have conducted fraud, such as the Piltdown Man hoax or Bernie Madoff's Ponzi scheme. It is not something the Office of Research Integrity should investigate. That is what makes the false facts all the more difficult to identify and expose. They are championed by well-intentioned, honest, hardworking people who are ill equipped to deal with complex, modern puzzles.

The work of another psychologist may help explain the behavior of Shonkoff and friends. Dr. Stephan Lewandowsky, an Australian cognitive psychologist, has conducted many studies to try to understand why people embrace beliefs that are contradicted by evidence. In one study, he asked students from Australia, Germany, and the United

States about events related to the Iraq War.[86] The researchers posed three types of questions. The first type was about events that were known to be true. An example was that US troops fired on a van that approached a checkpoint and killed some women and children. The second type was about events that had been reported in the media but were later retracted as false. An example was that Iraqi soldiers executed soldiers who were captured as prisoners of war. The third type of question was about fictional events that had neither happened nor been reported. An example was that Iraqi soldiers poisoned a water supply after they retreated from a position. This third type of fictional event was included in the study to make sure that students had relatively good knowledge of the Iraq War.

The issue the researchers were interested in was whether students could stop believing in something that had once been reported as true but was now confirmed to be false. American students reported significantly higher truth ratings for retracted items compared to the Australian and German students.

The researchers did not stop there. After asking the students if they believed the items were true, they also asked the students if they were aware that the retracted items had actually been retracted. The Australian and German students who were aware of the retractions had lower truth ratings for the retracted items. But not the Americans. The American students who were aware that the items had been retracted still believed the events were true.

The researchers took it one step further. They also asked a question about how suspicious the students were about the motive for the war. They did this by asking how strongly they believed the war was fought to destroy Iraqi weapons of mass destruction. They were able to show that while Australian and German students were suspicious about the motive for the war, that is, they did not believe it was fought to destroy weapons of mass destruction, they had lower truth ratings (i.e., believed less strongly) in events that had been retracted for being false. Not so the Americans. For the American students, being suspicious about the motive for the war had significantly less impact on their truth ratings for retracted items, and so they continued to have relatively higher truth ratings and belief in events that had been retracted. Overall, the authors concluded that being suspicious was indeed helpful for acknowledging that retracted items were not true even though this tempering effect of suspicion was less strong in the Americans.

The researchers were able to come to a straightforward conclusion. Australian and German students were able to make corrections in their minds when they were presented with new information that events that had been reported as true were actually false. The American students had substantially more difficulty making those corrections. The American students could not, or would not, stop believing in events that had been retracted as false, probably because they were relatively less skeptical for some personal reasons that are not hard to fathom.

The researchers summarized at least two main findings. First, repetition of new stories can create false memories, even when those stories are later proved to be false. That is not new knowledge, and human societies have probably known that for centuries. Second, suspicious people are able to self-correct their beliefs once they are presented with information that something is false. In contrast, people who show no inclination to be suspicious go on believing false events even though they have been told they are false.

We can probably safely assume that Australian, German, and American students all have the same innate capacity to be suspicious. The Australians and Germans however, were able to activate and/or listen to their suspicions, while the Americans were less willing or able to do that. The key finding seems to be that the Americans needed to be less suspicious in order to maintain some ideological belief about the war.

Dr. Philip Tetlock is another social psychologist who has spent a lot of time trying to understand why humans believe that what they think is true. Dr. Tetlock has noted many ways in which psychological research is often driven by ideological agendas. Further, he has noted how psychologists often seem to be only partly conscious of how their ideology drives their research.

In one commentary, Tetlock cited a literature review of research studies showing that male researchers often found different results than female researchers in regard to how easily men versus women could be persuaded and how much each gender conformed.[87] For example, in one of the dozens of reviewed studies, a researcher found that females seated in a scattered arrangement in an auditorium were most likely to be persuaded to change their opinion and be against nuclear testing after listening to a speech against nuclear testing, whereas males seated in a compact, shoulder-to-shoulder arrangement were least likely to change their opinion after listening to the same speech. The researcher who conducted the experiment was male.[88] The implication is that the male researcher possessed an ideological bias (either about nuclear testing or about the sexes) that led him to unconsciously select a topic (nuclear testing) and/or a testing method (social distance) that could change females' opinions more often or change males' opinions less often.

Tetlock cited another body of research in which researchers with different socioeconomic backgrounds found different sizes of racial differences in intelligence. He also cited a body of research in which industrial-organizational psychologists who worked for academic institutions tended to report results critical of questionnaires that measure personality characteristics that might predict future job performance of potential hirees, compared to industrial-organizational psychologists who worked in the private sector and depended on these questionnaires in making hiring decisions.[89]

Self-deception is inevitable

Human brains generate hatred, lust, rage, love, joy, pleasure, trust, mistrust, sadness, and anger. Our brains see, listen, perceive, process, compute, compare, contrast, remember, conclude, decide, reason, and believe. Our brains direct walking, running, eating, talking, hugging, loving, hitting, killing, and uncountable other motor actions. Each unique brain performs variations of these things thousands of times a day. Human brains are massively complicated. No one's brain is the same as any other person's brain. We all have different strengths and weaknesses. Being rational is only one of our skills, and some are able to employ rational thinking better than others. There has been an avalanche of psychological and psychiatric research that seems to show that human minds are enormously powerful but, paradoxically, incredibly deceptive to their users at the same time.

In his book *The Tipping Point*, Malcolm Gladwell described how the individuals who make social epidemics happen by tipping little things into becoming bigger things have certain skill sets that are innate. The individuals who serve as hubs to connect people do this automatically because they have natural talents of remembering things and connecting interpersonally with others. The individuals who are influential at making things popular are natural salespeople. They have innate skills at being persuasive. The effect is that the types of social epidemics of little things becoming big things that Gladwell described are not really surprising; they are destined to happen because of these few types of people who exist in the world. The specific things that tip are perhaps not destined; it depends on circumstances and who decides to tackle certain causes.

The same might be said of the way the false facts around neurobiology and trauma were destined to be weaponized and leveraged for social purposes. There are many individuals who feel compelled to help those who are more disadvantaged in society. In order to persuade others to join them in a course of action, they must have a persuasive argument. The arguments they use internally to persuade themselves of what is true must be seamless with their perceptions of the outside world. Their beliefs must become facts, and it is inevitable that they will. It seems destined that some neuroscience will be pressed into service for policy making, whether the neuroscience is true or not.

The toxic stress activists are smart, thoughtful people, and they cannot be dismissed as flawed outliers. As I noted earlier in the book, evolutionary biologist Robert Trivers observed that we humans are constantly in the mode of self-inflation in social circles. In order to be good at deceiving others, we have to deceive ourselves. The inevitability of self-deception and misuse of false facts is one of the guarantees of human life, right up there with death and taxes. Beliefs *must* become facts in our complicated modern world. The false facts were not originally created for the social agenda. They were discovered while studying Vietnam War veterans. Researchers were just trying to understand a new disorder, PTSD. We are, however, belief engines, and the small false facts were always going to be misused. The trouble with trauma is that the goal of the activists was never to arrive at true facts; their goal was to sustain useful beliefs.

The cognitive mechanisms that allow individuals to believe false facts so easily will be explained in Chapters Three and Four. Those chapters will explain the second and third rules of how beliefs become facts—Stokers and the Power of the Clan.

Prescriptives for Recovery:
Thought and Visualization Practices

The findings of this chapter are not intuitively uplifting additions to our knowledge about the human mind. The first of the two main findings may be summarized thus: many humans are born with neurobiological differences that make them vulnerable to developing psychiatric disorders. In other words, the neurobiological differences that are so often found in research participants were not caused by what happened to them. The second finding is that humans are designed for self-deception, which creates a paradox. The instrument we are trying to understand—the human mind—is the same instrument we must use to understand it, but that instrument is trying to deceive us as we do so. Every effort to understand the human mind is hard fought, and every lesson learned tends to easily vanish. That, in a nutshell, is why psychotherapy and other roads to recovery often take so long.

- The practices that take advantage of these two findings nevertheless are practical and reassuring. When you are in psychotherapy for trauma, or in recovery for some other problem that has been complicated by trauma, or working through issues on your own, you don't have to understand yourself as a damaged product that was altered by your experiences. In fact, it will be counterproductive to understand yourself as damaged goods at all.

- Instead, visualize yourself as someone born with strengths and weaknesses. Some of those are similar to the strengths and weaknesses of your mother and father because you share the same genetic material. Some of those were randomly generated by the mixing of your mother's and father's DNA or by random occurrences in growth and development. The point is that your personality and your neurobiology were largely determined at birth. As an individual, you are robust. You are not a fragile victim who can be permanently altered by stressful experiences. Stress can cause you rough patches and knock you down sometimes, but stress doesn't mold you.

- You don't have to pay attention to the writers and gurus who have been convincing everyone that stress is toxic, your neurons were killed, your neural circuits were rewired, and the DNA that you're passing on to your children is full of harmful genetic instructions that were created by your life experiences. Don't blame yourself so much for living a pretty normal life that happened to include some life-threatening experiences. The toxic stress gurus have been telling you to imagine every negative thought and feeling you have as a product of psychological stress that has embedded itself into your body. That advice is overrated and overpromises what can actually change.

- Research does not show that neurobiology can be permanently altered by psychological stress. The cross-sectional research could be interpreted that way, but it could also be interpreted as showing that the neurobiology was different before any trauma experiences occurred. The prospective longitudinal research, the only research that can make claims about causation, does not support the toxic stress model.

- Research and clinical experience often use a concept called *acceptance*. If patients can accept their flaws and weaknesses, this is often a crucial step toward learning how to manage them better. In fact, the existence of problems without acceptance is a surefire recipe for lack of recovery. The best road to recovery is to acknowledge that you may have been born with vulnerabilities of neurobiology, such as emotional dysregulation, tendency to ruminate, or overattention to threat. You may be able to learn ways to manage those, but it can be equally productive to not beat yourself up as a failure when you can't manage them. It is better to focus on the things you can change, to maximize the strengths you do have, and to stop spinning your wheels on things you can never change. Focus on believing that you are a good-enough person who has both strengths and weaknesses. Focus not on achieving unrealistic changes in yourself by reprocessing trauma experiences but rather on more realistic recovery plans for things you can actually change.

Chapter Three

STOKERS AND THE RISE OF COMPLEX PTSD

The birth of complex PTSD

In the late 1980s, two psychiatrists affiliated with Harvard University in Boston, Judith Herman and Bessel van der Kolk, embarked on a campaign to change the way the world thinks about a certain class of people. The audience they tried to persuade was initially their fellow clinicians and researchers, but it was really the whole world. Their method was to publish and speak through the scientific channels of journals and science conferences. Their aim was to give special recognition to the experience of repeated and prolonged trauma at the hands of perpetrators. Their aim was based on an unprecedented idea in medicine that patients should be recognized by what has happened to them rather than the types of symptoms they show. Their message was that repeated and prolonged interpersonal trauma, as opposed to single-blow traumas such as accidents and random injuries, was uniquely harmful and needed our special attention. It was an attempt to weaponize science to fabricate a narrative that nurture, not nature, dictates character, and to spread a narrative about the very core of ourselves as human beings.

Herman and van der Kolk started out together in the late 1980s and produced writings and lectures to promote this message with a new disorder they called complex PTSD. Herman would soon focus it on adults, as opposed to children, and give it a new name: disorder of extreme stress not otherwise specified, abbreviated as DESNOS. After DESNOS failed to be officially recognized in the 1990s, van der Kolk rebranded it in 2005 for children and called it developmental trauma disorder. After developmental trauma disorder failed to be officially recognized too, Herman and van der Kolk circled back together and embraced the original name of complex PTSD. Along the way, they would be joined by many stokers and succeed with one of the most incredible strategies in the history of psychiatry to convince much of the world that a new disorder existed despite the absence of the most basic scientific evidence.

Complex PTSD was not discovered through scientific consensus around a body of empirical evidence. Judith Lewis Herman invented the idea of complex PTSD. Herman is a psychiatrist who spent all of her career in private practice in Boston and was also affiliated with Harvard University to do some teaching. Herman was born in 1942 and graduated in 1964 from Radcliffe College, where she had been involved in the civil rights movement and the antiwar movement. She graduated from Harvard Medical School in 1968.

Then in 1992, she published the landmark journal article titled "Complex PTSD: A Syndrome in Survivors of Prolonged and Repeated Trauma," and also a book that called for recognition of a new psychiatric disorder she called complex PTSD.[1] Before this article, her scholarly career was focused mostly on describing the impacts of father-daughter incest, including two papers published with van der Kolk claiming that borderline personality disorder and self-harm behaviors were entirely caused by childhood stressful events.

Herman had been vexed because she was seeing patients in her office and reading about patients who had histories of trauma she described as "prolonged, repeated victimization" and showed more symptoms other than PTSD. She believed these victims were being impacted differently than victims of, say, car accidents, accidental injuries, or natural disasters. Herman was puzzled because these patients did not seem to respond to treatment as did patients with PTSD following traumas that were not repeated and did not involve victimization.

With her 1992 article, for the first time, a psychiatrist had proposed a disorder based primarily on a certain class of people defined by specific types of experiences as opposed to the types of symptoms patients showed. Complex PTSD, according to Herman, applied only to victims who suffered prolonged and repeated trauma, such as concentration camps, prisons, coerced prostitution, and chronic childhood abuse. Herman wrote that "the diagnostic concepts of the existing psychiatric canon, including simple PTSD, are not designed for survivors of prolonged, repeated trauma, and do not fit them well."[2] Other experts had loosely articulated some of these ideas previously, but Herman was the first to package them into a concise, sticky narrative.

In order to explain the wide variety of symptoms these victims showed, Herman claimed that such victims of repeated trauma show symptoms of problems in more fundamental and broad personality aspects that are not symptoms of PTSD. The main justification for this new disorder, Herman stated, was that the current system (i.e., PTSD and comorbid disorders) did not capture the multitude of clinical symptoms in one disorder. Her new disorder lumped all of these symptoms into one diagnosis. Herman wanted to formally recognize a broader number of symptoms beyond those that are identified for PTSD. She created the myth that these types of patients show a "prodigious array of psychiatric symptoms" that are all due 100 percent to their trauma experiences and nothing else.[3]

She called it "deformations of personality" by an alteration of all "the structures of self—the image of the body, the internalized images of others, and the values and ideals that lend a sense of coherence and purpose."[4] She claimed explicitly that if the complex PTSD diagnosis were used, it would improve recognition and treatment for this group of victims.

Her paper provided no standardized data; her theory was based on her speculations from recollections of treating some patients. To this day, no one has published a single case report that has documented a patient's symptoms and personality prior to their prolonged and repeated trauma and then captured the changes in the symptoms and personality that fit with complex PTSD.

Herman would not go on to publish more frequently, and never conducted large research experiments on complex PTSD. Complex PTSD would never be validated by the most basic standards of scientific evidence. But because of her work on complex PTSD, she would be given the International Society for Traumatic Stress Studies Lifetime Achievement Award in 2000.

Stokers seek moral status

This type of persuasion campaign, tinged with the moral foundation of caring for the vulnerable, coupled with weaponized false facts, would follow a familiar pattern in the modern world. It was nearly exactly the same pattern of persuasion used by supporters of toxic stress who convinced the world that trauma and stress alter the brain and create massive social disparities. While this is not to equate complex PTSD with the criminal fraud of Theranos, it is noteworthy that this was the same pattern exploited by Elizabeth Holmes, who convinced investors that Theranos would create "a world in which no one ever has to say goodbye too soon." In addition, though not to equate complex PTSD with the serious implications of taking a country to war, this was the same playbook the Bush administration officials used to persuade Americans that invasion of Iraq was justified because "we don't want the smoking gun to be a mushroom cloud." Herman mastered this strategy to convince the world that helpless victims at the hands of perpetrators had their personalities deformed to fundamentally alter the core of their selves and send them onward to disadvantages of massive proportions. This crusade would be the lifelong road to Traumaville for Herman and many other stokers.

The successes of each of these persuasion campaigns were made possible by stokers—a relatively small legion of like-minded supporters who held status and respect. How are stokers so successful at persuading others to believe along with them? Why do stokers act on the belief so passionately when the facts are not on their side?

As noted earlier, Elizabeth Holmes, the young founder of Theranos, was able to assemble an all-star team. A key aspect, and perhaps the aspect that blinded these individuals to the technical flaws of the company, was Holmes's apparent moral purity. George Shultz described her thus: "Everywhere you look with this young lady, there's a purity of motivation. . . . I mean she really is trying to make the world better, and this is her way of doing it."[5] James Mattis described her this way: "She has probably one of the most mature and well-honed sense[s] of ethics—personal ethics, managerial ethics, business ethics, medical ethics[—]that I've ever heard articulated."[6]

The moral appeal of complex PTSD

Herman believed regular PTSD was deeply flawed because it was supposedly based on victims of circumscribed events. PTSD "fails to capture the protean sequelae of prolonged, repeated trauma. In contrast to a single traumatic event, prolonged, repeated trauma can occur only where the victim is in a state of captivity, unable to flee, and under the control of the perpetrator."[7] Examples include prisons, concentration camps, slave labor camps, religious cults, brothels, institutions of organized sexual exploitation, and, for battered women and abused children, some families.

The main point worth noting about Herman's definition is how the creation of complex PTSD is more of a narrative of human development than it is a dry description of symptoms typical of medical disease. She used emotionally valenced words such as *survivors, interpersonal, perpetrators, captivity,* and *exploitation,* which are not medical terms typically used to describe symptoms.

The fundamental appeal of complex PTSD is moral, not scientific. To believe in complex PTSD is to believe in a mission to save weaker, disadvantaged people from being victims of stronger perpetrators. *By supporting this mission, the believer is imbued with higher moral status. That is the true value of complex PTSD.*

The concept of complex PTSD holds the promise that there is a secret explanation for so much of why unsuccessful and disadvantaged people are unsuccessful and disadvantaged. The idea that regular PTSD is wrong feeds into the hope of a victimhood model based on the notion that there is another explanation that can provide a cause for patients' faults. It slips like a hand into a glove perfectly for the view of nurture versus nature. Instead of people being less equal at birth, they are all born equal and pristine, and it is only external events that change them. The fact that the symptoms vary so widely over nearly every domain of human functioning makes the concept of complex PTSD a complicated weapon when arguing that nurture causes all our problems.

Herman made this clearer in her 1992 book, although I do not think she understood exactly what she was doing. In the longer format of a book titled *Trauma and Recovery: The Aftermath of Violence— From Domestic Abuse to Political Terror*, Herman had more space compared to her article in which to speculate about the ramifications of her creation.[8] Her book is highly political, explicitly feminist, and straightforward about the goal of trying to influence public policy. Herman uses up relatively little space on matters of data and scientific evidence to support any part of her theory.

What is complex PTSD?

Complex PTSD deviates from PTSD in two main ways. The first is that they use completely different definitions of trauma. In PTSD, the definition of trauma is very specific and clear—the experience must be life-threatening. It can be a car accident, accidental injury, combat, a natural disaster, rape, child abuse, or many other things. In complex PTSD, however, the definition of so-called trauma is expanded to include experiences that are not life-threatening, including neglect, emotional abuse, workplace or school bullying, indentured servitude, human trafficking, sweatshop work, being a prisoner of war, solitary confinement in prison, and being a defector from an authoritarian religion. The experiences all have to be repeated multiple times and must be of an interpersonal nature, but they may or may not be life-threatening.

Research is very clear that the life-threatening aspect of trauma experiences is what causes PTSD. The experiences also tend to be sudden and unexpected. Experiences that are not life-threatening, sudden, and unexpected may cause other problems, such as depression, anxiety, or temporary stress, but they simply do not cause PTSD.

The second way that complex PTSD deviates from PTSD is that the types of symptoms that individuals can show with complex PTSD are much more numerous than in PTSD. In PTSD, there are twenty symptoms that describe reactions that are triggered by reminders of trauma, and alterations in mood and behavior that have connections to vigilance and response to stress. In complex PTSD, there are many more than twenty possible symptoms. The exact number depends on which version of homemade proposed criteria you are looking at. The extra symptoms in complex PTSD focus on various dysfunctions in affect regulation, self-identity, attachment, and interpersonal relations.

Complex PTSD is not validated by evidence

Complex PTSD has met none of the traditional, well-defined criteria that validate proposed medical or psychiatric disorders. The description of a new disorder should always begin with case reports. A case report is about a single, real individual with detailed descriptions of his or her symptoms, a detailed history that includes the absence of the symptoms in the past and the new appearance of the symptoms, the change in symptoms over time, if any, and responses to traditional treatments. The constellation of symptoms must be different from those of known disorders, and the new disorders must usually, but not always, respond differently or fail to respond to treatments that work for known disorders. If doctors cannot provide case reports of real patients with different symptoms and different treatment responses, there is no point in conducting more expensive and time-consuming group studies.

The conventional method to define a new syndrome starts with clinicians in their offices who write up case reports, then some good detective work to connect the dots that varies with each case. The discovery of Lyme disease is a good example. In November 1975, a mother from Old Lyme, Connecticut, contacted the state health department to report the strange clustering of twelve children who had all been recently diagnosed with juvenile rheumatoid arthritis and all lived close together on the same road. Investigators gathered detailed histories on the cases and then embarked on a methodical study of the surrounding area for more cases. This type of slow, methodical detective work uncovered that the pattern and time course of symptoms did not fit juvenile rheumatoid arthritis. At the time of the first report in 1977, the investigators were not yet aware that a tick was spreading the disease, but they suspected an insect or spider, so they labeled it with the temporary, generic title of Lyme arthritis.[9]

There is not a single case report in the world that shows a pattern of causation for complex PTSD. There is not a single case report that shows the initial absence of personality deformations, followed by experiences of prolonged and repeated victimization, followed by the appearance of new personality deformations.

After case reports, the next steps involve face validation to get all experts in the field to agree on the proposed symptoms; convergent validation to show that things that theoretically should be related to the new disorder are, in fact, related to the new disorder; and discriminant validation to show that things that theoretically should not be related to the new disorder are, in fact, not related to the new disorder. Proponents of complex PTSD have not achieved any of these validation steps.

Herman's 1992 paper provided not a single description of a real patient, and provided absolutely no standardized data. Yet, this paper has been cited 1,766 times (Google Scholar, accessed February 4, 2017), and complex PTSD has become one of the most influential notions in the field.

At about the same time that Herman's article appeared, changes were being considered for one of the periodic revisions of the *Diagnostic and Statistical Manual*. The third edition had been published in 1980, and the fourth edition, *DSM-IV*, was to be published in 1994. The planning committee for *DSM-IV* decided to test Herman's theory, so they helped to fund a research study. They used standardized interviews with adult survivors of sexual and/or physical abuse. Interestingly, out of 118 adults who qualified for the complex PTSD diagnosis, 113 also qualified for PTSD. Because the PTSD diagnosis captured nearly all of those who would get this new complex PTSD diagnosis, the developers of the *DSM-IV* refused to include complex PTSD. In turned out that in terms of identifying this population with a diagnosis, the existing *DSM* actually did fit them well, and they were easily recognized. The mythical new diagnosis of complex PTSD failed to gain traction with most experts after the failure of this study and the rejection by the *DSM-IV*.

Bessel van der Kolk, however, had a new strategy. In 2005, he gave complex PTSD a new name, developmental trauma disorder, and claimed that it applied to children and adolescents. There was little, if any, mention of the old complex PTSD. It was as though complex PTSD and its failures never existed. Developmental trauma disorder appeared out of thin air, based on no solid evidence, exactly as complex PTSD had appeared in 1992. Van der Kolk and his fellow stokers appealed to the planning committee of the fifth edition of the *DSM*, the *DSM-5*, to include developmental trauma disorder as an official disorder. Failing to provide the basic level of evidence for diagnostic validation such as case reports or standardized group data, developmental trauma disorder met the same fate as complex PTSD. Just as the developers of the *DSM-IV* had refused to include complex PTSD as a new disorder, the developers of the *DSM-5* refused to include developmental trauma disorder as a new disorder. The *DSM-IV* debacle had been repeated all over again with the *DSM-5* as if nothing had been learned.

To the great fortune of the stokers, there was another taxonomy of medical and psychiatric disorders that was used mainly in Europe called the International Classification of Diseases, or ICD. The planning committee for the eleventh edition of the ICD, ICD-11, had no such reservations about the lack of scientific data, and they agreed to make complex PTSD an official disorder in 2019. The planning committee for the ICD-11 was either stunningly candid or wrote with unintended clarity when describing why they would consider making complex PTSD an official diagnosis. As the ICD Working Group on the Classification of Disorders Specifically Associated with Stress explained, "The inclusion of complex PTSD is partly a response to demands from clinicians for a greater recognition of the effects of enduring severity of some post-traumatic reactions."[10]

Persuasion by stokers was more powerful than science

By 2019, something amazing had happened. A disorder that had twice been rejected by the DSM was nevertheless enormously popular. As of this writing, most trauma experts believe that complex PTSD is real even though the official taxonomy of United States psychiatry has refused to endorse it for lack of evidence. Many science writers, journalists, and laypersons who have heard of it also believe it is real, and there has been relatively little pushback about it in the media. The story of how Herman, van der Kolk, and the other stokers convinced much of the world that complex PTSD is real is one of the greatest marketing campaigns in the history of psychiatry. The trouble is that none of it is true, and it lacks the most basic scientific evidence of validity.

This chapter is the story of how a large group of respected stokers spread a narrative about complex PTSD with a set of small false facts over twenty-five years to convince the world that disadvantaged people are made that way by certain types of trauma. At some level, most likely an unconscious one, the stokers knew their mission was about persuasion, not evidence. As will be explained, their writings are full of valenced moral imperatives, narratives of saving the disadvantaged, and denigration of anyone who did not believe as they believed. The stokers had an agenda to persuade others.

In fact, because they did not have the evidence they needed, all they could possibly do was persuade with moral imperatives. Paul Cairney, a professor of politics and public policy at the University of Stirling in the UK, has summarized this playbook. In his book *The Politics of Evidence-Based Policymaking*, Cairney's aim was to summarize a general process of how to use evidence to persuade policy makers, not how to deliberately dupe them.[11] However, it seems that in nearly all cases, facts are not the most valuable commodity. Policy makers, who are generally politicians and career bureaucrats, not scientists, need information from scientists in digestible formats. Opposing groups must compete "to present the most compelling narrative," not the most-proven facts.[12] Cairney seemed to perfectly describe the situations for both toxic stress and complex PTSD: "Events are treated primarily as resources, used to construct narratives and apportion blame. The emphasis is on persuasion—in the context of uncertainty, ambiguity, and the role of 'fast and slow' thinking—rather than the 'objective' use of evidence." The stokers create events with lectures, articles, and webinars to persuade, not present evidence.

Cairney understood that in complicated situations of uncertainty, people need shortcuts to think fast, and in so doing they tend to draw on moral foundations such as caring for the vulnerable, punishing cheating, rewarding loyalty, respecting authority, and protecting families and other social groups.[13] Policies about health inequalities almost inevitably "involve moral choices about who should benefit from public policy."[14] Hence, if your narrative contains a victim class, your narrative is likely to be more compelling.

Cairney described a framework for advocacy that details how individuals simplify the world through their belief systems, engage in politics to turn their beliefs into policies, and form coalitions with people who share their beliefs. The dynamics of groupthink bond these coalitions ever more tightly as like-minded colleagues converge to act on ideas that may or may not be based on good evidence. The danger, or perhaps the intended outcome, of effective persuasion, Cairney wrote, is that "scientists may exaggerate scientific consensus on 'the evidence' when they become advocates."[15]

Cairney used the term *knowledge broker* to describe a scientist who can translate the evidence to attract the attention of policy makers.[16] While policy makers try to reconcile their own beliefs with the beliefs of the competing sides, they must rely on scientists to focus on evidence.[17] When scientists misunderstand the evidence, such as

Shonkoff in the case of toxic stress, or Herman and van der Kolk in the case of complex PTSD, this may be problematic for the policy makers.

Status and heuristics: the innate underpinnings of complex PTSD

How did the believers and stokers of complex PTSD convince themselves about its existence? In complicated situations of uncertainty, people need shortcuts to think fast, as Paul Cairney explained, when scientists try to persuade policy makers. But exactly the same process applies to the scientists when they have to make up their own minds. In all cases, when individuals must think fast, or just make any decision at all in the face of uncertainty, their minds must grasp for and draw from existing foundations.

This process of thinking fast and drawing on existing foundations is what psychologist Daniel Kahneman popularized as heuristics. In his best-selling book titled *Thinking, Fast and Slow*, Kahneman described how people make fast judgments, what Kahneman called System 1, partly through a heuristic, or what could be more intuitively called a "substitution."[18] A heuristic is a procedure to find answers to difficult questions. *A key aspect to remember about heuristics is that they are, above all, practical methods. The method is not meant to be perfect, and certainly not rational. The method is meant to be sufficient for immediate, short-term approximations in situations where finding an optimal, perfect solution is impossible or impractical.* Heuristics are, in other words, mental shortcuts that keep the brain free from being stuck so that it can focus on hundreds of more important things such as survival, reproduction, and social relationships, or perhaps just focus on more enjoyable things.

There are many subtypes of heuristics. Anchoring is one type. For example, when children were asked to guess the number of jelly beans in a jar, researchers gave the children a suggested number as a starting point. This starting number was the anchor. Children who were given high anchors guessed the number of jelly beans to be higher than the children who were given low anchors.

This fast System 1 method of thinking works with cognitive ease but does not generate a warning sign when it becomes unreliable.

This fast method of heuristics is always confident. The only way to determine whether the fast method is wrong is to engage System 2, which is a slow method of thinking to more systematically evaluate the evidence. System 2 is what we call reason, or rational thinking. The problem, Kahneman wrote, is that "there is no simple way for System 2 to distinguish between a skilled and a heuristic response."[19] The way System 2 overrides System 1 is nonsimple, slow, energy costly, and, to many people, plain boring.

Kahneman and other heuristics researchers have focused primarily on determining how well people make judgments in artificial experiments in labs. They have concluded that people are poor at making judgments, particularly in uncertain situations. These researchers have tended to conclude that heuristic thinking is a flaw of the human mind. They have been criticized for this by other researchers who do not view heuristic thinking as a flaw, but as the human mind working exactly as it is meant to.[20]

Heuristics outside the lab

How do heuristics serve us in the real world? Kahneman's research showed how the mind functions in controlled and artificial laboratory situations (mostly with undergraduate college students) but was thin on extending the work into the real world. Jonathan Haidt, in contrast, is a social psychologist who studies the psychology of morality in the real world. The necessity of moral judgments in the highly social human world makes for a productive extension of Kahneman's System 1 of fast heuristics into the real world of complicated problems. Haidt states that moral judgments are done rapidly. "We make our first judgments rapidly, and we are dreadful at seeking out evidence that might disconfirm those initial judgments."[21]

Haidt used the analogy that if moral judgment was a dog, moral reasoning would be its tail. Judgments drive reasoning, not the other way around. "Intuitions come first, strategic reasoning second" is the summary of his social intuitionist model.[22]

What issues do people make judgments and form beliefs about? Haidt's research showed that "people care about their groups, whether those be racial, regional, religious, or political."[23] The primacy of beliefs is so strong that "we can believe almost anything that supports our team." The brain is not a balanced seeker of truth. The brain is partisan, with emotion and intuition "running the show and only putting in a call to reasoning when its services are needed to justify a desired conclusion."[24]

Haidt explained that our brains are wonderfully efficient at making these judgments (or beliefs) but rather poor at seeing how they are made. In what Haidt called the rationalist delusion, humans believe "that reasoning is our most noble attribute, one that makes us like the gods," yet we cannot see how reasoning has little influence on our decisions.[25] He described other research that suggests reasoning "evolved not to help us find truth but to help us engage in arguments, persuasion and manipulation in the context of discussions with other people."

Haidt noted that reasoning functions more like a press secretary than an impartial judge. Humans "are obsessively concerned about what others think of us, although much of the concern is unconscious and invisible to us."[26] When our status with others is challenged, conscious reasoning steps up "like a press secretary who automatically justifies any position taken by the president." Our brains have only dim awareness, if any, of the steps of this process. Our mental press secretary facilitates our capacities to lie and cheat, and then cover it all up so that we convince even ourselves that there is nothing wrong here. Haidt wrote, "When we want to believe something, the press secretary essentially says, yes you can. When we do not want to believe something, the press secretary says, no you do not have to." Having faith in our capacity to reason for the sake of impartial truth makes little sense.[27]

Heuristics can fuel self-deception

The work of Haidt and others may be summarized as a blueprint for why self-deception is common in humans. Heuristics launch beliefs with a hair trigger. Rational thought rarely catches up. This understanding of our minds is consistent with the work of nonpsychologists in other fields. Robert Trivers explored the topic as a biologist in his book *The Folly of Fools: The Logic of Deceit and Self-Deception in Human Life*. Trivers examined self-deception in animals, sex, disasters, war, and religion. His conclusion was this: "The central claim of this book is that self-deception evolves in the service of deception—the better to fool others."[28] Trivers concluded that there is no deeper theory to explain self-deception beyond the need for deception in our social lives.

Michelle Baddeley explored the topic as an economist in her book *Copycats & Contrarians: Why We Follow Others . . . and When We Don't*. Baddeley approached the topic with the rather narrow purpose of explaining why we follow others, or why we tend to act in herds. Her main conclusion is that we act out of self-interest to raise our own stature. Whether we are conformists going along with the herd or mavericks who are rebelling against the herd, "both types are rationally maximizing their own self-interest—they just balance the incentives to come up with a different sort of decision."[29]

Trivers and Baddeley may not agree on the underlying cause of our need for self-deception, but it seems that it must be largely, or perhaps completely, innate. The ultimate explanation of our tendency to act out of self-interest is most likely found in our genes. In his 1976 book *The Selfish Gene*, which some have called the most influential science book of all time, biologist Richard Dawkins used the term *selfish gene* as a shortcut to claim that the behaviors of humans to reproduce and act preferably toward their closer relatives is embedded at the genetic level.[30] Dawkins received enormous backlash from critics who, upon reading *The Selfish Gene*, were outraged to be told they were not inherently altruistic beings.[31]

Instincts, heuristics, and trauma

How does this apply to trauma? It is of somewhat secondary importance whether your beliefs help unfortunate victims you appear to be trying to help. In fact, your actions driven by your beliefs may actually hinder the victims you are trying to help, while your beliefs may actually help only yourself. There are three real reasons the activists went to battle for complex PTSD, all of which had nothing to do with science.

1. **Enhance their moral status**: To enhance their moral status, activists made a very public show of trying to help a class of disadvantaged victims. In order to provide a target for their own efforts and those of fellow stokers, they needed to have vulnerable victims designated as a special class.

2. **Define and justify the victim class**: To define this class, the activists set their sights on a particular type of trauma experience they called interpersonal, or polyvictimization, trauma that occurred at the hands of stronger perpetrators. To justify the uniqueness of this class, they were forced to attempt to scientifically explain why these victims had different symptoms than individuals with PTSD.

3. **Seize on anything that amplifies the victims' disadvantaged status**: One way to amplify the victims' disadvantaged status was to redefine the etiology of personality disorders, one of the most permanent and lifelong psychiatric conditions, as being a consequence of repeated and prolonged interpersonal trauma. The stokers created the narrative that this vast array of symptoms was caused by nurture, that is, trauma, as opposed to nature. They created the narrative that complex PTSD not only causes a vast array of symptoms but also explains a wide swath of social disparities found in disadvantaged populations in society.

Of these three reasons, the reason that gives the activists the most direct personal benefit, and the one that kick-starts the other two reasons into action, is the need to enhance one's moral status. Once the need for moral status is invoked within the mind, the mind must find something for which to battle that gives the person moral status among his or her peers and in his or her own mind.

Heuristics were the mechanism that came into play to rapidly and unconsciously find a class of disadvantaged victims who needed the most help. To be clear, heuristics were not the cause of the entire effort; they were simply the mechanism to guide it to a certain conclusion.

The cognitive guideposts for moral thinking for many people are often about helping disadvantaged people. Who are the disadvantaged people? Those are the people who suffer victimization at the hands of stronger perpetrators.

Next, the way to supercharge this mission, and thereby supercharge the activists' moral status, is to find a narrative that describes the victims as not just a little bit disadvantaged, but as massively, comprehensively, and permanently damaged goods. That is accomplished by saying all the symptoms and all the social disadvantages these victims suffer are caused by what happened to them. A key piece of this narrative is the simultaneous claim that they are not born disadvantaged. Instead, they were born equal to everyone else. All of their disparities are because of the interpersonal victimization they suffered at the hands of stronger perpetrators.

The natural argument in the sciences that gets automatically triggered for this narrative is the age-old debate of nature versus nurture. For the believers of complex PTSD to convince others, and to convince themselves, they must believe nurture is a far stronger force than nature, and perhaps the only force worth considering that molds character. In other words, people are not born unequal; they are made unequal by external events. This belief is doubly effective for elevating moral status because at the same time it does so for those who believe, it can diminish the moral status of those who do not believe. As will be explained later, those who do not believe this argument have been repeatedly accused of causing additional harm to victims by denying them the help they allegedly need.

In this explanation, (1) a cognitive instinct, the need for self-inflation through moral status, appears to be the underlying driving force, (2) which then finds its cognitive guideposts from heuristics to focus on the disadvantaged as a certain class of interpersonal trauma victim, (3) which then uses another heuristic to supercharge the issues by automatically triggering nurture explanations over nature explanations. All of these cognitive processes get cemented in place by the workings of the mind as a belief engine, and the inevitability of ignoring facts in favor of having the most useful beliefs. These three steps are fleshed out next.

1. Enhance their moral status

As noted previously, in order for the activists to enhance their moral status, there must be a hidden victim class that needs rescuing. Enhancement of status appears to be the underlying driving force. This gives clinicians moral status to themselves and among their peers and positions them squarely on the road to Traumaville. A strategy of rescuing a hidden victim class serves the dual functions of raising your own status while lowering the status of those who disagree with you.

> I imagine that the unconscious narrative inside the brain of a believer in complex PTSD goes something like this: We believers in complex PTSD are morally superior humans compared to our peers because we are better at identifying the hidden victims. When the victims are rejected by incompetent professionals, they are ostracized from society and their dysfunctions deepen; this explains their victimhood and nearly all of the disparities within society.

This mode of thinking was first articulated clearly in Herman's 1992 article, which would be referenced hundreds of times by future stokers. She claimed that this special class of victims was hidden to most professionals, and the moral failure of these professionals to see them causes further harm.

This was a fundamental principle that all future stokers would copy—the notion that one of the key problems is that this special class of victims appears to be hidden to most professionals. Ignorant professionals in particular fail to recognize that repeated trauma could cause personality deformations. According to Herman, "Misapplication of the concept of personality disorder may be the most stigmatizing diagnostic mistake."[32] This idea was echoed by van der Kolk, who wrote in his 2005 reworking of complex PTSD as developmental trauma disorder: "When professionals are unaware of children's need to adjust to traumatizing environments and expect that children should behave in accordance with adult standards of self-determination and autonomous, rational choices, these maladaptive behaviors tend to inspire revulsion and rejection."[33]

There is, however, no evidence that patients with complex PTSD are harmed in any way from being treated by clinicians who attempt to treat their PTSD.

It is instructive to look more closely at Herman's scientific contributions even before her landmark 1992 paper because they tell us two things, and they illustrate at the earliest stages what the complex PTSD campaign is really all about. First, the bulk of her early papers were about defining people by what happened to them rather than what their symptoms were. Nearly all of her papers prior to 1992 that she wrote as first author were qualitative descriptions about father-daughter incest and how to help its victims.

Trying to define people by what happened to them rather than by what symptoms they show or how they respond to treatment seems, in retrospect, inevitable once the PTSD diagnosis was formalized in 1980. Once a disorder like PTSD was identified—a diagnosis that includes an event as part of the diagnostic criteria, which it needed to do—it was inevitable that clinicians and researchers would dive deeper and ask whether certain types of trauma events had different consequences than other types of trauma events. This is natural and appropriate. However, the imbalance of how this occurred is what is troubling. All of the efforts have been geared toward interpersonal, repeated victimizations at the hands of perpetrators, such as rape, violence, and childhood abuse. None of the attempts have been focused on understanding motor vehicle accident trauma, accidental injury trauma, workplace accident trauma, or natural disaster trauma. All of the events that happen at random in the world did not seem worthy of special consideration.

Second, Herman teamed up with van der Kolk in 1989 and 1991 for two papers on self-destructive behaviors such as those seen primarily in persons with borderline personality disorder.[34] These papers had the intention of defining personality disorders as consequences of nurture rather than nature.

Herman's work never advanced to more-rigorous group studies or standardized assessments or clinical trials. Her role was more that of someone sounding an alarm and leaving the heavy-lifting research that is needed for scientific progress to others. That is a fine role. There is nothing wrong with that role. But sounding an alarm with qualitative stories cannot be considered the end of research to make definitive conclusions about a topic. The heavy-lifting research has to follow for the alarms to be considered anything more than speculative theories.

After the rejection of DESNOS by the *DSM-IV* committee in 1993, Herman went silent. She published only two journal papers as a first author in the next twenty-five years. She was, after all, not really a researcher. She was a private-practice clinician who did not have the skill or desire for the heavy lifting of research. However, she was about to receive an enormous amount of help from a small army of stokers who were researchers.

Stokers find their spiritual footing

In contrast to Herman, Bessel van der Kolk was one of the most distinguished researchers in the trauma field. He had founded the Trauma Center in Boston in 1982. He had been president of the International Society of Traumatic Stress Studies in 1990–1991. He had been part of the investigative team in the 1994 DESNOS field trial. He was not about to give up, and he invented a new plan to get attention.

After the debacle with the *DSM-IV*, the mythical new diagnosis of complex PTSD failed to gain traction with most experts after the 1994 study. Few researchers wrote about DESNOS, and no funded studies were conducted. DESNOS and complex PTSD seemed to be dying a death by being ignored.

In 2005, van der Kolk, who is not a child psychiatrist, repackaged complex PTSD as a disorder of children and adolescents, which he christened developmental trauma disorder.[35] Recycling many of the same arguments that Herman had used for complex PTSD, van der Kolk claimed that children were being diagnosed with inadequate and misleading diagnoses from the *DSM-IV*, which led to them receiving the wrong treatments.

The lack of evidence for harm to patients did not seem to slow down the stokers. In fact, if anything, the lack of evidence makes it easier for stokers to scream more loudly. As we saw with the run-up to the Iraq War in 2002–2003, the inability to properly investigate the situation on the ground actually made it easier for the Bush administration to make unsubstantiated claims about false facts. In 2005, when van der Kolk published his redefinition of complex PTSD for children, he made a clarion call for large-scale and urgent social action. He asserted, in the absence of facts, "Childhood trauma, including abuse and neglect, is probably our nation's single most important public health challenge, a challenge that has the potential to be largely resolved by appropriate prevention and intervention."[36] He yoked repeated and prolonged interpersonal trauma to the toxic stress narrative, and claimed that childhood trauma makes profound alterations of both "the mind and the brain." Furthermore, this hidden public epidemic is the cause of many other social disparities: "Developmental trauma sets the stage for unfocused responses to subsequent stress, leading to dramatic increases in the use of medical, correctional, social, and mental health services."[37]

A commentary coauthored by a group of stokers in 2012 made it explicit again that the new diagnosis was needed in order to drive social policy. In an article titled "Understanding Interpersonal Trauma in Children: Why We Need a Developmentally Appropriate Trauma Diagnosis," the stokers—Wendy D'Andrea, Julian Ford, Bradley Stolbach, Joseph Spinazzola, and Bessel van der Kolk—explicitly stated this new diagnosis was needed because "unfortunately, it may be the case of current events that a broad, but accurate, categorical diagnosis to describe developmental posttraumatic adaptations is a necessary step in moving toward more transactional frameworks."[38] It was never made clear what "moving toward transactional frameworks" meant exactly, but it had something important to do with preventing juvenile delinquency and aggression. It is noteworthy that diagnoses are not created in other branches of medicine—say, for cancer or heart disease—in order to drive social policy.

As the concept of complex PTSD gained increasing acceptance, other groups of stokers published a steady stream of studies that linked complex PTSD to more and more types of experiences. One study linked complex PTSD to individuals in jails, implying their trauma histories caused them to become violent criminals.[39] Another study implied that complex PTSD caused adolescents to become gang members who engaged in a spiral of juvenile delinquency and drug dealing.[40] Individuals with complex PTSD were found in another study in, of all places, the surprisingly traumatic society of Finland; complex trauma caused young people to grow up to become violent offenders.[41] Other studies found complex PTSD in civilians caught in the crossfire of the war in Kosovo, prisoners of war from the 1973 Yom Kippur War between Arabs and Israelis, and incarcerated women.[42]

The stokers seemed to show no caution about publishing entire books on the subject. In 2014, psychologist Christine Courtois wrote a book with the title of the movement's catchphrase: *It's Not You, It's What Happened to You.*[43] The subtitle was *Complex Trauma and Treatment.* The slim book was basically an extended version of descriptions of the massive array of symptoms and the unique treatment approach that is supposedly necessary but is not grounded in science. To date, stokers have published over fifteen books on complex PTSD.

Attacks on the moral status of opponents

Stokers also mastered the status game of tarnishing the status of those who disagreed with their agenda. The stokers seemed to intuitively understand the importance of personal tarnishing because the bad-mouthing was evident in the earliest writings on complex PTSD. Herman wrote, "Failure to recognize this syndrome" of complex PTSD by mental health clinicians contributed to the victims' misery. Herman even had the audacity to throw down the gauntlet of the Nazi Holocaust as a warning shot to those who would disagree with her. If clinicians deny the existence of complex PTSD, it is akin to blaming the passivity of Jews for having complicity in their fate.[44]

Julian Ford asserted in 1998 that traditional psychotherapy for PTSD "may inadvertently expose patients with DESNOS to overwhelming affects," which retraumatizes them in therapy sessions and causes them to dissociate.[45] Van der Kolk and Courtois wrote in their 2005 editorial that clinicians "may, in fact, be harmful" if they fail to diagnose complex PTSD and instead diagnose them with regular PTSD.[46]

In 2012, Judith Herman rose from her solitude of private practice in Boston to forge a heated reply to researchers who challenged complex PTSD. Psychologist Patricia Resick had led a group of researchers in critiquing a major trial of a new complex PTSD treatment, and they had thoroughly dismantled the poorly conceived study.[47] Herman, who had not been part of the maligned study, retorted, "Although a comprehensive and even-handed review of the literature on complex posttraumatic stress disorder (CPTSD) would be very timely and useful, unfortunately, in my opinion, the Resick et al. (2012) review is neither comprehensive nor even-handed. Rather, it reads like a position paper, marshaling whatever arguments it can against inclusion of CPTSD as a distinct subtype in the DSM-5."[48] The irony is amazing that Judith Herman, who never marshaled any evidence for complex PTSD and had perfected the art of position paper as a stand-in for a scientific paper in 1992, criticized Resick and her group, who actually knew the evidence, asserting that they were in fact the guilty position paper writers.

Stokers seemed to know they had little true evidence to fall back on, and instituted proactive tarnishing. When one realizes that the primary motivation for the stokers is to enhance their moral status, the tarnishing makes perfect sense. The lower the status of the opponents, the relatively superior the status of the stokers.

The drive to find a hidden victim class does not mean the motivation is wrong or flawed. This is the same drive we see in other extreme causes that have humanitarian considerations at their hearts, such as animal rights, leniency for death row inmates, and extreme versions of civil and women's rights. The problem arises when they are taken too far beyond the realm of any factual basis.

There is, in fact, no real evidence that victims of interpersonal trauma are systematically ignored or mistreated by mental health professionals. There are also no reports of patients feeling rejected because their symptoms were not recognized as trauma related, at least no more than the rejection felt by patients due to the insensitivity of therapists in dealing with dozens of other complicated issues. Herman and the stokers have failed to explain how all of the patients' other disadvantages follow from inadequate treatment. There are no good prospective data to show that early trauma causes deformations of personality or widespread social disparities. As noted in Chapter Two, violation of the principle of exchangeability explains these disparities, which cannot be proven by cross-sectional studies.

2. Define and justify the victim class

Once stokers were activated by their drive for moral status, they had to prove that the hidden victim class suffered from a real, special disorder in order to create the perception of scientific confirmation. Heuristics guided the stokers to focus on interpersonal trauma, as opposed to other types of trauma.

> *I imagine the unconscious narrative inside the brain of a believer in complex PTSD goes something like this: I want to be a good and righteous person, but I have failures. To make myself feel better, I must protect the vulnerable and care for the sick. This is the belief for which I must find some facts.*

When challenged with the decision of what to do and what to believe in order to enhance one's status, the believers of complex PTSD invoke the available heuristic of an archetypal hero figure, an ethical protector who tends to believe life should be fair and all humans are created equal. In contrast, the available heuristic for a thinker who does not reflexively believe in complex PTSD is probably a different type of archetypal figure who accepts that life is not fair and humans are born with different strengths and sometimes with profound weaknesses.

The strategy fitted to the stokers' heuristic was a campaign to diagnose individuals by events rather than by symptoms. This was nearly unprecedented in medicine, which diagnoses individuals by symptoms, not events. This strategy dictated that they align themselves with a cause to champion vulnerable people, and the danger they had to battle was interpersonal trauma. This strategy dictated that they focus on interpersonal and polyvictimization trauma events.

Stokers attempt to gain scientific acceptance

In order to make their case that interpersonal trauma victims were different from noninterpersonal trauma victims, they had to show that interpersonal trauma victims showed different symptoms from noninterpersonal trauma victims. They had to show that the symptoms of interpersonal trauma victims impacted a greater number of areas, were more severe, and were longer lasting than the symptoms of regular PTSD. They had to do this with actual data in order to appear to possess scientific confirmation. The stokers would attempt this with dozens of poorly designed and confusing studies.

Psychologist Julian Ford was one of the most prolific stokers who published studies and commentaries about interpersonal and polyvictimization trauma. After Judith Herman and Bessel van der Kolk, Julian Ford was perhaps the first major stoker to publish on complex PTSD, starting with his 1998 paper in which he suggested that traditional psychotherapy for PTSD may overwhelm patients who have complex PTSD, retraumatizing them and causing them to dissociate.[49] Since then, Ford has authored or edited twelve books and over 250 articles or book chapters. He was the president of the International Society for Traumatic Stress Studies in 2020. He serves as an associate editor for two international journals that specialize in trauma and serves as chair of a task force on child trauma for the American Psychological Association.

Ford's publications include a 2006 study, published appropriately in the *Journal of Interpersonal Violence*, which claimed interpersonal trauma had special effects. He showed that undergraduate college females showed more symptoms of complex PTSD if they had experienced more interpersonal trauma events.[50] He made a causal connection between the events and symptoms that was inappropriate because the data came from a cross-sectional study.

In 2011, Ford published a retrospective chart review of child and adolescent outpatients claiming that polyvictimization had special effects. He showed that a subgroup of persons who experienced polyvictimization showed more severe symptoms and a wider range of symptoms that may cause naïve clinicians to overlook the patients' true problems, misdiagnose them, and harm them by giving them the wrong treatment. Characteristically, Ford and his coauthors attributed the severity of the patients' symptoms to their experiences of polyvictimization and made no mention of the possibility that other factors, such as genetics or other nontrauma factors, could have caused any of their problems.[51]

In 2013, Ford published a repeat of his 2011 study except he used a sample of youths incarcerated in a juvenile detention facility. Again, he and his coauthors concluded they had found a subgroup of the youths who had experienced polyvictimization and showed more severe symptoms, but it was based, again, on the weak design of a cross-sectional study and made no mention of the possibility that anything other than their victimization might have caused their symptoms.[52]

A work group, but no real work

To make it appear they had scientific evidence, they had to justify all those extra non-PTSD symptoms being included in the definition of complex PTSD. The extra symptoms included affect dysregulation, as well as self-identity, attachment, and interpersonal impairments. They needed research evidence in order to convince their skeptics, which is where they failed in 1994 with the *DSM-IV* and failed in 2013 with the *DSM-5*.

The stokers went to work. In 2005, the National Child Traumatic Stress Network formed a work group of experts to solve this challenge for complex PTSD diagnosis in children. They called the work group the Developmental Trauma Disorder Collaborative Group, and they put Bessel van der Kolk in charge. I was invited to be a part of the work group. In 2005, I had not yet figured out what the stokers were doing. I was skeptical of the whole idea, but I was neither friend nor foe at the time, so I flew to the National Child Traumatic Stress Network conference to meet with the work group.

The meeting was enormously frustrating. There were about a dozen people around the table in a hotel meeting room, with van der Kolk sort of loosely running the meeting. The general agenda was to discuss strategies to validate the proposed disorder of complex PTSD in children. The group included Julian Ford, Joseph Spinazzola, Marylene Cloitre, Glenn Saxe, Bradley Stolbach, and several others. One after the other, individuals offered their ideas for data sets they could look at or statistical tests they could run. It was apparent that each speaker talked about the concept of complex PTSD in a different way, with different definitions of trauma or stress and different definitions of which symptoms to include. Hardly anyone followed up on the ideas of the previous speakers.

To me, at least, it seemed quickly to resemble a high school student-government meeting where students with no experience and no real authority cast about for any ideas to improve the school. Hey, let's demand vending machines outside the cafeteria! Hey, let's put reclining chairs in the senior lounge!

They were all very smart researchers and clinicians, but none of them had training or experience in how to validate a disorder. I had more experience than anyone else at the table in validating a new disorder, which I suppose is why I was invited. I had spent the past twelve years conducting multiple studies to validate developmentally sensitive criteria for PTSD in children six years of age and younger. I was familiar with the traditional steps of how to validate a disorder and the different types of construct validation that would need to be addressed.

I explained that the place to start is to develop a plan to get everyone on the same page and develop a plan to agree on what the criteria should be. That means to start with individual case reports. You describe several real individuals who are believed to have the disorder. There ought to be a consensus among experts that several cases represent a new disorder before proceeding to more expensive group studies and fancy statistical tests.

Next, you proceed to face validation. Using the detailed case reports of a larger group of individual patients, you describe the symptoms in clear terms, as opposed to creating symptoms out of one's imagination or memory that may or may not match any real person's symptoms. Then you do very simple calculations to determine how frequently each symptom appears in the group. Then you do more very simple calculations to determine the best combination of different symptoms that efficiently diagnoses every individual believed to have the disorder. The process does not require fancy statistical techniques.

During the discussion, Marylene Cloitre suggested using the Q-sort technique to decide which symptoms to keep, even though the Q-sort had never been used to validate disorders. The Q-sort technique was a method invented by social scientists to try to objectively study how people subjectively view situations. In this technique, researchers write some presumed qualities of a situation on index cards. Two or more participants then independently sort the stack of cards by putting the quality they believe best represents the situation on top. The quality that is second best at describing the situation is second from the top, and so on. The Q-sort is never used to validate diagnostic criteria because it does not capture the process of testing different combinations of symptoms, which I explained to the group. At the time I thought Cloitre did not understand Q-sort. In retrospect, I think she understood it perfectly. The Q-sort is all about opinions. If someone wanted to create misdirection and confusion about the diagnostic criteria, the Q-sort was a perfect suggestion. The meeting ended with nothing concrete decided and no plan of action.

After the meeting I wrote out my recommendations as a blueprint they could follow. I sent it unsolicited to van der Kolk and the other work group members. I did not expect to hear from them again.

To my surprise, I did hear from them again. The work group decided to collect detailed case reports, as I had suggested. They were asking the sixteen work group members to follow a standardized format and write up detailed histories of five children, each of whom had experienced multiple interpersonal trauma events. To incentivize clinicians, they would pay them $100 for every case report. I presented the proposal to a team at my university who work with abused and neglected young children in foster care. Several of the clinicians agreed to participate. The clinicians collected detailed data on symptoms and history on seven children. I sent the data to van der Kolk's group and waited. I had to bug Spinazzola and van der Kolk several times to get them to pay my clinicians, and they finally did. I never heard anything back about the results. One of their emails said they had collected thirty cases, but no report on the data was ever published.

Much more public controversy would strike van der Kolk and Spinazzola later. In 2018, both were terminated from their jobs at the center van der Kolk had founded due to allegations of creating a hostile work environment.[53] The details were not made public, so it is not clear whether this incident bears any relevance to the story of complex PTSD. But prominent mental health professionals who are champions for the vulnerable being removed from their posts is so rare that it seems at least worth mentioning. The incident does seem relevant in revealing the dismissive behavior that may be involved in the moral dynamics of the more extreme complex PTSD supporters.

A dismissive behavior of van der Kolk was known before this incident and is apparent in many of his lectures. During one lecture in 2015 he informed the audience of his importance in discovering the impact of trauma: "My colleagues and I sort of invented this trauma stuff in the late 1970s, early 1980s, and then we thought the world would become a better place."[54] It was he and Judith Herman, he said, who may have been the first clinicians in history to discover how to talk to patients to take their trauma histories. All the other clinicians, he implied, were too ignorant to realize the impact of trauma.[55]

But, he explained, other people who didn't know what they were doing came behind him and screwed everything up. Instead of the world becoming a better place, his colleagues ruined things, van der Kolk said, with "an *insane* diagnostic system that ignores the realities of people's lives. We got an *insane* diagnostic system that ignores the fact that we are all part of a larger universe, that we are part of each other, the way you behave affects the way I am, and that most mental illness is the result of the environment and the individual being at odds with each other."[56]

It probably doesn't help that supporters of complex PTSD often treat van der Kolk with reverence. He is viewed with awe by many clinicians because of his deep knowledge, insights, and vision of humanity. The organizer of the conference for his 2015 lecture introduced him to the audience this way: "It was our deep desire to invite Dr. van der Kolk to be our keynote speaker. And do you know what? I feel like an Oscar speech acceptance person, but dreams can happen, and the evidence is that he is sitting right here."[57]

Van der Kolk rewarded the audience with a personal revelation about his vision of the current world. Once he got to the microphone, he declared that the US bombing of Baghdad at the start of the 2003 Iraq War was what finally made him lose faith in humanity.[58] As I watched this on YouTube, I found myself a bit bewildered, wondering, what is the point of disclosing that personal information? It struck me as odd for a scientific presentation. It also struck me as odd that a man who studied incest and child abuse, and who had Dutch relatives impacted by the Nazis' attempted genocide of Jews, had maintained his faith in humanity all the way up until 2003. But it makes sense when viewed through the lens that van der Kolk is promoting a morality, not science. His personal revelation sent the message to his audience that the horrors of humanity are with us today more than ever. And even though the present time is the worst of all horrors, he is here for us with his message of a set of small false facts, weaponized neuroscience, and dismissal of those who can't see what he sees.

Treatment protocols used as misdirection

But back in 2005, van der Kolk and some other stokers came up with their own plan to "validate" the complex PTSD disorder, which was to ignore the process of validation altogether and create misdirection with other types of research. One method of creating misdirection was to create new psychotherapy protocols for complex PTSD. Marylene Cloitre was the first to jump the gun when she published a study in 2002 on a sixteen-session psychotherapy model she called Skills Training in Affective and Interpersonal Regulation (STAIR).[59] This was followed in 2006 by an entire book on the technique.[60] Julian Ford was next when he published a paper in 2008 to describe his nine-week protocol called Trauma Affect Regulation/Guide for Education and Therapy (TARGET).[61] In 2009, he and Christine Courtois published an entire book that they edited, called *Treating Complex Traumatic Stress Disorders: An Evidence-Based Guide.*[62]

Fancy statistical tests used as misdirection

Other stokers bypassed traditional validation by going straight to fancy statistical tests that have nothing to do with validation of disorders. The statistical tests they used most frequently came from a class of tests called latent analysis. The idea behind latent analysis is that there are one or more hidden groups the human eye cannot see because of the large number of symptoms they share in common in different combinations. The hidden group is latent because it cannot be directly measured. Even though the group is hidden from view, we can directly measure the individual symptoms we can see, such as sadness, irritability, or insomnia. The fancy statistical tests work in the background to find associations between these individual symptoms. Individuals who share common symptoms are lumped together into latent groups. There are statistical rules of thumb about how many symptoms individuals have to share before they are declared to be in discrete groups.

In latent analysis, the hidden group is, of course, complex PTSD. For example, Cloitre and her coinvestigators used data that had been previously collected at a clinic for adults in New York City that specialized in trauma. Their latent analysis produced three groups—one they called Complex PTSD, one they called simply PTSD, and one they called Low Symptoms. The Complex PTSD group had PTSD symptoms, just like the PTSD group, but also showed symptoms of affective regulation, worthlessness, guilt, and interpersonal problems.[63] Keep in mind that even though they called this group Complex PTSD, and claimed these data provide evidence for the validity of complex

PTSD, they did not describe a single individual who actually met the diagnostic criteria for complex PTSD. It is possible that none of the individuals in their Complex PTSD group actually met the full criteria for complex PTSD.

Stokers have published over a dozen of these types of latent analysis studies. Cloitre, Philip Hyland, Mark Shevlin, and Thanos Karatzias often collaborate. Writing as coauthors in different combinations, they have published at least seven of these types of studies.[64]

The major problem with latent analyses is that they are often circular, self-fulfilling prophecies. If a researcher only inputs data on symptoms believed to be part of complex PTSD, the computer will always find a group that shows these symptoms in common. The computer can only find what it is given to work with.

For example, I could claim that I have discovered a new disorder called complex heart failure. Complex heart failure, according to my new definition, is defined as the symptoms of traditional heart failure plus symptoms of kidney failure, liver failure, and dementia. If I collected the symptoms from a large group of patients on heart failure, kidney failure, liver failure, and dementia and subjected them to latent analysis, the statistical test would always find a group that has all of those symptoms in common. It has to find this group because that is what the test is programmed to find. The test would also find groups that have only heart failure, only kidney failure, only liver failure, and only dementia as long as I included those kinds of patients in the study. I would then use the result of the test to claim that I have validated complex heart failure. Obviously, this test in no way validates a disorder of complex heart failure because it tells you nothing about the onset of symptoms, the course of symptoms, and how the symptoms responded to treatment. I could do this all day and create dozens of new disorders.

Complex PTSD can have nothing to do with trauma

The strategy to focus on interpersonal and polyvictimization events created another challenge for the stokers. Many of the interpersonal and polyvictimization events they felt were important to include were not actually trauma events. They were stressful events, but not life-threatening ones as typical trauma events are defined. These non-life-threatening events included emotional abuse, neglect, living in violent neighborhoods, bullying, property crime, foster care placements, and poverty. These non-life-threatening events are clearly excluded from the types of events that cause PTSD, and this has been proven by research studies repeatedly.

By expanding the definition of trauma to include non-life-threatening events, the researchers drastically changed the type of individuals who might be diagnosed. Victims could have experienced one or the other type of event, and did not have to experience both. Victims diagnosed with complex PTSD therefore could have experienced only non-life-threatening events and zero life-threatening events. This potentially makes the samples of true PTSD victims noncomparable to those of complex PTSD victims.

How did the researchers address this challenge that their different definition of trauma created a disorder that could have little to do with actual trauma? They didn't. They never felt compelled to address the issue head-on because they realized they did not have to. In its everyday use, the word *trauma* is one of those words, like *torture*, that can mean almost anything to anybody. Trauma can mean life-threatening physical harm, painful stretching exercises in physical rehabilitation, a loss by a favorite football team, or being stuck in traffic. As long as the world used the word *trauma* interchangeably for a wide variety of situations, the researchers could fly under the radar and few people would challenge them. The ease with which stokers mixed non-life-threatening events in with life-threatening events in their unique definition of complex trauma reflects another one of the complications of this entire issue. Outside of PTSD research, *trauma* can mean almost anything to anybody.

Violation of the principle of exchangeability
Another major flaw of all latent analysis studies is that they are cross-sectional and violate the principle of exchangeability. As I described in Chapter Two, a cross-sectional study is a study in which the individuals

are studied once, and only once. Cross-sectional studies have no power to determine causation between two variables.

With regard to complex PTSD, this means that all the extra non-PTSD symptoms that are supposedly part of the complex PTSD diagnosis could have been present before individuals experienced any trauma, or they might have developed regardless of whether individuals experienced trauma. Specifically, the extra non-PTSD symptoms of affect regulation, self-identity, attachment, and interpersonal impairments could have been already present prior to trauma or they were going to develop anyway in individuals who would later experience prolonged and repeated interpersonal traumas. In addition, it is likely that the presence of these extra symptoms is part of what makes these individuals vulnerable to being in living situations where repeated interpersonal victimization is possible. Individuals who do not possess those extra symptoms are less likely to live in the types of families or be in the types of situations where interpersonal victimization is likely to occur.

The stokers for complex PTSD have never acknowledged this flaw of cross-sectional trauma research or even the existence of the principle of exchangeability. I have read hundreds of studies by the stokers of CPTSD, and I have never seen them mention that they are even aware of this very basic principle of exchangeability as a potential limitation of their research.

Behind-the-scenes efforts were also common for stokers. In 2009, I was asked by planners of the *DSM-5* revision to prepare a review paper on the important issues for the diagnosis of PTSD in children and adolescents. Charles Zeanah and Judith Cohen were secondary authors on the paper. The planners passed a draft of our manuscript around to other experts in trauma including Judith Herman. Herman sent me a private email in which she wrote the following:

I work with adult patients in the outpatient psychiatry service of a "safety-net" hospital. Most of our patients have been multiply traumatized (mean # of separate types of trauma hovers around 4), but mainly they suffer from the effects of prolonged abuse and neglect by caretakers. Though they do manifest classic *DSM-IV* PTSD, their most salient symptoms are often their difficulties in self-care, affect regulation and interpersonal relationships. Many are self-harming. I would expect that similar or analogous symptoms would be manifest in chronically abused children and certainly in adolescents. Would it be possible to include more discussion of this issue in your paper? I realize this is a tall order, but I do think the issue needs to be addressed.

It was such a gentle, almost sweet request; one might think nothing of it. But in reality it was an attempt to do a complete end-around of science. She was, in effect, saying she doesn't work with children, and doesn't know whether they show these symptoms in relation to trauma, but she expects that they probably do. Would I please not ignore these vulnerable children? I politely declined her request.

In summary, heuristics guided the stokers to pay special attention to victims of interpersonal trauma, as opposed to other types of trauma victims. They could have selected any type of trauma—motor vehicle collisions, natural disasters, war, or burns. The stokers picked interpersonal trauma because fighting for alleged victims of perpetrators best served their need for moral status. There is no good evidence to support their argument that the symptoms of interpersonal trauma are substantially different from those of noninterpersonal trauma. The stokers have never provided case reports or group studies that support construct validation for this proposed disorder.

3. Seize on anything that amplifies the victims' disadvantaged status

Stokers tried to amplify the tragedy of victims of complex trauma by equating complex PTSD with severe personality and characterological problems typically seen in personality disorders. Personality disorders are a distinct type of psychiatric disorder. Personality disorders are different from other disorders such as depression and anxiety because they are permanent. They have a very strong genetic underpinning. All psychiatric disorders have a genetic contribution, but personality disorders are thought to be almost entirely due to genetics because the features are present so early in life, they remain stable throughout lifetimes, and they are largely intractable to psychotherapy.

I imagine the unconscious narrative inside the brain of a stoker of complex PTSD: I see that these extra symptoms look a lot like borderline personality disorders, so I need to dismiss any contradictory evidence and instead believe that borderline personality disorders as they are currently defined no longer exist. Instead, borderline personality symptoms must be caused by interpersonal trauma.

Once the stokers focused on the narrative that there is a special class of disadvantaged trauma victims who are massively, comprehensively, and permanently damaged goods, they were faced with a new problem. How do they explain the existence of these massive, comprehensive, and permanent symptoms? In order to remain on the road to Traumaville, the stokers needed a moral crusade to endlessly fight for. Thus, these symptoms could not be genetically inherited because they do not fit with the narrative that trauma caused them. They do not fit the narrative that some people are simply born with disadvantages. The stokers had to go with the theory that trauma caused them. They had to favor nurture over nature to explain the existence of this special class of interpersonal trauma victims.

Complex PTSD overlaps with borderline personality disorder

The DSM-5 recognizes ten types of personality disorders: paranoid, schizoid, schizotypal, antisocial, borderline, histrionic, narcissistic, avoidant, dependent, and obsessive-compulsive. Within this group of disorders, borderline personality disorder is probably the most distressing and dangerous. Individuals with borderline personality disorder are characterized by intense anger, hostility, and mood swings that push others away, unstable personal relationships, disturbances in self-image, intense fear of abandonment, difficulty trusting, and frequent suicidal thoughts.

Individuals with borderline personality disorder are often the victims of interpersonal trauma. Borderline personality disorder and trauma experiences often occur in the same individuals, probably because whatever causes them to develop borderline personality disorder also causes them to frequently be in unsafe situations where traumas can occur. It is also probable that the interpersonal problems of individuals with borderline personality, such as anger and hostility toward others, may precipitate violent interactions.

The stokers of complex PTSD, however, claim that trauma experiences *cause* the symptoms that look like borderline personality disorder. But there is no good evidence to support that. Many individuals with borderline personality disorder, perhaps most of them, have never experienced repeated interpersonal trauma. Thus, it is likely that the massive, comprehensive, and severe symptoms described in complex PTSD are actually symptoms of borderline personality disorder and are not due to trauma.

But in order to bolster the case that the problems are due to trauma, the stokers had to prove two things: (1) they had to make the argument that interpersonal trauma caused the types of symptoms normally found in borderline personality disorders, and (2) they had to show that individuals with complex PTSD were different from individuals with borderline personality disorders. The stokers have published many studies, which will be described, but none of the studies have been able to prove those things.

In other words, once the belief was ingrained that complex PTSD symptoms include symptoms that traditionally would be diagnosed as personality disorders, the false facts had to be found to support the belief. Any contradictory evidence had to be ignored or dismissed with the wave of a hand. The stokers had to construct a scientific narrative that trauma—a force of nurture—and not nature, explained the existence of this special class of interpersonal trauma victims.

The stokers constructed this narrative by publishing dozens of studies and commentaries that promoted the theory that interpersonal trauma caused deformations of personality. Herman seemed to intuitively understand this from the very beginning. In her 1992 paper on the subject, she started making the argument that interpersonal trauma caused personality disorder symptoms, or what are also known as characterological changes. As noted earlier, she wrote that PTSD fails to capture "the protean sequelae" of prolonged, repeated trauma, which include personality and characterological changes that are more diffuse and tenacious than PTSD. When van der Kolk expanded the complex PTSD concept to children, he also repeated these assertions many times, such as in this statement: "After a child is traumatized multiple times, the imprint of the trauma becomes lodged in many aspects of his or her makeup."[65]

There are numerous problems with these arguments. It is well-known that personality disorders have strongly, if not entirely, genetic origins. This probably explains why the stokers never explicitly mention the phrase *personality disorders*. Instead, they call them "personality and characterological changes" and hope it goes unnoticed.

While promoting the idea that interpersonal trauma causes deformations of personality, the stokers needed to simultaneously convince others that complex PTSD was not simply misdiagnosing, or perhaps changing the diagnosis of, individuals who have personality disorders. The stokers turned again to the fancy statistical tests of latent analysis. Marylene Cloitre published a study that claimed that latent analysis found a complex PTSD group that was distinct from a borderline personality disorder group.[66] This was, of course, unsurprising, and it was a completely irrelevant study because complex PTSD includes symptoms of PTSD that are not found in borderline personality disorder. The question is not whether latent analysis can distinguish the two because no one has ever proposed that the two are identical. The question is whether complex PTSD encompasses borderline personality disorder and overlaps with it.

Julian Ford and Christine Courtois published a review paper in 2014 to try to address this issue.[67] They acknowledged that the overlap of diagnostic criteria for complex PTSD and borderline personality disorder raised questions about the scientific integrity of complex PTSD. Their lengthy review is full of the same type of logical errors as Cloitre's latent analysis paper. Ford and Courtois list all the ways that complex PTSD is different from borderline personality disorder. What they never mention is that no one has ever claimed that complex PTSD is identical to borderline personality disorder. The criticism of complex PTSD is that it has subsumed many of the symptoms of borderline personality disorder. Individuals who are being diagnosed with complex PTSD are likely individuals who have both borderline personality symptoms, which are unrelated to trauma, and symptoms of PTSD, which are related to trauma. Ford and Courtois never entertained that idea, as if they were saying, "Do not pay attention to the fact that complex PTSD and borderline personality disorder massively overlap. Move along, folks, nothing to see here."

Instead, Ford and Courtois focused on all the ways they differ. Ford and Courtois concluded, as expected, that "although BPD and cPTSD overlap substantially, it is unwarranted to conceptualize cPTSD either as a replacement for BPD, or simply as a sub-type of BPD."[68] Despite the illogic of this conclusion, I would agree with it. But that conclusion has nothing to do with the problem. The problem is that complex PTSD subsumed many of the borderline symptoms in order to support the narrative that interpersonal trauma deforms personality. Individuals who are being diagnosed with complex PTSD are really individuals with two separate diagnoses—borderline personality disorder plus PTSD.

All the misdirection is difficult to follow

Trying to untangle all of the stokers' arguments is dizzying. I found it incredibly challenging while trying to write this book to tell the stories in an organized and concise fashion. I am sure many readers have found it frustrating to read. The complexity of the issues is, I think, one of the things that keeps more professionals from challenging the whole thing.

The effect on many skeptical clinicians is that they are not sure what to believe. They may not have totally bought the argument, but at the least they are a bit confused. They go along with the argument because they do not have the time to dig into the evidence and they do not want to appear like outsiders. For example, Todd Grande, a psychotherapist in Delaware who posts YouTube videos on many mental health topics, generally appears to be a level-headed, low-key, nonmelodramatic clinician trying to present both sides of every issue. Grande posted a video to discuss the evidence for and against complex PTSD.[69] He noted that some believe that trauma causes borderline personality disorder, but also noted the conundrums that not everyone with borderline has experienced trauma and that borderline personality disorder is largely heritable. Grande voiced his opinion that he thinks complex PTSD is distinct from BPD, or that it might be a subtype of it, but overall, he was not certain. His conclusion was "I don't know" and the issues should be studied further, which, one could argue, is exactly how the stokers want every clinician to feel—confused enough about a complicated issue so that they face no real opposition. But Dr. Grande should be commended for at least having the capacity to say, "I don't know."

The stokers needed to promote a set of false facts that were close enough to the truth to be believable, and, ideally, based on situations that were so difficult to observe that they could be neither verified nor disproven. This turned out to be easy. Stokers have been able to take advantage of the complicated relationships among life events, the wide array of psychiatric symptoms, and the vagueness of psychiatric taxonomy where many things are uncertain. Complicated situations can create a vacuum of uncertainty, and also create fertile ground for groupthink, in which like-minded colleagues converge around bad ideas in the face of conflicting evidence.

We can see some similarities with the Iraq War. The highly respected members of the Bush administration cabinet engaged heavily in stoking with speeches, editorials, interviews on news shows, and speeches at the United Nations.

We can see some similarities with Theranos. The highly respected members of the board of directors were largely what compelled investors to trust the company and pour millions of dollars into it, and also what attracted talented professionals to work there.

We saw a similar situation with toxic stress. The false facts about neurobiology and brain alterations were tirelessly promoted by Jack Shonkoff and his private council. Without the highly respected Dr. Shonkoff and his other highly respected colleagues from highly respected Harvard University doing the stoking, it is likely that toxic stress would not be nearly as popular as it is today.

For a belief to be considered true even though it is false, there needs to be a set of small false facts. But if no one knows about the set of false facts, they cannot serve their function. That is where the stokers came in.

The mythical diagnosis is enormously popular

What the stokers accomplished for complex PTSD was one of the most successful persuasion campaigns in the history of psychiatry. The mythical diagnosis has become enormously popular. Nearly every major professional organization and every major US governmental agency that deals with mental health issues today publicly expresses confirmation of complex PTSD.

The usually respectable National Center for PTSD includes a page on their website for complex PTSD.[70] While mentioning that the disorder was rejected by both the *DSM-IV* and *DSM-5*, the website nonetheless stated there is "abundant evidence" to support the notion of complex PTSD and described how to treat it.

The American Psychological Association (APA) sells a DVD of a training workshop on how to treat complex PTSD called "Complex Posttraumatic Stress Disorder."[71] The Clinical Practice Guideline for the Treatment of PTSD endorsed by the APA acknowledges the controversy around complex PTSD with a footnote stating that it was rejected by *DSM* but accepted by ICD.[72] Yet, the guideline treats complex PTSD as a possibly real thing that deserves further study.

In 2010, the American Academy of Child and Adolescent Psychiatry published a practice parameter for clinicians which mentioned complex PTSD as a proposed new disorder but stopped short of criticizing the complete absence of research evidence to validate it.[73] Complex PTSD was presented as an alternative explanation in an ongoing debate about how to diagnose.

The American Academy of Pediatrics (AAP) provides a free guide for pediatricians working with foster children that endorses the concept of complex trauma with no reservations.[74]

The National Child Traumatic Stress Network maintains a page on its website titled "Complex Trauma" that makes absolutely no mention of the controversy about it.[75] They endorse the TARGET and other new treatment protocols. They also distribute a webinar titled

"Developmental Trauma Disorder: Identifying Critical Moments and Healing Complex Trauma."[76]

The Substance Abuse and Mental Health Services Administration is all in. SAMHSA provides the funding for the National Child Traumatic Stress Network, which, among many complex trauma-related products, includes more than one million dollars to fund the creation of a Complex Trauma Treatment Network.[77]

The International Society for Traumatic Stress Studies published treatment guidelines in 2019. They took the middle road, but were not very critical. They seriously considered the topic of complex PTSD: "Rather than systematically reviewing the evidence for the treatment of complex presentations of PTSD, it would likely be more beneficial to undertake a narrative review of the current situation with respect to Complex PTSD."[78] The society also published a position paper specific to children and adolescents, which noted, "At this time there is only very preliminary evidence to support the existence of CPTSD in children and adolescents. . . . To date, there is not enough evidence to recommend a particular treatment for CPTSD in children."[79] Nevertheless, they recommended further research.

A Set of Small False Facts as misdirection

The selection of interpersonal trauma was an advantage for the stokers' cause. It was an advantage because the complicated issues of trauma exposure, symptom expression, and cause and effect gave them a wide field on which to practice misdirection and create confusion.

There is a saying among journalists that some stories are too good to check, which means, of course, that they are too perfect. The story of complex PTSD was too good to check because it fit seamlessly with the internal beliefs of the stokers. For good measure, the stokers flooded the literature with so much misdirection and so many irrelevant research papers that it was too difficult to check.

Perhaps the best way to summarize the large number of irrelevant arguments put forth by the stokers is to compare it to chaff from a plane trying to deceive an incoming missile. The chaff deceives the missile to follow the chaff and not the plane. The stokers want you looking the wrong way so you do not catch on to what they are really doing. I acknowledge that may mischaracterize what they are doing; it is conceivable that, as Trivers has so well explained, they are primarily trying to deceive themselves so that they can better deceive others.

A loosely coordinated opposition

A small group of trauma experts has sharply and publicly criticized the complex PTSD argument. Unlike the situation with toxic stress, where few researchers have dared to question it, the misdirections, inaccurate claims, and nonexistent scientific foundations of complex PTSD have been described in detail several times. The first known critique was in 2004, when Shawn Cahill and three colleagues published a detailed critique of Cloitre's first STAIR trial.[80]

In 2005, Dean Kilpatrick at the Medical University of South Carolina, one of the elder statesmen of trauma research, criticized many aspects of the complex PTSD agenda. In addition, he has been one of the few to recognize the influence of belief systems that were at work. He wrote, "We should not believe everything someone tells us just because they believe it strongly or because they are an authority figure."[81] Kilpatrick referred to the belief systems as dogma, which contrasts sharply with the role of scientists to work from true facts. The contrast between dogma and science is that a dogmatist accepts the belief system as a given, and facts are irrelevant, whereas a scientist works in facts and views belief systems as tentative. Kilpatrick wrote: "I say the traumatic stress field needs more science and less dogma. We owe it to ourselves, to our clients, and to the professional reputation of the traumatic stress field to base our clinical practice on the best science available and to be skeptical of claims that appear to have limited empirical support."[82]

In 2012, Patricia Resick led a group of nine other researchers to critique the entire concept of complex PTSD. Patricia Resick is a psychologist who created prolonged exposure therapy, which is one of the most widely used treatments for PTSD in the world. She has probably conducted studies with more adult PTSD patients than anybody in the world. Her group noted the amateurish attempts by the stokers to claim that diagnostic validation exists for complex PTSD and to provide a blueprint for how validation ought to be done.[83] The researchers noted that there is no precedent in psychiatric taxonomy for the proposal to split off a new diagnosis. Resick and colleagues exploded through the loopholes of the argument that complex PTSD would neatly bring "parsimony," whatever that means, to diagnosing. They noted that there are no studies of neurobiology of complex PTSD. They noted the flaws in the argument that new treatments are needed to replace existing treatments. They noted that at the time, despite the high level of certainty voiced by stokers, there had been only one treatment study that actually involved patients with complex PTSD. They noted the confusion created by the different conceptualizations of the stressor criterion. Resick and company noted the claimed overlap of complex PTSD symptoms with borderline personality disorder with no satisfactory justification. Last, they noted the rather simple but glaring problem that the stokers never proved causality; there has never been a case study or a group study that has tracked the onset of all the extra symptoms of complex PTSD to the traumatic and/or stressful events.

In a commentary in the same issue as Resick and company's critique, another trauma expert, Ramón Lindauer, a Dutch psychologist at Amsterdam University Medical Centers, wrote that he agreed with Resick and colleagues about all the evidence, but he did not really care. He asked, "What would be the clinical, political, and social consequences of not including it?"[84] He explicitly stepped over the line and went from an impartial researcher to an advocate for political reasons when he wrote, "The inclusion of a clinical diagnosis developmental trauma disorder in the DSM could also help keep the issue of child maltreatment on the agendas of politicians, insurance companies, and funding bodies. Clearly the scientific basis should also be adequate, but aren't we sometimes being too strict?"[85]

I think Lindauer summed it up more explicitly than anyone else, even though he has not been one of the more active stokers. He acknowledged that the evidence does not stack up, but the evidence is not what is important. The really important issue is that politics and social advocacy should trump evidence.

In 2016, Ad DeJongh, a Dutch psychologist, along with twenty coauthors, published a scathing critique of guidelines published by a special task force of the International Society of Traumatic Stress Studies (ISTSS). The Complex Trauma Task Force had toiled over a document called "The Expert Consensus Treatment Guidelines for Complex PTSD in Adults." DeJongh and his colleagues noted the lack of evidence for the phase-based treatment recommended by Cloitre, Ford, and others. The specific criticisms were that there existed no rigorous research to support the view that phase-based treatment led to better outcomes for complex PTSD, and there was no evidence that traditional PTSD treatments cause harm to patients with complex PTSD.[86] DeJongh's detailed critique included many studies that the task force failed to cite for unknown reasons.

Cloitre, as the lead author of the task force being criticized, led the defense against DeJongh and colleagues. Cloitre and her team never really replied to any of DeJongh's specific criticisms. Instead, they countered that complex PTSD had been validated in five latent class studies.[87] As I mentioned earlier, latent class studies do nothing to validate a disorder. The employment of latent analyses was just misdirection to make your head swivel. Who can argue with something that sounds as important as latent class analysis? The gist of Cloitre's argument, much like Lindauer's argument in 2012, was to shrug and ask, "What's the harm of another therapy?"

In 2017, ISTSS was working on revisions to a third edition of their popular book titled *Effective Treatments for PTSD*, which influences treatment for trauma victims all over the world. I was asked to write or cowrite one of the chapters. By this time, I had woken up and realized how the toxic stress and complex PTSD believers had dominated all levels of clinical work, research, professional organizations, and social advocacy.

I replied to the invitation thus:

I appreciate the invitation. I could accept your invitation with a contingency. I am concerned with the direction a subgroup of trauma experts has taken with their persistent efforts to promote complex trauma, complex PTSD, and developmental trauma disorder. In my opinion, those concepts have no empirical basis. It has been disappointing to watch the proponents of these concepts ignore the basics of scientific validation and publish and promote these as if they are facts. I would not feel comfortable coauthoring a chapter that sidesteps this issue. I anticipate that a chapter that is critical of complex PTSD is going to meet resistance from the editors because I see that complex PTSD is already reified in at least one of the chapter titles. I am a little wary of putting in a lot of work on a chapter and then [having] the editors demand to have criticism censored. I look forward to your thoughts.

Unfortunately, one of the coauthors wrote back: "I wouldn't want to do a full-blown 'hatchet job' on the notion of complex PTSD in a chapter like this—though such an effort may be [a] VERY helpful opinion piece in another publication, maybe a journal." Not wanting to appear complicit with the complex PTSD stokers, I declined the invitation.

In 2018, ISTSS was putting the final touches on the first treatment guideline they had developed for complex PTSD. ISTSS created an online portal for any person to provide feedback on the guidelines. I submitted feedback of more than 1,100 words. My first sentence was: "The development of treatment guidelines for the proposed complex PTSD is premature because there is no evidence that this proposed disorder meets the most basic criteria for diagnostic validity for any age group." I explained in detail the lack of case reports and diagnostic validation research. I explained my history with the developmental trauma disorder work group in 2005 and their complete lack of interest in proper diagnostic validation. I explained that the campaign to recognize complex PTSD is driven by an ideology that is dangerous because it violates the public trust in scientists.

It appears that all of the criticisms from Cahill, Kilpatrick, Resick, DeJongh, myself, and others have had little to no effect. Stokers continue to conduct biased research. Journals continue to publish it. ISTSS continues to promote the concept of complex

PTSD. All of our criticisms have been uncoordinated, lonely voices with no consistent traction.

This situation is reminiscent of the run-up to the Iraq War of 2003, when the drumbeat for war was overwhelming. The individuals who questioned the drive to war were not effective in preventing it. They were ineffective because the desire for war was so strong, but they also were ineffective because they were uncoordinated, lonely voices.

Brent Scowcroft, who was a highly respected national security advisor under Republican US presidents Gerald Ford and the first George Bush, published a strong protest against going to war in the *Wall Street Journal* in August 2002, seven months before the invasion.[88] Weapons inspector Scott Ritter loudly protested against a war. US Representative Dennis Kucinich protested by organizing forums on Capitol Hill for diverse bipartisan voices to speak out. Other lone voices made their dissenting opinions known, including House majority leader Dick Armey, State Department official Richard Armitage, and former administration officials Henry Kissinger and Lawrence Eagleburger. But as a *New York Times* article described them, they were putting forth what "appeared to be a loosely coordinated effort."[89] They were no match for the highly coordinated and persistent efforts of those who wanted a war.

Conclusion

In his book titled *The Righteous Mind: Why Good People Are Divided by Politics and Religion*, psychologist Jonathan Haidt took readers on a tour of human nature through the perspective of moral psychology as a way to think about the two most divisive topics in human life: politics and religion. Divisiveness arising between belief systems is inevitable. Haidt understood that the foundations for divisive morality are partly learned but are also substantially innate. Building from eighteenth-century philosopher David Hume, who was perhaps the first to clearly note how humans are driven by intuition, Haidt explored "how the righteous mind was 'organized in advance of experience.'"[90]

Haidt mined social psychology research for insights on motivation, and cognitive psychology research for insights on errors of reasoning.

This research showed that our capacity for reason is not our main operating system. Reason is just one of many tools in the brain, and not even one of the most commonly used tools. Many of the bizarre decisions made by humans actually make perfect sense "once you see reasoning as having evolved not to help us find truth but to help us engage in arguments, persuasion and manipulation in the context of discussions with other people."[91] Those who are skilled at arguing, Haidt said, often "are not after the truth but after arguments supporting their views."

Why it matters to understand this is the same as why it matters to understand the history of toxic stress. A subgroup of ideologically driven individuals is trying to redefine a disadvantaged class of people as victims who are not different at birth. The ideological individuals must see their professional external world to be seamless with their internal world. The complex PTSD stokers do not have quite the same social-engineering focus as the toxic stress activists, which probably explains why no organized group like Shonkoff's council arose to promote complex PTSD.

Why can't they unbelieve things later?

To be fair to the stokers, they are very smart people trying to do good things in the world. Unfortunately, they are clever writers, too. And it was probably inevitable that someone would propose something like complex PTSD given the way human nature works. As Donald Rumsfeld wrote in his autobiography about his actions that helped to launch the Iraq War, he and his colleagues were not misleading anyone on purpose. Rumsfeld wrote, "The President did not lie. The Vice President did not lie. Tenet did not lie. Rice did not lie. I did not lie. The Congress did not lie. The far less dramatic truth is that we were wrong."[92]

Rumsfeld stops short of saying he might have been deceived by his own mind—by his own belief systems or instincts or cognitive biases—but his conclusion is clearly in line with the arguments of this book. When presented with a complicated conundrum of the modern world, our human minds can get it very wrong, even on a big stage with a big spotlight and lots of data.

Humans have instincts that serve them well under normal conditions but can cause problems when we are bamboozled by more complicated conditions. Psychologist Deirdre Barrett wrote an entire book on the subject titled *Supernormal Stimuli*. The concept of supernormal stimuli, coined by the Dutch Nobel Prize winner Niko Tinbergen, explains the problems instincts create when they are disconnected from their normal environment.[93] Barrett's aim was to apply the concept of supernormal stimuli to sex, health, international relations, and media.

Examples provided by Barrett included a bird who will take care of an egg placed in her nest by a different species of bird because her instincts tell her to take care of eggs. A male beta fish will knock its head against the glass of an aquarium wall when it sees its reflection. A male barn swallow will find a mate easily if his chest feathers are darkened with a marker. Baby-faced criminals get lighter sentences because they appear less threatening. Humans are attracted to puzzles and games because of our innate curiosity that was helpful for survival during evolution on the savannah, even though solving puzzles provides us no survival advantage today. In all these examples, the animals followed instincts that helped them survive, but when they were placed in situations in which they did not evolve, their instincts caused unintended consequences.

If we replace the term *instincts* with *heuristics*, we see the same conundrum. Human minds possess heuristics, which is simply another name for mental instincts. The heuristics serve us well under normal, everyday conditions. But when we are faced with modern, complicated problems for which the heuristics were never intended, the heuristics cause unintended consequences.

Social psychologists Les Ross and Richard Nisbett phrased it a different way. Ordinary physics explains the world around us very well in everyday situations. But when we venture into more complicated domains such as space and the realm of quantum physics, ordinary physics is inadequate. Psychology is the same way. Ross and Nisbett wrote, "Lay psychology, like lay physics, generally gets the job done reasonably well." But there are times when lay psychology fails to serve us well, and it is for very understandable reasons connected to how our minds work.[94]

The phenomenon we have seen with complex PTSD happens over and over in the world. We have seen it with the initial embrace of chronic traumatic encephalopathy by many who tried to ban youth football. Merrill Hoge has documented heavy-handed stokers at Boston University and their CTE research program.[95] We have seen it with the initial embrace of cold fusion. Early supporters, very smart people all, believed cold fusion was a fact. We have seen it with the misdirection about weapons of mass destruction in the run-up to the Iraq War.

One thing that is different about those examples and complex PTSD is how relatively short-lived those beliefs were. CTE research has received severe criticism in less than ten years. Cold fusion was debunked in about five months. The weapons-of-mass-destruction belief was proven wrong in less than a year after the war started. Belief in complex PTSD has existed for over twenty-five years and is only picking up steam.

This time frame suggests that in terms of anything to do with psychology, persuading people to believe something is incredibly easy. Solomon Asch, one of the pioneering social psychologists, showed in 1955 just how easy it was to influence individuals.[96] He showed groups of seven to nine male college students two large cards. The first card showed a single straight, vertical line. The second card showed three lines of different lengths. The students' job was to pick the line from the second card that was the same length as the line on the first card. The task was not at all difficult. Under normal conditions, people would pick the correct line nearly 100 percent of the time.

The trick was that all but one of the students were collaborating in secret with Dr. Asch. When collaborators picked the wrong line on purpose, the lone subject who was not collaborating started to pick the same wrong line. When only one collaborator picked the wrong line, the subject was hardly ever swayed. When two collaborators picked the wrong line, the subject accepted this wrong answer 14 percent of the time. When three collaborators picked the wrong line, the subject accepted this wrong answer 32 percent of the time. When more than three collaborators picked the wrong line, this had no further influence on the subject.

Consistency of opinions also appears to play a role in persuading people to believe something. Another social psychologist, Romanian-born Serge Moscovici, performed a variation of Asch's test. He showed groups of people thirty-six slides that were different shades of blue. If his collaborators said green every single time, subjects accepted the wrong answer at least once about one-third of the time. But if his collaborators said green inconsistently, subjects accepted the wrong answer much less often.[97]

But why can't individuals slow things down and pull themselves out of these situations to figure out the correct answers? Yet another social psychologist, Timothy Wilson, and his colleague Elizabeth Dunn summed it up succinctly. They wrote, "Because of personal motives and the architecture of the mind, it may be difficult for people to know themselves." We can talk about how much of their self-deception is due to conscious attempts to block out unwanted thoughts and how much is due to unconscious suppression of unhelpful thoughts. But perhaps the most common cause of self-deception is that much of the mind is simply inaccessible to examination. As Wilson and Dunn said, "Introspection cannot provide a direct pipeline to these mental processes" much of the time.[98] That does not mean that introspection and self-correction are impossible. It means it is often slow and hard work, which they compared to "an archeological dig." This makes perfect sense when we remember that successful psychotherapy requires months or years.

There are obstacles to this archeological dig, many of which have already been discussed in this book. Our instincts were developed for survival of the clan and enhancement of individual status, not for introspection. Heuristics were developed to make rapid and efficient decisions, not the most accurate decisions. In a way, our minds are actually better designed for self-deception than for accurate perception of reality.

There is no single term that can neatly sum up all of the moving parts that contribute to this self-deception as though it were a single natural law of the mind. But one that comes close is naïve realism. The notion of naïve realism is that "people persist in feeling that their own take on the world enjoys particular authenticity, and that other actors will, or at least should, share that take, if they are attentive, rational, and objective perceivers of reality and open-minded seekers of truth."[99] Naïve realism explains in a nutshell not only why individuals have great difficulty with self-correction, but why they double down when they are wrong.

The stokers are like an inverted version of the three wise monkeys who see no evil, hear no evil, and speak no evil. The stokers created the narrative of a false evil in the world, and then promoted it by see no truth, hear no truth, and speak no truth. When others do not agree with them, their minds automatically double down to believe even more strongly in order to enhance the self-deception, to enhance their faith with their fellow believers, and to tarnish the nonbelievers. It is not a malicious activity. It is not due to a lack of information. It is not being lazy. It is a self-protective strategy to maintain the status of their clan vis-à-vis an opposing clan. To ask why believers can't unbelieve, we may as well be asking why conservatives don't stop being conservatives, and liberals don't stop being liberals.

This naïve realism slips out frequently in the statements of the complex PTSD stokers. They did not like the existing trauma-related disorder, PTSD, because it was not well suited to their ideological agenda of seeing human nature through the lens of nurture rather than nature. Their efforts to displace PTSD with a different disorder that was better suited to a social-engineering agenda began soon after the PTSD diagnosis was created. Their mission was not about science. Their mission was about advocating their ideology by weaponizing whatever science they could for social change. As one stoker put it, "Advocates for these female patients, like Herman, argued that there was a *moral and psychological imperative* to agree upon a new diagnosis that actually made sense of these patients' experience"[100] By giving a name to the interpersonal victimization suffered by these women, this name—complex PTSD—would grant a status recognition the victims somehow deserve. This recognition would also somehow unlock the door to the endgame of social engineering. Were complex PTSD to be officially recognized, "its supporters believe it would be a game changer. Just as the creation of PTSD 'transformed the health care system for individuals exposed to traumatic stress and led to an explosion of specialized research and practice,' says psychologist Bradley Stolbach, 'the inclusion of DTD in DSM-V . . . will be a powerful catalyst for transformation of the systems that serve children.'"[101]

When faced with conflicting viewpoints, rational minds would slow things down and consider the possibility that maybe they do not know something for certain. Naïve realism, however, takes the possibility of "I don't know" completely off the table. The richest discovery on the road to Traumaville may be that the three hardest words in the English language for many people to say are "I don't know."

Heuristics, however, guard the concept of "I don't know" locked away in a deep dungeon of the mind, and we have trouble getting past the guards. A difficult thing about heuristics is that we don't want to challenge them too much because we depend so much on them. Any lessons learned from challenging heuristics lack stickiness. Humans like to believe they are rational. We love characters like Sherlock Holmes and Ayn Rand's heroes of logic. But whenever we are confronted with the reality that we are not consistently rational, and are much more influenced by beliefs, the lesson is never retained. We quickly forget to be rational, and can be rational only with immense hard work. It is easier to lapse into the economical heuristics of beliefs. My most important purpose with this book is to show this function of how our complicated brains really work.

Complex PTSD is divisive

In 2019, a woman sent an email to me about one of my blog posts on the *Psychology Today* blog site. She argued that I was wrong and she believed complex PTSD was a real diagnosis. Because she was a survivor of interpersonal violence herself, she said she knew better than me and all my academic research and clinical knowledge. I wrote back to her, "Your argument seems to be that since you are a victim you have special knowledge about diagnostic categories that nonvictims cannot comprehend. . . . I think special recognition is fine; if that helps you, I'm glad. But your special recognition does not have to be a diagnostic category in official taxonomy. If your experiences deserve a special diagnostic category, then perhaps every type of trauma deserves a special category, e.g., Car Accident Trauma, Plane Crash Trauma, Desert War Trauma, Jungle War Trauma, and Firefighter Burn Trauma, ad infinitum."

The need for the status of moral superiority drives the seemingly inevitable separation into tribes based on psychological ideology. It has absolutely nothing to do with science. The strategy is the result of instincts that were baked into the DNA of the human mind for long-standing needs of living in clans. Maybe researchers and clinicians will form their own tribes. There is already an informal split between one group that is inclined toward activism, social engineering, belief in nurture over nature, and victimhood and one group that is inclined toward hard science and sticking to facts. The split is just not formal. We've already split into tribes based on religion, culture, country, and politics. Why should we think scientific and psychological ideologies will result in anything different?

Prescriptives for Recovery
Thought and Visualization Practices

- Daniel Kahneman provided a prescription to deal with heuristics and to save people from their bad choices. The main solution is to slow down and enlist System 2 more energetically. Because it is so difficult to analyze our own thinking processes, he suggested analyzing the thinking process of others. That is easier said than done, so Kahneman suggested using a visualization of coworkers gossiping around the proverbial water cooler. Specifically, apply System 2 to the choices of others because it is easier to see the mistakes of others than your own mistakes. Further, he believed that organizations can do this better than individuals because organizations inherently move more slowly and can impose orderly procedures. Thus, if decision makers in organizations are forced to remember the mistakes of others (around the proverbial water cooler), they will have those voices in their heads to stop them from making mistakes in the future. Voices in our heads of others' mistakes are preferable, he believes, because we seem incapable of learning from our own mistakes.

- Think of the underlying motivation before you believe. Beware the universal need for moral status. A belief that seems based on true facts at first can actually be based on false facts that are driven by the pursuit of moral status. To help understand the bases of morality, Jonathan Haidt, along with Craig Joseph, developed the moral foundations theory. The six foundations of the theory can be thought of as a toolbox to draw upon when trying to understand some of the true motivations of others.

  The Care/Harm foundation motivates individuals to cherish and protect others. In many, this may extend strongly toward helping, and not harming, disadvantaged groups. The Fairness/Cheating foundation believes in rendering justice according to rule, and takes a strong stance against cheating. The Loyalty/Betrayal foundation arouses the tendency to want to stand with your group, family, and/or nation, and contains a strong posture against betrayal. The Authority/Subversion foundation believes in traditions, and takes a strong stance against rebellion. The Sanctity/Degradation foundation abhors disgusting actions, and includes a strong posture against immoral activities that could desecrate the body. The Liberty/Oppression foundation reacts sharply against those who attempt to dominate others and restrict their liberty.

When the Care/Harm foundation carries excessive importance, and is not balanced by the other moral foundations, we can see how this creates Stokers who focus disproportionately on disadvantaged groups. So, instead of trying to parse complicated situations by the facts alone, consider also that skewed moral foundations might be motivating individuals or driving cultural movements. The more fervently individuals appear to support a belief or a cause related to victims, the more it might indicate a hyperfocus on the Care/Harm foundation operating strongly beneath the surface.

- If you experienced repeated, interpersonal trauma, and believe you have symptoms of complex PTSD, I acknowledge that visualizing yourself as having complex PTSD can feel like an attractive solution. It is likely to be helpful in the short term. A single diagnosis is less frightening than twin diagnoses of PTSD and borderline personality disorder. A treatment plan for one diagnosis seems simpler than a plan for two diagnoses. Believing problems were caused by external events is often easier to accept than admitting that you may have been born with psychological vulnerabilities.

- Some people may say, "I don't care if complex PTSD is validated scientifically or not. It's been a useful way for me to think about myself after what I've been through. I feel better about myself with this diagnosis. My psychotherapy based on this diagnosis has helped me." All those things may be true. There are many examples in psychotherapy and in other areas of life where truth is not necessary for people to feel better. The placebo effect is a real effect. Believing in something desirable is often more comforting than the facts.

Consider the long-term objective, however. Do you simply want to feel better, even if it is based on a false narrative, or are you trying to achieve a deeper, truer understanding of your problems? Will you be satisfied with a short-term fix, or are you committed to a longer-term peace with yourself?

- The alternative to complex PTSD is nothing novel. Instead of visualizing yourself as a person whose problems were all caused by certain types of external events, visualize yourself as a more complicated person who has two or more issues to deal with. One issue is your reactions to those external events, which most likely manifest as PTSD symptoms. Another issue is your personality that has been with you all your life and includes difficulties with affect regulation as well as self-identity, attachment, and interpersonal problems.

- An accurate understanding of the nature of the problems is key. In psychotherapy, we call the process of arriving at an accurate diagnosis psychoeducation. In recovery models for addiction, the process is more explicit about acceptance of one's limitations. I see patients who are relieved to receive the diagnosis of borderline personality disorder, and I see patients who are relieved to receive the diagnosis of high-functioning autism. In both cases they are relieved because it means they haven't been dumb about interpersonal relations; it means they've been working with major handicaps. Instead of beating themselves up because they feel like failures for doing it wrong, they feel better about themselves because they realize they've been battling against limitations they didn't know they had. It sounds counterintuitive, but just receiving an accurate diagnosis often brings relief and a profound sense of enhanced self-worth.

- Instead of working on an unrealistic treatment plan under the pretense of one unvalidated disorder that oversimplifies your problems, develop a realistic treatment plan based on two or more validated disorders. With an accurate understanding and humble acceptance of one's true limitations, it is easier to put together a treatment plan. For individuals with PTSD and features of borderline personality disorder—or what has been called complex PTSD—you can follow strategies that are based on interventions that actually have evidence behind them. For PTSD, there is cognitive behavioral therapy. For borderline personality disorder, there is dialectical behavior therapy. Both therapies are well researched and effective.

- Some victims of trauma are able to work past the pain of their experiences to achieve a type of transformation called posttraumatic growth. In addition to managing the negative symptoms, they experience an openness to reconsidering their belief systems. The school of positive psychology would call this technique "change the narrative." Instead of viewing being fired from a job as destruction of a career, the event is viewed as the opportunity to start a new career path—perhaps even a blessing to try the career you have always wanted but were afraid to try. Parents of children born with severe developmental disabilities often view their children as gifts instead of burdens. These parents view their children as signposts to show them their purpose in life. Using this technique, victims of interpersonal trauma can see their experiences not as something that destroyed their life plans and fragmented their personalities. They can see their experiences as something that started them on a new path.

Victims may become advocates. They may create nonprofit organizations to prevent violence. They may become motivational speakers to reach out to other victims.

Posttraumatic growth is a relatively new term in psychotherapy work, but the understanding that suffering can yield positive change is thousands of years old. Elements of the transformative power of suffering are evident in the teachings of Hinduism, Buddhism, and Islam, and have been noted in the writings of ancient Greeks, Christians, and Hebrews.

How does one achieve posttraumatic growth? It appears that most of the growth occurs spontaneously in individuals outside of psychotherapy offices and treatment programs. Individuals appear to have a natural inclination to find meaning in their experiences, which may be viewed as another one of the benefits of humans being belief engines. Humans will find meaning almost anywhere in order to help them adapt in the world.

Here we see the multifaceted utility of our being belief engines. You can opt to believe the gurus telling you that trauma has deformed your personality by altering your fragile capacities for affect regulation, self-identity, attachment, and interpersonal problems. Or you can accept those problems as wired into you from birth, and believe that traumatic suffering can be mastered and can even be channeled into transformative growth.

Chapter Four

THE POWER OF THE CLAN AND THE INFLUENCE OF PARENTING

Of the eighty-three journal articles and book chapters I have published, one of my most cited articles is one I wish I could take back. In 2001, I and my coauthor were the first to review all of the studies that assessed the post-trauma problems of both children and parents.[1] Our aim was to understand whether there was a connection between children who developed more symptoms following traumatic experiences and the parenting they received following those experiences. At the time, there were seventeen studies that met our review criteria. In sixteen of the seventeen, we found that children who showed more trauma-related symptoms had parents with more symptoms or marital problems.

Sixteen out of seventeen studies was impressive. This finding begged for interpretation. How were children's symptoms and parents' problems connected? We offered four theories that might explain this extremely consistent connection. Three of the theories were variations of blaming the influence mothers might have over the emotional regulation of children. These three theories focused on different ways parents could act cold or insensitive toward their children. We used this to propose a new construct called relational PTSD, wherein the behavior of one partner in a relationship, usually the mother, makes the symptoms of the other partner, usually the child, worse.

I now know that relational PTSD does not exist, and I have apologized elsewhere for ever suggesting it. The vast majority of the paper presented a narrative that made it sound like parents were to blame for making their children develop PTSD symptoms following traumatic experiences. As a young, naïve investigator, I thought we were on to something. So did many other researchers, apparently, and, unfortunately, I am one of the most commonly cited sources to support mother blaming for PTSD. This paper has been cited nearly six hundred times by other scholars and is the second-most cited of all my papers.

The fourth theory was not relational at all. The fourth theory suggested that maybe parents who possess genes that make them vulnerable to developing psychiatric symptoms pass those genes on to their children. These shared genes make both parents and children more symptomatic, and it has nothing to do with how they relate with each other interpersonally. We devoted only two sentences to this shared-genes theory.

If I were to write that paper today, I would give the genetic theory much more attention. I would never have coined the term *relational PTSD*, although to absolve myself of a little blame, I can say that my coauthor, who was my mentor, coined it and I went along. Instead, I wish I had explained that these studies provided absolutely no good evidence for mother blaming. As the famous saying goes, "Correlation is not causation." I have learned over time that it is highly unlikely that parents cause children to develop PTSD symptoms. But in 2001, I was overly influenced by the Power of the Clan.

Mothers and normal child development

The modern view that parents possess enormous influence over child development, which has been fostered by experts for decades, is surprisingly little different at its core from the ancient tribal belief system in terms of the importance of parents. Of course, we now know much more about how normal child development proceeds. The natural biological, psychological, and emotional changes that occur in stages throughout childhood are now known to occur on a precisely predictable schedule—so predictable that pediatricians can track whether children reach developmental milestones on schedule by following a development chart. The major domains of development are generally agreed upon to be physical (learning to sit, learning to walk, and eye-hand coordination), cognitive (understanding language, speaking, and overall intellectual function), and psychosocial (ability to interact and get along with others and learning to express and manage different emotions).

Consistent with ancient beliefs, the majority of people believe that parents can have a major influence on these trajectories of child development. It must be stated that this is an extraordinary belief. Child development is a hardwired function of genes that progresses in nearly the same way for every single human. Child development has occurred on the same schedule for millions of years. The notion that something as temporary and external as parenting practices can take over the controls of child development is an extraordinary theory. Yet the majority of people believe it.

The majority of psychologists, psychiatrists, social workers, and professional counselors believe this theory to some degree. But mental health professionals are far from being unique in this belief. The theory is also widely believed by the vast majority of the general human population. One of my acquaintances is a successful businessman who is well liked by all and has traveled the world. He has two sisters and a brother. His brother is almost the opposite of him. The brother graduated from law school but was never successful at anything, feels entitled that his parents should still support him, and is not well liked by anyone. My acquaintance theorized aloud to me one day as to why his brother was so different. He believed that his brother was different because their parents always treated him differently. The parents coddled him. If the parents had drawn a hard line with the brother early on, my acquaintance thinks, the brother would have turned out a much different, better person.

But, I said, you, your brother, and your two sisters had the same parents who provided essentially the same childhood and the same parenting to all of you. Isn't it possible that your brother was simply born to be different, with a different mix of genes, and your parents' habits of parenting had little to do with it? I told him that I see it all the time in my practice. Siblings turn out wildly differently with the same parents, and it is evident from the time they can first walk and speak. My acquaintance looked down and away a bit with a distant stare, seemingly unable to consider that this was even a worthy possibility.

The belief that parenting molds children's development is widespread in all walks of life, and it is easy to find. It can be found in most biographies of famous individuals. For example, Charles Darwin allegedly was shaped permanently by the parenting he received after the death of his mother. Darwin lost his mother to illness at the age of eight years. He was largely raised by his older sisters, who thereafter maintained silence about their mother. Since Darwin lacked a proper way to mourn, this supposedly impacted his emotional development and contributed to his lifelong mysterious, psychosomatic illness.[2]

Renowned musician Louis Armstrong lacked a stable home during his childhood, living at various times with his mother, with his grandmother, and in group homes. He supposedly developed a character trait to live life with determination from a Jewish family he worked for who temporarily fed and nurtured him.

Marilyn Monroe was raised mainly in foster homes and group homes because her mother was often mentally unstable. Supposedly, this grim childhood molded her into an unstable personality who aspired to be an actor where she could play out imaginary lives that were better, while she was unable to maintain stable relationships in real life.

This type of belief permeates normal child-development beliefs of experts. A typical illustration of this belief comes from a college textbook titled *Child Psychology: A Handbook of Contemporary Issues*: "Overall, research on how families influence children's social development has shown that the quality of relationships within the system is of critical importance. . . . Parents (i.e., primarily mothers) characterized as low in responsivity and sensitivity and high in control, intrusiveness, and harshness have children who are less socially competent."[3]

The belief that parenting is a foundational basis of child development, and perhaps the most important foundation, is like talking about one of the "big beliefs" of human societies—race, religion, politics, or sex. Everyone, no matter their training or station in life, holds their own deep-rooted beliefs. The prevailing belief among both experts and parents is that parents have a powerful influence on their children's normal development and future personalities. The belief is so strong within most people that to claim otherwise amounts to radical heresy.

Mother blaming is the natural extension of this theory of child development. Mother blaming is the extraordinary theory that parents, especially mothers, possess the power for both tremendous good and tremendous harm simply by interacting with their children on a daily basis. They can mold their children's personalities into moral, kind, and thoughtful human beings, or they can alter their brains to make them psychiatrically disordered for life. Of course, when children turn out well, it is not called mother blaming; it is called excellent parenting. It is only when they turn out poorly that it is called mother blaming.

The trouble is that it is not true. Mothers are incredibly important for many things for their children. The evidence, however, does not support the idea that mothers can drastically mold the fundamental character of individuals.

The nurture assumption

In 1995, Judith Rich Harris published a dense, thirty-two-page review article in a journal called *Psychological Review* that described her new theory of child development.[4] Harris's article challenged this dogma about the importance of parenting. She backed up her theory with mountains of evidence and put a knife through the heart of the commonly believed theory to demonstrate that parents did not possess these extraordinary powers, and, in contrast, children's peer groups likely had a much stronger influence on their social development than their own parents.

Harris's article received the American Psychological Association's George A. Miller Award for an Outstanding Recent Article in General Psychology. The reactions of other psychologists to her article were modest and cordial. It is likely that most of the experts who disagreed with her viewed her as a nonthreatening one-off. You see, Harris was a nobody and had no professional status. She had no advanced degree, and she was not a licensed clinician. She had been in Harvard's graduate psychology program but was kicked out at the age of twenty-two for failing to meet their doctoral standards. (In a bit of sweet irony, her letter of termination was signed by the same George A. Miller for whom the award for her paper had been named.) At the time she published her 1995 article, she was fifty-seven years old and had only two prior publications as a first author in peer-reviewed journals. She was not even employed at a university. She made a living by working from home as a writer of undergraduate psychology textbooks full of other people's research. In the byline where authors usually list their prestigious university employment, she was forced to simply list her hometown address—Middletown, New Jersey.

But this unlicensed, non-degreed grandmother from New Jersey had the bit in her teeth. She knew she was on to something big. She was physically limited by a chronic autoimmune disorder, but mentally, she could thunder like a thoroughbred. She kept writing about her new theory and in 1998 published a book titled *The Nurture Assumption: Why Children Turn Out the Way They Do.*[5] This time, she got a much different professional reaction. The book was well-done and persuasive, and was getting publicity. Her book had hit a nerve with the licensed and degreed experts of the world.

This time, the experts came after her with knives out. They determined that Harris ought to pay a price for her audacity to challenge the cherished theory of mothers' influence over their children's development. Jerome Kagan, the dean of child development experts, a psychologist at Harvard University, and perhaps the most respected voice in the field, attacked Harris repeatedly for years.

He told one journalist, "I am embarrassed for psychology."[6] He told another journalist, "What she says is just silly. . . . Any parent knows that intuitively."[7] He told yet another journalist that Harris's work is "total nonsense." Her book, he said dismissively, "was a media event. It had nothing to do with science. If the media had not hyped it—partly because it was so crazy—nobody would know about her."[8]

Frank Farley, a psychologist at Temple University, past president of the American Psychological Association, and an expert on child development, told a journalist, "She's all wrong. . . . Her thesis is absurd on its face, but consider what might happen if parents believe this stuff! Will it free some to mistreat their kids since 'it doesn't matter'?"[9] Wendy Williams, a psychologist and later the founder and director of the Cornell Institute for Women in Science, told the same journalist, "By taking such an extreme position, Harris does a tremendous disservice." Wade Horn, a clinical child psychologist and director of the Fatherhood Institute, said, "This book is not just silly, but dangerous."[10]

These experts were willing to take drastic and public steps to put Harris in her place. They needed to scare the world and persuade it that Harris was wrong.

The belief in mother blaming also had to be defended because social policies related to children, including child care, education, social services, public health, and medical intervention, are shaped by conceptions about childhood. These "ideologies of childhood," even when voiced by psychological researchers, "are not chaste scientific productions," but rather reflect the prevailing political and social atmosphere.[11] Social programs that were built on promoting maternal guidance, and the funding for those programs, which are viewed as critical to children's lives for those who fought for the programs, would be at risk if Harris was right.

Many others, however, have supported Harris, and personally, I believe she is right. But whatever you choose to believe about child development, my point is that the ferocity of attacks on Harris, many of them personal, demonstrates the innate force of the Power of the Clan for supporting mother blaming. These academic experts were harsh, but they were simply saying what most of them intuitively believed.

In Chapter Two, we saw the power of a Set of Small False Facts for making a belief sound like a fact. In Chapter Three, in the stories of complex PTSD and the rise of Theranos, we saw the importance of the role of Stokers; in order for the small false facts to do their work, respected individuals have to lend their status to the beliefs. We've looked at the type of facts—true facts and false facts—and we've looked at the characteristics of individuals—self-inflating stokers. But the subject of this chapter—the Power of the Clan—explains why the mental mechanisms that churn belief into fact exist in the first place. The Power of the Clan is what sets individuals on the road to Traumaville. Our ancient brain, which developed from living in small clans, is designed to be deceived when that serves a useful function, but this can go sideways in modern times when we are faced with more complicated situations.

The Power of the Clan

The Power of the Clan, as it pertains to psychological trauma, is a confluence of several instinctual mental mechanisms that were baked into the DNA of our ancestral brains through millions of years of living in small clans. The Power of the Clan is the power of instincts that helped us thrive in social groups, and it is the driving force behind mother blaming.

The first mental mechanism is based on the selection of caring parents. In ancient times, caring parents were more likely to give birth to caring children by passing on the genes that make people caring. Before modern medicine, when survival of children depended much more on parents to provide safety, healthy habits, and medical treatment, children with caring parents were more likely to survive and grow up to be caring parents themselves. Over thousands and thousands of years of this pattern occurring, it is likely that the proportion of caring parents increased compared to noncaring parents. Judith Rich Harris made the obvious evolutionary point: "Babies whose parents took good care of them were more likely to survive than those whose parents were negligent, and the surviving babies inherited the mental mechanisms that impelled their parents to provide that care."[12]

The qualities of caring individuals were essential within clans for another reason. Caring individuals have a conscience. Christopher Boehm, a cultural anthropologist who studied primates under renowned field researcher Jane Goodall, explained how having a conscience is of immense importance to human social life. Boehm studied how clans deal with bullies and agitators who refuse to cooperate. In the politics of clan social life, a key issue is how to deal with upstarts and bullies who try to upset the power balance. The most effective way to deal nonviolently with upstarts and bullies is with public shame and ostracism. To avoid being pegged as an upstart, and to avoid the possibility of shame and ostracism, tribal members learn to be humble. And so, as Boehm described, "people are careful about extolling their own success."[13] He reported an anecdote about a hunter who would not admit to killing a big prey directly, but with humble hints and clever twists of language, he could let his tribe mates know what he did without bragging.

Boehm wrote, "The killing, wounding, social exclusion, and social avoidance of aggressive (or cunning) deviants who do not rein in their predatory tendencies could have influenced earlier human gene pools, affected them so profoundly that a uniquely human conscience was able to evolve."[14] This ancient process for the development of a highly developed human conscience explains the origins of morality.

Psychologist Jonathan Haidt, who studies the origin and utility of morality in humans, seems to find much overlap with Boehm's observations of primates and human tribes. Haidt has noted, much like Boehm, that some of our earliest understanding of how social groups survive is that they have a mechanism to rein in the bad actors. The basic social unit is not the individual, it is the hierarchically structured family, which cannot function well if individuals act only for themselves. There must be strong forces to compel cooperation. According to Haidt, a society that could not rein in bad actors would be a network of "many nested and overlapping groups that socialize, reshape, and care for individuals who, if left to their own devices, would pursue shallow, carnal, and selfish pleasures."[15]

The forces that are most effective to constrain selfish impulses are shame and guilt. The development of shame and guilt as innate traits helps to explain why humans are altruistic. Prehistoric humans who were better at inhibiting their own antisocial tendencies would obviously make better tribe mates for all the activities that required cooperation. Shame and guilt were excellent mechanisms for social control, particularly for ostracizing bullies who could feel shame.

As noted previously, Haidt and several colleagues developed the Moral Foundations Theory as a way to codify their finding that systems of morality have many similarities and common themes across widely separated cultures.[16] They proposed five foundations of morality, which are all grounded in "our long history as tribal creatures."[17] One of these five, the Care/Harm foundation, appears to overlap entirely with Harris's emphasis on how caring parents beget caring children, and hence caring people populate the clan.

Thus, when children turn out well, the entire clan gives the parents credit. But it is a double-edged sword, as Harris pointed out: "The flip side of parent power is parental culpability—the idea that if anything goes wrong with the kid it's the parents' fault."[18] Social forces are everything in this context. Believing that parents are to blame doesn't have to be true. It just has to be useful for the clan.

The second mental mechanism is the need for status. In previous chapters, we have seen how the need for status influences beliefs and behaviors, but we have not addressed the question of why the need for status exists in the first place.

Following the controversial success of The Nurture Assumption in 1998, Judith Rich Harris published her second and last book in 2006, called No Two Alike: Human Nature and Human Individuality. Her aim in the second book was to explain why no two people have the same personality. She put forth a theory to explain the variations in personality not due to genetics. Harris theorized that humans are born with several instinctual systems for storing information about people and social groups.[19] These instincts are our inborn, automatic ways of learning about and thinking about other humans.

As described in Chapter One, Harris theorized in *No Two Alike* that humans are born with three mental systems for understanding the social world. These are the Relationship System for evaluating individuals, the Socialization System for learning the rules of how to behave in groups, and the Status System for comparing oneself to others in order to maximize one's status.

One huge area of status is, of course, child care. How your children turn out is constantly compared to how your neighbors' children turn out. Your children are a direct reflection on you as a parent. Your status, both how you view yourself in relation to others and how others view you in relation to themselves, is largely determined by how you are perceived as a parent. Thus, according to Harris, this instinctual system, which is baked into our DNA, explains why the need for status exists in the first place.

We constantly strive for status because we must live in social groups. Status is not only the way to maximize the amount of good things you can acquire in the clan, it is, in the modern world, the main determinant of how we perceive our own value as an individual.

The third mental mechanism is the primal instinct to protect the safety of the clan. Instincts developed from our long ancestral existence in dangerous worlds. Safety was essential at both the individual and clan levels. At the clan level, social organization was responsible for every facet of life—survival, safety, shelter, food, reproduction, and medicine. Before modern civilization, clan life was heavily embedded in predator-and-prey relationships, diseases were more fatal, and weather events were more deadly. Life required cooperation and coordinated social skills. It was dangerous and mysterious. The human brain developed massive skills of memory, executive functions, future planning, and cooperation that no other species has or will achieve largely in order to master these social arrangements.

Before scientific explanations were available, meaning and intentions had to come from somewhere else, and, for lack of anything else, these often had to be mysterious powers. The clan believed in higher powers that shaped their fortunes because they had no other explanations. The higher power could be animal spirits, totems, gods, inanimate forces, or other clan members with special powers. The higher powers either favored them or disfavored them. If they were lucky enough to find an excellent cave near good hunting grounds, it was because they did something to please the higher power. If a clan member fell ill, it was because the clan did something to displease the higher power. If they had a successful hunt, they paid homage and gave thanks to the higher power. If a blizzard nearly froze the entire clan, it was because they forgot to pay homage to the higher power. And so on.

Mother blaming is a way to give an etiology to mysterious child problems. This is the Power of the Clan. The need to raise good children baked instincts into us that included having a conscience. The need to cooperate socially and inhibit bad actors baked instincts into us to acquire status. Add to these a third component of safety and the need to explain mysteries that might threaten the clan: if there are deviations, there must be someone or something to blame. Mothers are the natural target. Blaming others is by definition only possible in a group. If we lived solitary lives, there would not be such a need to assign blame.

These compelling urges have been recognized for a long time, but the true origins of the urges were mysterious for most of history. The eighteenth-century Scottish philosopher David Hume was one of the earliest to try to explain our unique predicament in the world. Hume observed that we are put in a world where the true causes of many events are concealed from us. The continuous dangers of death, sickness, and other threats have unknown causes. He wrote, "These unknown causes, then, become the constant object of our hope and fear; and while the passions are kept in perpetual alarm by an anxious expectation of events, the imagination is equally employed in forming ideas of those powers, on which we have so entire a dependence."[20]

In times of extreme danger, the urge for the clan to pull even closer together is a powerful vortex. As Montseratt Guibernau wrote in her book titled *Belonging: Solidarity and Division in Modern Societies*, the urge to belong to social groups in most individuals is so strong that they are willing to give up substantial individual freedom. The attractions of security, protection, and companionship are so strong because "the emotional appeal of belonging to the nation, as a political community, stands as the most powerful agent of political mobilization, one able to establish a sharp distinction between those who belong and those who are regarded as enemies and aliens."[21]

A side effect, or perhaps an intended effect, is that we find it useful to attach meanings to events. When a clan member falls ill, it is useful to have a reason for it. When bad weather strikes, it is comforting to feel there is a reason for it. We are, after all, belief engines.

This "need to defend a shared nest,"[22] based on fundamentals of morality, caring, and social cooperation, very nearly explains all one needs to know about America's military responses following 9/11. This hits the nail on the head of why Cheney and Rumsfeld and the majority of the United States' citizens were willing to go to war. Any war. They just needed a country to invade. They needed to send two messages. One message was to their fellow clan members that the shared nest would be defended. The other message was to the enemies of our clan that we were not weak.

Most of the functions of social life of early clans are taken care of for us now by others in modern life whom we never see and who are highly specialized. Our leaders are elected officials, most of whom we never meet personally. Titans of business are CEOs of huge corporations whom we never know. Food is provided from states and countries that we may never visit. Medicine is taken care of by highly trained groups of doctors, nurses, and technicians. War is handled by highly trained soldiers.

But one function of social life remains in the hands of individuals. Child care is nearly alone as a daily function of survival that is the primary responsibility of individual parents. When something mysteriously goes wrong with children, all eyes turn to parents.

One unintended consequence of automatically finding someone to blame for mysterious problems in children is that the belief must have as its starting point the idea that children are not born bad. In other words, all children must be born equal, and the only reasons for deviations have external causes. It is straightforward to see how this provides one of the fundamental mental and instinctual underpinnings, if not the only one, that drives the always-rollicking nature-versus-nurture debate.

The confluence of these three mental mechanisms is what provides the enormous heuristic force to give parents blame when children turn out poorly. According to the first mechanism, the selection of caring parents, humans have a highly developed sense of caring and nurturance because those are beneficial qualities to have in a clan for protecting and raising children. According to the second mechanism, the need for status, we are wired at birth to monitor social status and to enhance our social status whenever feasible. Being a good parent is one of the most common ways social status is measured. These two factors chug along like clockwork on a daily basis, barrels loaded, trigger cocked in anticipation of any mysterious problem that needs explaining. Then, children develop problems that we cannot easily explain, such as PTSD, and the third mechanism, protect the safety of the clan, is triggered to find meaning where there is a vacuum, to assign blame to maintain the structure of the clan, and to assign status, good or bad. Mother blaming automatically occurs like a runaway train, and we can't even find the brake. The Power of the Clan is an invisible, sucking vortex that is so automatic that it is difficult to see it happen and so strong that it is difficult to resist.

In summary, the Power of the Clan is a confluence of mental mechanisms. This makes for a difficult story to remember, and for me, a difficult story to write. The mind is infinitely complicated, and there are no simple, single-cause, linear relations in the brain. I find it difficult to write these things concisely in a sticky narrative, and I imagine readers have a difficult time following my writing. That is an apology for the denseness of this chapter, but it is also an explanation of how trauma researchers have such an easy time persuading others of false beliefs. Who can keep track of it all?

Bernie Madoff's Ponzi scheme and the Power of the Clan

We've seen how heuristics work well in everyday life but not so well in complex situations; it is also apparent that the Status System works well in the simple world of clan survival. But in complex, modern situations it often has unintended consequences.

Bernie Madoff masterminded the largest financial crime in history, involving $65 billion, and his story provides an extreme example illustrating the Power of the Clan. Madoff was clearly the singular villain in the crime, but it is fascinating that the whole thing was made possible only by tapping into the Power of the Clan. Harry Markopolos, an accountant who tried to expose Madoff years before he was arrested, wrote a book that explained how Madoff was able to pull off the Ponzi scheme for more than twenty years. The book, titled *No One Would Listen: A True Financial Thriller*, begins with a four-page glossary that lists all the characters involved.[23] It is telling that so many individuals had to collude as a clan to make themselves believe that nothing illegal was happening. Investors wanted to be in Madoff's clan. Watchdogs of the financial markets were too closely connected to this clan. All played important parts in allowing the fraud to happen. These four pages of a cast of characters are the essence of how this could only occur in the dynamics of a clan, and speaks to the realization that while Madoff was a master manipulator, this was not just one man running a con. It was a clan of people who wanted to believe that one special man in their special clan had mysterious and magical powers to master the stock market. Madoff was simply immoral enough to capitalize on that belief system.

The key for the Power of the Clan to work is that the clan has to believe certain individuals can have special powers. The narrative of Markopolos's book begins with a scene after Madoff had been caught. An investigator for the Securities and Exchange Commission (SEC) went to interview Madoff in jail and was expecting Madoff to be tight-lipped. Instead, boasting of his close connections in the financial industry, Madoff gave expansive answers for three hours. "He claimed to know so many important people—'I knew this one,' that one 'was a good friend,' this one he 'knows very well,' that one he 'had a special relationship with.'"[24]

Those who were not part of his special clan were dismissed with a patronizing wave of the hand. When the investigator asked Madoff about Markopolos's efforts to expose the Ponzi scheme, Madoff was dismissive. Markopolos is "really a joke in the industry," Madoff said.[25] This is the same strategy we have seen with Bessel van der Kolk, who offhandedly dismissed anyone who disagreed with him, and the consistent refrain of the complex PTSD stokers who claimed that clinicians who cannot see what they see and believe what they believe are actually harming patients. In other words, do not bother yourself with the evidence; those people outside my clan are fools. Madoff said, "All you have to do is look at the type of people I was doing this for to know it was a credible strategy. They knew the strategy was doable. They knew a lot more than this guy Harry."[26] Madoff was signaling that he was a man with special powers within a clan of important people.

Clan relations were key to Madoff's success even before he started the Ponzi scheme. From the earliest days of his career, a portion of his money-management business was based on personal, private, clan-like relationships. When Madoff was starting out as a money manager, his father-in-law, Saul Alpern, who ran an accounting firm, gave him an inside track. Alpern created a limited partnership of clients and family members. Individuals deposited money into the partnership, and then Alpern passed the money on to Madoff to invest. This cozy little family affair was probably illegal as an unlicensed mutual fund, but it was not yet a Ponzi scheme.[27]

This pattern of clan and insider status grew and evolved over time. One of Madoff's early clients was a wealthy businessman named Stanley Chais.[28] Chais had trust funds with Madoff for his three children, and would eventually have more than four dozen Madoff accounts. Starting in 1970, Chais took the extra step of setting up three formal partnerships that raised money from other people and invested it with Madoff. None of these funds was registered. They were called feeder funds, and they would become the model for how Madoff got his investors later after the Ponzi scheme kicked in. The model evolved from wealthy individuals setting up the feeder funds to respected firms setting up the feeder funds. For example, "lawyers at several New York City firms set up formal partnerships so their clients could invest with Madoff," and the same thing occurred at prominent accounting firms.[29]

Madoff, who was Jewish, used his Jewish-ness to prey on the Jewish nonprofit world of New York City. He had contacts with Jewish philanthropists. Madoff's relationship with J. Ezra Merkin "helped to cement Madoff's reputation among Jewish philanthropists. The allure was poignantly simple: his investment skill would amplify their generous impulses."[30] Noted Jewish author and Nobel laureate Elie Wiesel invested his entire endowment with Madoff.

Madoff accumulated additional respect because he was one of the pioneers in computerized trading on the markets. He became a member of the National Association of Securities Dealers (NASD) board of governors. The board of governors is the controlling body that sets policy on a national scale. The NASD is a self-regulating organization that operates the NASDAQ stock market. He was chairman of the NASDAQ market for three one-year terms. He gained prominence as a reassuring voice during the 1987 stock crash.

Ironically, it may have been the 1987 stock crash that drove Madoff to ignore whatever moral guardrails he possessed and start the Ponzi scheme. In her book, Diana Henriques provided evidence that during the 1987 crash, investors withdrew so much money from their accounts that Madoff needed cash in a hurry to cover the losses, avoid public embarrassment, and maintain his golden reputation.[31]

In jailhouse interviews, Madoff seemed to reveal without really knowing it that the genesis of the Ponzi scheme was all too tied in to his sense of narcissism. Two of his biggest individual investors, Jeffry Picower and Carl Shapiro, withdrew huge sums of cash after the 1987 crash. This was described by Madoff as a personal betrayal. Madoff claimed he had personal understandings with his investors that profits would be reinvested, not withdrawn. He stated that these men "changed the deal on me. I was hung out to dry."[32] Other customers withdrew funds, but nowhere near as much. Madoff is masterful at misdirection and making it sound like a simple and impersonal situation of investors who violated his practice guidelines, which forced him to do something he did not want to do. Of course, it was all just about the business. But it sounds like Madoff was not about to have his reputation stained in such a personal way. It seems that the entire Ponzi scheme was less about the money than it was about Madoff's massive and narcissistic need for status in the clan.

During the early years of the Ponzi scheme, investors came mainly through a network of wealthy individuals and the feeder funds set up by some of the clients, what Henriques called the "friends and family" network. Most of the investors did not invest directly with Madoff. The middleman organizations had to be lucky enough to have personal relationships with Madoff. These organizations would round up their existing customers to pool their cash, and they would pass the cash in bulk to Madoff. The individuals had to be lucky enough to be a customer of one of the few middleman organizations that were working with Madoff. Most individuals who lost money in Madoff's Ponzi scheme never gave cash directly to Madoff. It was all about the clan of Madoff's groups, and the clans within those groups whose members all felt they had special status to be included.

When one of the feeder funds, run by Frank Avellino and Michael Bienes, was investigated by the SEC in 1992 for being run as an unregistered mutual fund, the SEC demanded the feeder fund return $400 million to investors. Madoff covered this hole by taking funds from other accounts,[33] but this likely created a bigger hole that needed even bigger investments, which is the inevitable outcome of every Ponzi scheme when the money going out starts to outweigh the money coming in.

This forced Madoff to turn to larger, professionally managed sources of cash called hedge funds. Hedge funds are relatively risky money-management products limited to wealthy investors. In return for having a genius manage the money in the hedge fund, investors pay huge management fees. The hedge funds would turn over a portion of the money from their investors to Madoff. Madoff would in turn send back handsome returns, obtained of course falsely through the Ponzi scheme, to the hedge funds, which would then send handsome returns to the wealthy investors.

The hedge funds, however, were run by professional money managers, and, unlike the friends-and-family network of nonexpert investors, they demanded an explanation from Madoff for how he produced such incredible returns before they would hand money over to him. This is where Madoff learned to master the set of small false facts. Madoff told the managers that he used something called the split-strike conversion.

The split-strike conversion strategy is a real strategy sometimes used by money managers, but is too complex for the average person to truly understand.[34] The strategy involves the purchase of stocks and then bracketing the stocks to be either purchased or sold depending on which direction the market moves. The bracketing involves a call option to create a ceiling on gains and a put option to provide a floor on losses. It was plausible because Madoff held such a large volume of stocks that he might be able to leverage the strategy better than others, or even create market movements that only he could anticipate. It sounded plausible, but not quite believable because there would have to be equally large buyers to handle the amount of trading Madoff would have to do to make such large sums of money.

When SEC inspector general David Kotz met with Madoff in jail, "Madoff kept assuring Kotz—accurately—that the investment strategy he pretended to be using all those years could have worked, could have been real, was 'not that exotic.'" Big Wall Street firms might be claiming now that they saw through him, but his clients had included several former top executives at Merrill Lynch and Morgan Stanley, he said truthfully. "Credible people knew it could be done or they wouldn't be clients."[35] His split-strike conversion story was just plausible enough to be believed.

By 2005, enough suspicion had reached the SEC that they began investigating Madoff, three years before he was eventually arrested. Two SEC agents investigated Madoff for three weeks in 2005 and tried to make sense of what he was doing. They eventually seemed to believe his split-strike conversion pitch and stopped investigating.

A lot of people probably surmised that Madoff was a fraud. Markopolos believes that other fund managers thought Madoff was cleverly front-running, not doing something as stupid as a Ponzi scheme. Front-running makes money by trading stocks with insider knowledge. Front-running, while it is illegal, does not have the catastrophic end of a Ponzi scheme, and many turn a blind eye to it. After all, this was Wall Street, where arcane rules are bent or sidestepped all the time. The SEC disciplines dozens of individuals every year for insider trading.

Harry Markopolos also focused on a different dimension of the clan. As he described in his book, he submitted detailed reports to the SEC on what he believed was Madoff's fraud in 2000, 2001, and 2005. Incredibly, the SEC never acted on those reports. It was not just investors who were deceived by Madoff; the SEC turned a blind eye to his obviously outlandish reports of success. Just as the public and repeated criticism of the evidence, or lack thereof, for the concept of complex PTSD has had little impact on diminishing its luster, the evidence of a Ponzi scheme had little impact on the SEC watchdogs.

The real terror of the story, according to Markopolos, is not the gullibility of investors; it is the incompetence of the SEC. The individuals in our clan who are supposed to protect us failed to do so. I think Markopolos is right. It is inevitable that bad actors will try to bamboozle honest people; that is not tragic. But the watchdogs of our clan are supposed to protect us, and the failure of our watchdogs is more terrifying.

With the split-strike conversion strategy and the arcane rules of the stock market, we can see parallels with complex PTSD and the weapons of mass destruction in Iraq. The complex details can't be understood. They are used as misdirection to make your head swivel and take your eyes off the real problem.

Not everyone was misdirected, however, and possibly none of the professional investors ever believed Madoff's actions were completely legal. They knew something was too good to be true. But, as Markopolos wrote, "even those people who had questioned his strategy had accepted his nonsensical explanation—as long as the returns kept rolling in."[36] In other words, as long as there was not a large risk of getting caught, they wanted the status of money and Madoff.

The Power of the Clan says you don't have to possess the true facts to persuade people. Our socially inclined brain is grasping for useful beliefs to navigate the social clan, not necessarily true facts. Markopolos was one of the few who were certain it was a Ponzi scheme. But even Markopolos's closest coworkers wouldn't believe him that it was a Ponzi scheme. Markopolos wrote that for a long time his coworkers "just couldn't get beyond Madoff's reputation. He was a respected public figure who had served on major securities industry boards; he had tremendous credentials."[37]

Henriques understood it was all about the social relationships. "What was it about Madoff that made all these smart, analytical people trust him so much, so easily, for so long?"[38] She explained that unlike other con artists, he was never showy. "Instead, without saying a word, he seemed to create a quiet but intense magnetic field that drew people to him, as if he were true north, or the calm eye of the storm. One associate called it 'an aura.' Like a gifted actor, he drew one's attention simply by stepping onstage, by entering a room. He wore his expertise casually—'he had the decoder ring,' one former regulator recalled—and he seemed seductively unflappable in times that felt messy, chaotic, and scary to everyone else."

Madoff helped create the image of exclusivity. Henriques stated, "For some time he had cultivated the impression that new investors simply couldn't get in—he had all the money he wanted: he wouldn't even discuss the business with would-be clients. It was akin to winning the lottery if he agreed to add your hedge fund to his coterie of institutional clients. The approach was masterful, of course. It proved that Groucho Marx's famous rule also worked in reverse: everyone wanted to join the club that wouldn't let them in."[39] The spiel worked so well that in 2001, a story revealed Madoff surprisingly to be perhaps the world's largest money manager, holding assets totaling $6 billion.

Markopolos tells an anecdote about an investor who sees the news of Madoff's arrest by the FBI in 2008 on a TV screen in a plane. The investor turns to his wife and tells her about the arrest and that they just lost millions. She, under the Power of the Clan, does not believe him. "That's not possible," she says, and returns to her magazine. What's not possible? It is not possible that Madoff deceived them? It is not possible that the FBI arrested an innocent man? The anecdote is light on details, and perhaps portrays only the woman's temporary state of mind, but it tells the whole story in a nutshell. The woman believed in her mind that Madoff was trustworthy and had magical powers, and she had to disbelieve reality so that the outside world would be seamless with her internal world. She had to deceive herself in order to maintain her belief.

The history of mothers with special powers: autism

At the end of the nineteenth century in the United States, a feeling had grown within society that would lead to the emergence of the first professionals in child mental health. As one modern writer looking back on that era observed, the feeling was "a moral panic over the behavior of the urban poor," which fostered new notions of childhood.[40] This gave rise to the earliest child psychiatry clinics, which were curiously called child guidance clinics. The clinicians were not treating children; they were guiding parents to be better parents.

These efforts were focused on children with disabilities or low intellectual ability, street children, and juvenile delinquents. The efforts have been described as "a child-saving movement funded by the upper class and staffed by the middle class, particularly middle-class women. United in their vision that poverty, immorality, and antisocial behavior could best be attacked by reshaping childhood," these reform movements intended to save wayward children included "compulsory education, settlement houses, juvenile courts, reform schools, welfare departments, child protection organizations, and research centers." Central to many of these efforts was the theory that parenting had the extraordinary power to either cause or prevent these problems.

Leo Kanner is considered to be the first child psychiatrist in the world before child psychiatry was an official specialty. In 1943, Kanner published the first description of autism in children.[41] He published a follow-up paper in 1949 on what he believed caused autism. He quite bluntly suggested that autism was due to a lack of maternal warmth. He observed that children were exposed from "the beginning to parental coldness, obsessiveness, and a mechanical type of attention to material needs only. . . . They were left neatly in refrigerators which did not defrost. Their withdrawal seems to be an act of turning away from such a situation to seek comfort in solitude."[42] Kanner coined the famous phrase *refrigerator mother*.

Thus, from the very first days of child psychiatry, from the very first child psychiatrist, mother blaming was invoked to explain why children turned out poorly. Recently, others have come to Kanner's defense to explain that he never meant to blame parents for autism and that he went out of his way later in life to not blame parents.[43] Perhaps. But in 1949, he wrote clearly enough that he does indeed need defending. Kanner, under the Power of the Clan, had mastered mother blaming.

Bruno Bettelheim took the baton from Kanner, and he did much more to make the refrigerator mother concept popular. Bettelheim, a self-taught psychologist, seemed to acknowledge that there was a genetic component to autism, but he strongly believed that autism was largely caused when mothers withheld affection from their children. In his 1967 book *The Empty Fortress*, which was highly regarded at the time, Bettelheim expressed his opinion that autism was not simply present at birth when he wrote, "My own belief, as presented throughout this book, is that autism has essentially to do with everything that happens from birth on."[44] He directly attributed those events "from birth on" to poorly responsive mothers: "If things go wrong because such anticipatory behavior is not met by an appropriate response in the mother, the relation of the infant to his environment may become deviant from the very beginning of life."

Bettelheim has been widely discredited since his death but not because of his promotion of mother blaming. He had misrepresented his credentials,[45] plagiarized material for his book,[46] and reportedly beaten his institutionalized child patients.[47]

Schizophrenia

A similar thing happened with schizophrenia. Schizophrenia is one of the most debilitating illnesses of the brain. Patients with schizophrenia are often paranoid, see strange and terrifying hallucinations, and hear hallucinations that are often threatening and violent. Patients with schizophrenia also usually have profound impairments to interacting in a smooth personal manner with other humans. They frequently end up unable to hold jobs and require assistance and supervision in their daily living.

Unable to understand what caused schizophrenia, proponents of early theories, of course, blamed parents. Theodore Lidz, who trained in psychiatry at the department run by Dr. Kanner and then worked at Yale University, became a leading authority on schizophrenia. In his 1965 book titled *Schizophrenia and the Family*, Lidz and his two coauthors frequently referred to the concept of "schizophrenogenic mothers" as "seriously disturbed and strange women" who caused schizophrenia in their children through cold and rejecting parenting.[48]

Fortunately, this theory is now widely discredited scientifically. Genetic studies and longer clinical experience have shown the absurdity of mother blaming for schizophrenia. It is too bad that simpler rational thought did not prevent mother blaming in the first place. How can any rational clinician look at a family that contains one child with schizophrenia and siblings who show no signs of schizophrenia and conclude that parenting selectively impacted one child but left the other siblings unscathed?

Nevertheless, the tendency to blame mothers remains a strong and ever-present force. In one research study, individuals who had one close family member diagnosed with schizophrenia were asked to explain their feelings about various aspects of genetic research on schizophrenia.[49] Their narratives were recorded and then rated by researchers. These individuals clearly understood that genetics played a leading role as the cause of schizophrenia. Despite this understanding, the individuals still felt pulled to blaming themselves. As one participant said, "I suppose mothers blame themselves for everything."

It seemed that the manner in which these family members talked about genetic causes of schizophrenia was a counterweight to "weaken the grip of a historically dense and still culturally prevalent ideology of motherhood as the crucible from which psychopathology issues." In other words, talking about genetics was a path for "absolution from a sense of guilt" as much as a statement of fact.

Seventy-two types of psychopathology

The theories that mothers cause autism and schizophrenia were popular through the 1950s and 1960s, but have been scientifically discredited as we have learned more about genetic contributions to mental problems and the resilience of children to insensitive parenting. But the blame-the-mother theory keeps finding new homes. The weight of evidence that parenting does not cause children's mental illness is no match for strongly held beliefs. The theory that cold and rejecting parents cause children's problems has simply moved on to other disorders like a game of whack-a-mole.

Psychologist Paula Caplan captured the extent of this whack-a-mole game. Caplan wanted to know the extent of mother blaming in science journals. She undertook a survey of nine journals that focused on the etiology of psychopathology. She looked at every issue of these nine journals for 1970, 1976, and 1982 to determine whether there was any change over time coinciding with the new feminist movement.[50] First, she found an astounding seventy-two different kinds of psychopathology that mothers were blamed for. Second, the survey showed that this culturally dominant trend of mother blaming showed no signs of slowing down over the years.

In 2020, one of my patients was a four-year-old boy who had difficulties with defiance and disruptive behaviors. His legal guardian and caregiver was his grandmother on his mother's side. The grandmother and I were discussing why the boy might be acting defiant. The grandmother explained that the boy's mother—her daughter—had many problems. She was a drug addict and a horrible parent. The grandmother blamed herself for being a poor parent to her daughter and blamed herself for her daughter's problems.

But she had raised another daughter who was completely different—successful, happy, and stable. How could it be possible, I asked, that you were the same mother for both daughters but you blame yourself for one turning out poorly? She paused quietly, as though she could hardly comprehend such a theory.

I need to be clear. I am not saying that parents are unimportant. Far be it from that. Parents are enormously important for keeping their children safe and alive, teaching them language, and instilling the countless things that go into culture. But parents can neither mold their children's characters to make them better (e.g., more moral, smarter, wiser, or more ethical) nor mold their characters for worse (e.g., cause psychiatric disorders). They cannot alter the neurons and architecture of their children's brains for either good or bad. Harris had to explain the same thing when the academics came after her with knives out.

I am not saying that mothers should feel stupid for blaming themselves. That is asking too much. As a parent, blaming oneself for how children turn out is one of those instincts, like Barrett's supernormal stimuli, that serve an incredibly important function under normal circumstances, but have unintended consequences in more complicated situations.

Mother blaming in PTSD as the extension of the clan

Judith Rich Harris made a groundbreaking contribution to decoupling mother blaming from child development. Mother blaming had been mostly removed from diagnoses of autism and schizophrenia, but it was too strong a heuristic to die completely. It would inevitably find new homes. PTSD was an obvious and easy new home. PTSD is the only major psychiatric syndrome that has an event as part of the diagnostic criteria. Just as the early clan experienced weather events and illness events that needed explanation, the changes seen in children following trauma events fit like a hand in a glove for mother blaming.

What exactly do stokers of mother blaming claim? Do they claim that parents cause PTSD in children? Do they claim that parents make PTSD worse? They rarely say with any direct clarity, which makes it all the better for misdirection. But they have pointed to many different parenting practices that supposedly cause children to be worse following traumatic events.

Due to the complex task of parenting, there is no one single way to measure the quality of parenting. As a result, nearly every study that investigates parenting blames mothers in slightly different ways. One research group blamed overprotective parents; their excessive parental control and infantilization of children supposedly harmed them.[51] Another group blamed parents who provided less emotional support following trauma.[52] A different group blamed parents who were more hostile and coercive, causing children to develop PTSD somehow.[53] Yet another group blamed depressed mothers but didn't bother to study how depression may have changed actual parenting practices.[54] Bessel van der Kolk chimed in with his opinion, and blamed bad parenting for causing attachment problems that harmed children following trauma.[55] The list goes on in all the different ways that researchers decide to measure parenting.

In addition, the concept of mother blaming has been expanded to a construct called social support. An insufficient number and quality of friends and family who are supportive has been blamed for worsening PTSD symptoms.[56] This has been taken even further to blame PTSD symptoms on the ridiculous concept that the quality of neighborhoods and media coverage create psychiatric disorders, just to cover the whole metaphorical village that supposedly raises children.[57]

Why mother blaming for PTSD is not true

In my previous book, *They'll Never Be the Same*, I provided the evidence that shows the mother-blaming model for children's posttrauma problems is not true.[58] I explained that when actual parenting (not just parental symptoms) has been observed or measured, the results have not supported a blame-the-mother model. I explained that when children's symptoms are tracked over time in prospective longitudinal studies, as opposed to cross-sectional studies, the appearance of parental symptoms does not precede children's symptoms. In fact, it may make more sense to reason that parents were being affected by their symptomatic children, not the other way around.

I explained that just because children with problems have parents with problems does not mean the parents caused the children's problems. There were two major flaws with all seventeen of those studies we reviewed in our 2001 paper. First, both children and parents were assessed at just one point in time, well after everybody's problems had developed. As noted earlier, cross-sectional studies cannot tell us what the children or parents were like before the children's problems developed, and cannot explain *how* the children's problems developed. We have a chicken-or-egg problem.

Second, none of those seventeen studies actually measured any type of parenting behaviors. The researchers in those studies never interviewed the parents or children and never observed the parents with their children to see if the parents were cold and insensitive. Those parents with PTSD and depression symptoms and marital problems could have been warm, sensitive parents.

I explained one of my studies, which was the first research to measure actual parenting and followed subjects prospectively in a longitudinal design. We measured maternal sensitivity several different ways, and we followed the children for nearly two years. Instead of finding evidence to blame mothers, I found a surprising result that was the opposite of what the mother-blaming theory predicted. *The children with the most PTSD symptoms had the mothers who appeared the most sensitive toward their children when they were measured on how they actually interacted with their children.*[59] Contrary to the popular blame-the-mother wisdom, poor emotional sensitivity of mothers did not seem to cause or worsen their children's symptoms.

After my study was published in 2015, a group of researchers in the UK conducted a similar study that observed actual parenting and followed subjects prospectively in a longitudinal design. Of the fourteen different ways they measured parenting, eleven showed no correlation with children's post-traumatic stress symptoms one month after trauma experiences. The results were slightly different six months after trauma experiences when eight of the variables showed no correlation.

Strangely, the authors convinced themselves that the "observational assessments broadly supported" the notion that parenting worsened their children's post-traumatic distress even though nineteen of their twenty-eight tests did not support it.[60]

Victoria Williamson and colleagues conducted a meta-analysis of studies that measured actual parenting behaviors and were unimpressed by the evidence for parents' influence on children's posttraumatic stress. They wrote, "Given the small number of high quality studies available, only provisional recommendations about the role of parenting in childhood PTSD are made."[61]

Mother blaming is baked into our DNA

The conclusion of this chapter is that mother blaming is a confluence of instinct and inborn heuristics. This view is consistent with Harris's theory that humans are born with three mental systems for understanding the social world: a Relationship System, a Socialization System, and a Status System. This view is consistent with that of psychologists Roy Baumeister and Mark Leary who, in an influential 1995 paper, recognized that the need to belong is an instinct, like eating.[62] This explains where mother blaming comes from and why we do it so easily, without even thinking, and why it is such a powerful sucking vortex that draws us in to believe things that are not true. In contrast to the toxic stress and complex PTSD situations, mother blaming is a more direct conduit to a heuristic. We do not like to challenge heuristics. They are somehow unassailable or, perhaps, not even visible.

This conclusion is different from those of many other psychology books that have described our cognitions. Most of those books provide excellent descriptions of how our brains work, but rarely ask the question of origin. In Malcolm Gladwell's popular book *The Tipping Point*, for example, he tried to explain how humans behave in the process of creating social epidemics. Gladwell attributed much of the cause to external circumstances having strong influence over human behavior. In writing "our inner states are the result of our outer circumstances,"

Gladwell seemed to credit nurture more than nature.[63] He gave several examples of experiments in psychology to illustrate that.

The situation is more complicated than that. Yes, our inner states can be influenced by outer circumstances, but this is possible only because of the innate nature of our inner states. Gladwell described how our brains make us behave, and he acknowledged that it is probably the result of the way evolution has structured our brain, but he never probed deeper for those details on why our brains behave like this in the first place. I think Gladwell missed the primary influence of the inner states. This is no criticism of Gladwell; he provided marvelous insights into our behaviors. It is simply a way of noting that instincts and heuristics can be difficult to grapple with.

A heuristic is a purely mental mechanism. It is an automatic mental shortcut to solve problems and make judgments. In the various definitions of *heuristic*, emphasis is often placed on a heuristic being rapid and efficient to allow humans to function without having to constantly stop and think. Personally, I am not sure a heuristic has to be rapid to be useful. I am not sure a heuristic belief is any more rapid than a rational thought. I think everything the brain does is rapid. I think the key difference between heuristic beliefs and rational thoughts is the order and the energy involved in each. Heuristics land first, and for any rational thought to land second, the heuristic has to be waved off the landing pad to make room for it.

An instinct is an automatic behavior. The behavior is usually performed in response to an external stimulus. There is no mental thought driving the behavior. Birds bring food to their babies in the nest but they do not have an underlying thought telling them to do that.

How is a heuristic different from an instinct? A heuristic is an automatic thought without a behavior. An instinct is an automatic behavior without a thought. If a heuristic is automatic, like an instinct, does that make a heuristic the mental form of an instinct? We could draw an arbitrary line and say that instincts describe behaviors and heuristics describe thoughts and not mix them together, just to keep our terminology clear.

The answer is not clear. An internet search of phrases such as "instinct versus heuristic" brings up very little. A search in PsycINFO, the major database of psychology literature, with the terms *instinct* and *heuristic* combined, returns literally nothing relevant. In Wikipedia, the description of instinct does not mention heuristic, and the description of heuristic does not mention instinct. Evolutionary psychologists, whose aim is to understand which psychological adaptations evolved from our ancestral past, should have an opinion if anybody would. They have discussed psychological traits as social instincts or cognitive instincts, but it is difficult to find any robust discussion.

Darwin used the term *instinct* to describe emotions. Babies learn to smile and laugh instinctively, he noted. Are emotions truly instinctual responses or simply the secondary result of the hardwired neural circuitry that fires when an instinctive behavior is completed? In the psychology business, you can't talk about thoughts and behaviors without emotions. It is the holy triad of human psychology.

The Power of the Clan is not one simple factor; it is a complicated confluence of factors. Likewise, the mother-blaming instinct is not one simple heuristic. That complexity is difficult to write about clearly, and probably difficult to read about, which makes it easy for stokers to exploit.

The confluence of mental mechanisms that create the Power of the Clan's influence with regard to trauma may be thought of as a "cloud of heuristics." When we are trying to solve a mysterious problem, multiple heuristics get triggered simultaneously with overlapping areas of agreement.

One of the heuristics in this cloud is likely the affect heuristic. The affect heuristic states that stimuli that elicit stronger emotions carry stronger power to influence decisions. Because we have strong feelings about mothers, and also about the mother-child relationship, we are likely to favor explanations that involve mothers.

Another is the availability heuristic, which says people make judgments in line with the ease with which examples come to mind. Because children generally spend more time with mothers than anyone, it is easy to think of mothers as the cause of children's problems.

Yet another is the familiarity heuristic, which states whatever circumstances explained past behavior probably hold true for the present. Because children appear to dress, talk, and behave as their mothers directed them to in the past, it is easier to blame mothers for any deviant child behavior in the present.

Still another is the peak-end heuristic, which says we think positively or negatively about an event based on whether the event ended positively or negatively. If our most recent recollection of mother-child relationships is negative, which it most likely would be when children have behavior problems, it is easier to attribute the children's behaviors to the maternal parenting.

The invisible sucking vortex

One interesting thing about the underlying cause of mother blaming is that so little criticism is written about it. This suggests, again, that mother blaming is indeed a composite of heuristics, which we know operate below the conscious level. It is a sucking vortex, but it is also so hard to see in motion.

The unfortunate history of mother blaming seems totally forgotten by modern researchers and clinicians if we are to judge by how often mother blaming keeps popping back up. It is likely they never really learned the lesson in the first place because heuristics do not like to be challenged. You can almost see the progression—attack the worst things (autism and schizophrenia) first; then, after losing a foothold with those, move on to softer targets.

Part of the reason that mother blaming keeps popping up is that the subjects, that is, mothers, are just easy targets. After all, mothers blame themselves too. If mothers don't push back, who else is there to push back? Why push back? The opposition is loose and uncoordinated. Mother blaming is another area where all three rules of how beliefs become fact were mastered. A key difference from toxic stress and complex PTSD is that hardly any arm-twisting was needed. The belief in blaming mothers is so widespread and so common in everyday life that it occurs automatically.

In a sense, everything comes back to the clan—everything, that is, that pertains to happiness and contentment. When old men and women are asked near the end of their lives for their accomplishments or regrets, they typically say the secret to happiness is something like "friends and family." Literally, everything about our survival, success, and happiness depends on belonging to others on whom we have to depend for so many material and psychological things. If you never have the feeling that you belong to someone or something, it seems more likely you can become a hermit or an anarchist, or commit suicide.

Montseratt Guibernau wrote, "A sense of belonging generates the strongest antidote against alienation and aloneness. Belonging offers a point of reference to the individual who is now able to transcend his or her own limited existence by sharing some common interests, objectives and characteristics with fellow-members."[64] The sense of belonging to a clan is powerful psychological support that helps block the feelings of anxiety, uncertainty, and alienation that can so easily creep into the human mind in day-to-day life.

This is the paradox of mother blaming. In order to create more and more caring parents who would benefit the clan by raising caring children, we had to imbue parents with enormous power, even if it was artificial. In order to create the image of caring parents, you have to live with the unintended effects of blaming parents.

I've written before about a mother who was blamed by her child's therapist for the child's PTSD symptoms as an example to show how easily and frequently it occurs. This is a common practice in psychotherapy that needs to stop. To be wrongly blamed for the unhappiness of your child is perhaps the most crushing blow possible, or it would be if mothers weren't so prone to believing it themselves.

Prescriptives for Recovery
Thought and Visualization Practices

- A prescription for better living can grow from gain of knowledge, and does not have to involve a step-by-step behavioral technique. When humans are armed with accurate knowledge, we can have some faith that they will figure out what to do with it on their own. The alternative to believing parents have the power to mold the most fundamental blocks of children's personalities and problems is accurate knowledge that the true source of children's personalities and problems is different from aspects of children that can actually be molded.

There is no good evidence that parents can mold their children at a fundamental level into being intelligent, moral, immoral, kind, mean, free from major psychiatric disorders, or inflicted with major psychiatric disorders. Parents can have temporary influences on all of those things, but they can't alter the core building blocks of those qualities. One only has to look at a family in which one child is a psychopath and the other children are not, or one child is a genius and the others are of average intelligence, or one child is an extrovert and another is shy, or one child has an anxiety disorder and the others do not. The children in those families received essentially the same parenting, and there is no good evidence that differences in parenting caused those different outcomes.

Parents are, however, incredibly important for other things. Parents are a primary source to mold their children in areas that are not hardwired by the genetics of human development. They teach their children the thousands of things that go into culture, tradition, manners, and wisdom, and instill in them a sense of being loved unconditionally. In this sense, parents have plenty to do. Their plates are full.

- We need to be able to slow down our process of making judgments in complex situations and identify the fast heuristics at work. We need to engage Kahneman's System 2 of rational thought to analyze the beliefs that

System 1 generated. Kahneman's prescription was to visualize conversations with others around the proverbial water cooler because it is easier to identify errors of judgment in others than to see them in ourselves.

- We need a way to constantly remember that we are innately designed to operate in small social groups. This means we are constantly geared toward self-inflation. We are constantly scanning our environment to evaluate others and our standing with others for the purposes of knowing how we fit in the social environment and how we can maximize our moral status in the clan.

Different experts have emphasized different aspects of this instinctive thinking in slightly different ways. Christopher Boehm and Jonathan Haidt have emphasized how our minds are driven by moral considerations. Judith Rich Harris developed her three-tier system that I find particularly memorable and useful. The Relationship System specializes in evaluating other individuals in terms of whether we can help them or hurt them. The Socialization System specializes in learning the rules of how to behave in groups so that we understand how to go where our group goes and do what our group does. The Status System specializes in comparing ourselves to others in order to maximize our status so that we know how to maximize the amount of good things we can acquire in terms of mates, security, and resources.

When you find yourself struggling to understand complicated situations, you can visualize yourself in an ancient clan. Literally imagine yourself in a clan of about twenty people, living in a cave shelter, dependent on each other for safety, food, mating, healing, and love. Imagine what your obligations would be to the clan and what your motivations might be to maintain your status within the clan. This can greatly simplify the process of trying to understand why others are doing what they do and what your obligations ought to be to do the best thing.

In this simplified situation, consider, as Boehm and Haidt have noted, how this kind of thinking can rein in bad actors who are not behaving in the clan's best interests, and how it might temper your own actions to avoid being pegged as a bad actor. Think of how others in the clan might be trying to promote false beliefs while trying to silence those who disagree with them, and how that would make you feel. Imagine what a person would say if they could have less extreme views. Think of whether someone's belief is trying to categorize people by what happened to them rather than by their true nature.

- A recovery plan for dealing with psychiatric problems, whether in professional treatment or self-help, based on the truest path is likely to stem from an accurate understanding of how you got to this point. Nearly all of you will, at some point, wonder about your childhood and the parenting you received. It is important to remember a key distinction between your *feelings* about your childhood and the *impact* of your childhood on your character.

  You can feel bad about your childhood and you can dislike things about your parents, and those are absolutely legitimate issues to process in psychotherapy. Childhood issues and parenting can leave lasting impressions of anger, hurt, guilt, and shame. But lasting impressions of anger, hurt, guilt, and shame are not the same as the fundamental building blocks of your character. Those have no bearing on whether you are fundamentally moral, kind, ethical, extroverted, introverted, smart, or psychiatrically disordered.

  Be aware that there exists the sucking vortex to blame parents for their children's symptoms, and it is largely based on false beliefs, speculation, and notoriously wrong clinical intuition. Many clinicians intuitively believe in an unproven power of parenting. When counseling isn't working, clinicians and patients alike tend to blame parents.

The best advice is not to engage in therapy that is aimed at the wrong source of the problem. I am reminded again of how Diana Henriques summed up the Madoff Ponzi scheme when she wrote that the most dangerous lies are those we tell ourselves. While I am not intending to draw parallels between a criminal fraud and parenting, the basic cognitive processes involved in both share similarities. You ought not lie to yourself that you caused your child's problems, or that your parents caused your problems, because that leads to the wrong interventions.

The alternative is to understand that problems you are struggling with likely have been caused in large part by vulnerabilities you were born with. The scientific term for this is the *diathesis stress theory*. Individuals can be born with certain vulnerabilities, called the diathesis. When I talk to patients, a way they easily understand it is for me to call it "how you were wired" or "the cards you got dealt at birth." I've found most patients actually find it a relief to understand their problems this way because it means they have not been failures for trying for many years to fix something they never had the power to fix.

This accurate understanding frees you up to focus more efficiently and realistically on the things you can change. The wisdom of this has been encapsulated in the most modern version as the Serenity Prayer, but has been known for centuries. This wisdom asks to be granted composure to accept the things you cannot change, courage to change the things you can, and wisdom to know the difference.

EPILOGUE

By the time I finished this book, I was surprised to realize it was nearly the nonfiction remake of Arthur C. Clarke's science fiction classic *2001: A Space Odyssey*. Clarke's book begins with the evolution of a hominid who is the first to learn new skills with weapons. The hominid is taught the new skills by a mysterious higher power. He learns he can kill, and this makes him master of the world. The hominid is not sure what to do with this new power. He stands over one of his victims and thinks, not quite sure what to do next.

Clarke's book comes full circle at the end when one of the astronauts has evolved too with the aid of the mysterious higher power. The astronaut returns to Earth as the immortal Star Child with new powers. He saves Earth by detonating a nuclear warhead with his mind before it strikes its target. The Star Child, with his new weapons, is the master of the world. Clarke wrote, "Then he waited, marshalling his thoughts and brooding over his still untested powers. For though he was master of the world, he was not quite sure what to do next. But he would think of something."[1]

Both the hominid and the Star Child evolved new weapons. How they used those weapons were their decisions.

Previous nonfiction works have described the powers of the human mind and what humans have decided to do with those mental powers, for good or bad, over broad landscapes of religion, politics, human relations, and everyday life. Jonathan Haidt's *The Righteous Mind* and Robert Wright's *The Moral Animal* are two of the closest examples that overlap with this book in noting how the inborn nature of the human mind intertwines with many problematic issues in modern life.[2] For example, Wright noted the misuses of social Darwinism to justify oppression through imperialism and racism. There are many other excellent books that have appeared in the last thirty years trying to find a "direct pipeline to these mental processes."[3] This book is different in being a long-form exploration of one topic—psychological trauma.

My book has been two stories that intertwine to tell a story of how a psychological concept has emerged as a new weapon. One story is about the rise of trauma ideology as a major force in human societies, and the other story is about the origins of how the extraordinary human mind works to turn belief into fact.

Story 1. Trauma is weaponized.

Trauma has become a powerful weapon to achieve social engineering. Activists on the morally inspired road to Traumaville have created a narrative that psychological trauma is the source of nearly all social disparities.

Toxic stress activists want government laws and policies to direct funding to prevent every possible source of stress and trauma. California is already spending $40 million for screening that has no promise of being effective. Complex PTSD activists want complex PTSD recognized in order to mold taxonomy and treatment plans to fit their version of truth that nurture creates all of our victim classes in society. Mother blamers want child care, child education, child social services, child public health, and child psychological treatment to conform to their beliefs so that the external world appears seamless with their inner world.

All of these efforts hinge to an increasing degree on messaging that trauma is the root danger that is in the same class as the snake in the grass that we must vigilantly watch out for.

The world is being divided by this ideology that is defined by belief in trauma as the root cause of why some people are disadvantaged and dysfunctional. Victimhood is a guiding heuristic in this ideology, in the sense that our moral status rises or falls based on our commitment to helping the disadvantaged. Believers in the ideology fuel the victimhood narrative and believe we've made sense of it all by favoring causal explanations based on nurture. According to this worldview, people are born equal instead of unequal.

Researchers who hear the call of victimhood ideology the most strongly ostensibly started out in the tribe of Scientists, but then switched to join the tribe of Activists. There is nothing wrong with scientists behaving as activists, as long as they do it based on accurate science. The problems arise when researchers use inaccurate science. Today's researchers are able to disseminate messages in a far more massive volume and breadth than lone individuals could ever have done in the past.

How are we to think of these researchers?

These researcher activists do not seem to be aware that they have the science wrong. Truth to a scientist ought to be like eyesight to a painter. You don't have science without truth. Explaining some bit of nature factually is literally why scientists exist. We have to wonder how something so fundamental to a profession is now so dysfunctional.

If there was such a thing as science crime, it would be when scientists violate the defining trait that science is about truth. It's almost a sacred thing. Like Prometheus stealing fire from Zeus, such violations seem like they should have tragic consequences. A case could be made that the stokers of complex PTSD, mother blaming, and, especially, toxic stress have committed crimes against science.

But these are such blundering crimes. They are committed in the name of trying to help disadvantaged victims. It is difficult for most people to be too hard on them. Aren't they just well-meaning individuals who pushed it a bit too far? Sure, they pushed too far, but isn't that what activists do, by definition?

Diana Henriques wrote about Bernie Madoff's crime, "It seems to be such a gentle crime. . . . Until the money runs out, people love the Ponzi schemer; they are grateful to him"[4]—just as believers in toxic stress and complex PTSD are grateful to Bessel van der Kolk, and awed to be in his presence. Hence a Ponzi scheme is uniquely suited to be a crime about status among clans. "Such is the Ponzi scheme. It is the crime of the egotist, not the sadist."[5] In a way, isn't a scientific scam such as toxic stress a type of literary Ponzi scheme? Isn't someone drawing in the intellectual capital of victims in order to pay off the original contributors and justify the continuation of the false narrative? They all know it might be false, but they keep contributing because they want to be part of the high-status group.

The Relationship System of Harris has a tough time figuring out these activist researchers within the clan of scientists. Are they the good guys? The bad guys? A complicated mixture of both? How can we trust them? When do we know to trust them and not trust them? It raises complicated issues that we didn't have to worry about thousands of years ago in a simpler world.

Even to single them out feels a bit awkward. Writing this entire book has felt a bit like a betrayal of my colleagues. Shonkoff, Herman, and their adherents believe the ends justify the means; they believe it is okay to puncture the integrity of science as long as it is for social good. Is that wrong or right? There is no universal law of nature about that, so the better question is, all things considered, the practical one: is it good for the clan? Perhaps even a level below that: is it acceptable to the clan? It is obviously considered acceptable because they did it, many others did it before them, and no great clamor was raised.

It is only psychology, after all. If it was cancer, a clamor would be raised. So if it's obviously acceptable, why write a book to explain and expose it? Because only about half the clan agrees with the ends. This half—the Shonkoffs and Hermans of the world—are trying to bamboozle the other half of the world to get funding for social programs. Once money enters the picture, or trying to tell other people what to believe, or trying to force people to do things, then it is not acceptable. It is a form of corruption that will become increasingly corrupted, as things always do once money gets involved.

I think we know how the stokers think about themselves. Henriques perhaps provides some insight from her jailhouse interviews with Madoff. In her second interview, Madoff looks thinner and frailer.

He has worked with a psychologist and has tried to gain insight. He claims he always wanted to please people.[6] He never thought of what he was doing as stealing; he was just taking risks. "The Madoff case demonstrated with brutal clarity another truth that we simply do not want to face about the Ponzi schemer in our midst: he is not 'other' than us, or 'different' from us. He is just like us—*only more so.*"[7]

Protecting the integrity of science is not the believers' and stokers' main concern. They just want to make the world better. It reminds me of a response I received from a journal reviewer recently. I had written a letter to the editor of the *Journal of the American Academy of Child & Adolescent Psychiatry* to express disagreement with a new series of articles the editor had launched called the *Master Clinician* series. I argued that handpicking one expert to write an article on a subject as a benighted "master clinician" was bound to include personal biases and propagate misinformation. I justified this by saying that nonscientists have to trust scientists for our knowledge of nature, and a journal shouldn't arbitrarily anoint one researcher to speak for an entire field. The reviewer, who was one of the deputy editors of the journal, disagreed with me and rejected my letter, writing back sarcastically and dismissively, "Are you kidding?"

I was not kidding. I believe scientists have a role to play in the clan as the explainers of nature, and truth is our only true calling card. The people we are beholden to are our fellow clan members, who are mostly decent, honest people, and we should not lie to them.

A danger is that skeptics may want to see the believers and stokers as evil. But they are not evil. There are fully human. As Henriques described him, Madoff "was not inhumanly monstrous. He was monstrously human."[8] Greedy for praise. Arrogantly sure of himself. Smugly dismissive of skeptics. Doesn't this sound like the stokers of toxic stress and complex PTSD? It sounds just like van der Kolk's arrogant smugness in dismissing his critics. It sounds like the complex PTSD stokers who were battered by criticism for lacking evidence but simply shrugged it off, because they felt a moral imperative to improve society.

What is the harm of exaggerating? The harm is that the best writers are good at spreading their ideology while the rest of us think it is science. I believe that's called propaganda.

I grew up loving the writing of Stephen Jay Gould on evolution. I subscribed to *Natural History* magazine just to get his monthly article. As Gould came under fire in later years for misrepresenting science to promote his personal theories, I felt bamboozled. Gould's battle to preserve biodiversity by demanding that humans change their attitudes toward other species now sounds psychologically naïve.[9] Gould was a believer in nurture, the idea that humans can be changed simply by molding them better. When I was younger, Gould's brand of activism fit neatly into my worldview, but I changed, and his real intentions became clearer.

I want to be mad at Gould, but I'm not sure he was malicious enough to warrant my anger. As one critic of Gould wrote, "Gould was not the only biologist who wanted to derive meaning from the facts of biology; in fact, he may have been typical."[10]

I want to be mad at Bush, Cheney, Rumsfeld, and the White House gang that engineered the Iraq War, but I don't think they were malicious. I think they were typical. I believe Rumsfeld when he wrote in his memoir that they did not lie; they were simply wrong.

I have to remind myself that it boils down to our wonderfully horrifying imperfections that are simply not designed for complicated, modern conundrums. As Kevin Simler and Robin Hanson wrote in their book *The Elephant in the Brain: Hidden Motives in Everyday Life*: "We, human beings, are a species that's not only capable of acting on hidden motives—we're designed to do it. Our brains are built to act in our self-interest while at the same time trying hard not to appear selfish in front of other people. And in order to throw them off the trail, our brains often keep 'us,' our conscious minds, in the dark. The less we know of our own ugly motives, the easier it is to hide them from others."[11] Self-deception is strategic.

What to do about it?

Can better education prevent this collateral damage? Carol Tavris and Elliot Aronson wrote an enlightening book, *Mistakes Were Made (But Not by Me)*, to explain how humans cling to outdated attitudes. They explained, "Most people, when directly confronted by evidence that they are wrong, do not change their point of view or course of action but justify it even more tenaciously. Even irrefutable evidence is rarely enough to pierce the mental armor of self-justification."[12] They noted numerous historical examples of mistaken beliefs driving ill-fated actions, including George Bush and the Iraq War and the Watergate cover-up. They discussed the infamous McMartin Preschool scandal in which the owners and teachers of the school were charged with abuse of forty-eight children. By the end of two trials, the case ended with no convictions because it came to appear the abuses never occurred. It was the longest and most expensive case in American history because of overzealous parents, psychologists, and district attorneys who could never come to grips with the possibility their beliefs were mistaken. Even Bessel van der Kolk makes an appearance in Tavris and Aronson's book as a single-minded expert witness in court defending the myth of repressed memory.[13] The answer to the persistence of scientifically unsound beliefs, the authors proposed, is that better education of our professional classes in methods of science and the vulnerabilities of self-justification could effectively rein in these self-deceptions.

I don't think so. I don't think humans can change that easily. Instead, one might reason, why fight it at the individual level? Maybe the popular book and movie *Divergent* is on to something a bit more realistic.[14] In a postapocalyptic reboot of society, individuals are divided into five factions based on their inherent strengths—Candor (for their honesty), Abnegation (for selflessness), Dauntless (for bravery), Amity (for the peaceful), and Erudite (for intelligence). Perhaps we need a faction for Skeptic.

The stories of toxic stress, complex PTSD, and mother blaming should teach us that the tribe of Science, at least in the domain of psychology, has failed us. Why should we care? The truth matters because that is essentially the role scientists have in society: to be the ones who speak truth against magic, superstition, and scams. If scientists don't tell the truth, why should we keep supporting them? Once one group of researchers gets away with untruths to support their ideological agenda, the public will lose confidence in all researchers, and they should. If researchers can't police themselves, they don't deserve the public's trust. The toxic stress cabal may believe that their means justify the ends of helping children in the way they believe they should be helped, but it will backfire sooner or later, and then the public will have good reason never to trust any researcher again.

Perhaps we should explicitly recognize the inherent skills (and weaknesses) of humans in the areas of science, skepticism, and reason. We could just be honest and recognize we need a tribe called Skeptics who are good at slowing down to think, mainly in Kahneman's System 2; who don't fret terribly about their moral status; and whom we can empower to judge important facts.

Forming into tribes or clans is natural. Each country is a clan. Each profession is a clan. We're in a battle for the soul of the psychological clan, and truth is often losing.

Story 2. How the mind works.

Human reasoning is not flawed. The deployment of reasoning is flawed.

Reason is a superpower that humans alone possess in the animal kingdom. Yet it seems to be deployed as a role player, not the main attraction. There are so many other interesting and vital things our brains need to do. As Hugo Mercier and Dan Sperber described humans, "They drink and piss, eat and shit. They sleep and snore. They sweat and shiver. They lust. They mate. Their births and deaths are messy affairs. Animals, humans are animals!"[15] Reason has little to do with any of those functions. Reason evolved, they argued, to help us justify our beliefs and make us better arguers.

Reason did not evolve to sort belief from truth. It turns out we're just not that interested in the truth. You want the truth? Good luck. As the reviewer of my letter to the editor said, "Are you kidding?"

This is the Ideology Age

In the Stone Age, early weapons and tools were made of stone. Then the Bronze Age became dominant, with better weapons and tools. Then the Iron Age produced even better weapons and tools. For the last thirty years, with the invention of computers and the internet, ideologies may be the strongest weapons. We've been living in the Ideology Age to some degree since writing and paper were invented, but it was never a dominant, large-scale weapon until books and electronic media could spread the messages so far, so reliably, and so constantly. Many thought the power of ideologies would be tempered by the democracy of the internet, but the power of ideologies seems only to be accelerating.

Trauma is fast becoming one of the keystone ideologies of this age. How one thinks of trauma divides the population into two camps, just like other big topics such as race, politics, and religion. Trauma is the psychological version of these controversial issues. Trauma is the version of ideologically driven social engineering that is figuring out rapidly how to weaponize neuroscience and weaponize complicated psychology, just as advocates on the other big topics have weaponized skin color, economics, foreign relations, and cosmologies of the universe.

In the ancient clan, one bad actor could be reined in by the rest of the clan with shame, guilt, and the threat of ostracism. This method is still effective in small groups today. But part of the trouble with trauma is that shame, guilt, and the threat of ostracism haven't worked well to rein in bad behavior when the internet and social media facilitate the spread of ideology so easily. Instead of one bad apple having a limited influence, belief systems have been able to fight to be master of the world and can be divisive for large populations.

Some type of counterbalance is needed to react to the spread of psychological ideologies. The response to it cannot be a simple, naïve mantra that says we need to educate people better, we need to train journalists better, or we need some sort of public-education program. We are talking about ideologically different ways that a large proportion of humans fundamentally think in contrast to different ways that others think. Reason, and hence education, has nothing to do with it.

One-half of the world will keep believing certain false facts, while the other half will be skeptics. The skeptics, however, need to stop being a loosely coordinated group of individuals and become a louder and better coordinated organization. The skeptics need to realize they're in an ideological war whether they want to be in one or not, and they can't score any points when they're on defense all the time.

Decency, respect, and truth matter, and they don't really need any other explanation. They are held up as fundamental qualities all humans should show because they are what make social cooperation possible. The stokers are not really engaged in social cooperation. They are engaged in social dominance. They have made it clear, with their own words, that they want us to believe what they believe, or at least not push back on them, so they can have our tax dollars to fund their social programs and our cooperation to alter society in a way that is seamless with their moral foundations. That's the opposite of free speech and free thought. That's the opposite of science.

Happy ending

The happy ending is that this book tells you a little bit about how to see through the misdirection, and perhaps even how to live a happy life. The secrets boil down to several simple ideas: Think like the clan. Slow down to System 2. Learn when not to double down. Find the friend group that can say, "I don't know."

These simple secrets ought to help you have a more realistic view of the messiness and complexity of decision making. Recognize that there are predictable mental mechanisms that almost always explain the confusing misdirections. There are appropriate rules for determining whether information is a false fact or a true fact. Individuals who don't follow those rules are probably trying to bamboozle you with a dismissive wave of the hand. If the attractive narrative is too good to check, or too complicated to check, it is likely not true. Simple, yet complicated.

A Ponzi scheme works only because of our human capacity to trust. I agree with Henriques when she wrote, "A world immune to Ponzi schemes is a world utterly devoid of trust, and no one wants to live in a world like that."[16] Likewise, mother blaming only works for humans because of our capacity to empathize. Despite all this messiness of human nature, I would not want to live in a world that did not include mother blaming. Mother blaming seems to be a necessary if undesired result of being moral and compassionate.

The next major Ponzi scheme is inevitable and is already being formulated. The same is true for psychology. The trouble with trauma is that the next belief system without any truth is already being formulated. The only thing that can stop it is others willing to slow things down, to dare to brush past the heuristics guarding the dungeons of the brain and entertain the lonely prisoner down there named "I don't know."

My idea of a good book is one that helps you see a tiny bit of how to play this game of life. I hope this book has done that by explaining how a bit of our thinking works. We'll tackle these troubles with trauma somehow, but the next ideologies are already percolating. You can't stop the ideologies from existing on either side of any issue. The bamboozlers will think of some new scheme. Skeptics will think of some new way to push back. Ideologies, the new weapons of this age, will battle to determine which one will be master of the world. Despite our flaws, we will always have an extraordinary and complex capacity for thinking. We may not be quite sure what to do next, but we'll think of something.

ACKNOWLEDGMENTS

I am grateful to the team at Central Recovery Press for maintaining a mission to create books that enlighten and help people. My special thanks to Patrick Hughes for his passionate support and constructive insights to improve the book's message and reach. My thanks to Valerie Killeen for her steady guiding hand. She was exceptionally organized and reliable through this whole process. I thank the editor, David Fulk, for his many valuable suggestions to make my writing clearer.

I want to acknowledge every library and anyone who makes libraries possible. I've always loved libraries. In college, I spent almost as much time squirreled away in a desk amidst the stacks on the less-trafficked top floor of the library as I did in my dorm room. During my research career, I blissfully stalked journal articles in the basement stacks of the medical school library (before everything was digitized) while my colleagues were seeing patients. Short of wild nature, there is no more peaceful, fulfilling place for me than libraries.

I used many vacation days for three years to research this book. I would pack my lunch and head out early in the mornings to either the Tulane University library or one of the Jefferson Parish public libraries. I would march in with a list of books to pull off the shelves and skim through them.

Sometimes I would skim through an entire book in five minutes. Sometimes I would be grabbed and read every word of the first chapter, and wonder why I would even try to write something better than that. I skimmed ninety-one books and typed a couple hundred pages of notes, inspired and enlightened by great thinkers. Many of the ideas for this book sprang from those long, quiet days in libraries.

It was there, in those temples of knowledge that the original ideas of this book changed into new ideas. Beliefs that I had trusted lost their traction in my mind and were pushed aside to make room for new, rational facts.

ABOUT THE AUTHOR

Michael S. Scheeringa, MD, currently works as a tenured professor at Tulane University School of Medicine in New Orleans, Louisiana, as an endowed chair and the vice chair of research. He has been active as both a practicing clinician and a researcher for over twenty-eight years as the principal investigator on five large, federally funded research projects on the topic of PTSD in children and adolescents. He has worked with over five hundred patients and families with PTSD. Much of this work has been conducted with very young children, which has given him a unique developmental perspective. This work has led to more than eighty scientific articles and more than 120 lectures and workshop trainings around the United States and for international audiences. He has developed multiple assessment measures that have been translated into seven languages. His CBT manual and DIPA diagnostic interview have been distributed to over one thousand clinicians in more than twenty countries. He has been a consultant to several national efforts, including the National Academy of Sciences and the DSM-5. He is the author of *They'll Never Be the Same: A Parent's Guide to PTSD in Youth* (Central Recovery Press, 2018).

NOTES

Introduction

1   Institute of Medicine and National Research Council, "Child Maltreatment Research, Policy, and Practice for the Next Decade: Workshop Summary," *The National Academies Press*, (2012).

2   Children's Bureau, "Child Welfare Outcomes 2009-2012: Report to Congress Executive Summary," *Children's Bureau*, (2012).

3   David Finkelhor, Richard Ormrod, & Heather Turner, "The victimization of children and youth: A comprehensive, national survey," *Child Maltreatment* 10 (2005): 5–25.

4   James E. Alcock, "The Belief Engine," *Skeptical Inquirer* (1995): 14–18.

5   Michael S. Scheeringa *et al.*, "Diagnosing PTSD in early childhood: An empirical assessment of four approaches," *Journal of Traumatic Stress* 25 (2012): 359–67; Michael S. Scheeringa *et al.*, "Trauma-focused cognitive-behavioral therapy for posttraumatic stress disorder in three through six year-old children: A randomized clinical trial," *Journal of Child Psychology and Psychiatry* 52 (2011): 853–60.

6   Malcolm Gladwell, *The Tipping Point: How Little Things Can Make A Big Difference* (Boston: Little, Brown and Company, 2000).

7   Charles B. Nemeroff, *Plenary: The Neurobiological Consequences of Early Life Stress: Treatment Implications* (Toronto: International Society for Traumatic Stress Studies, November 2005).

8   *60 Minutes Overtime*, 2017, "Oprah's 'life-changing' story." Aired March 11, 2017.

9   Judith L. Herman, "Complex PTSD: A syndrome in survivors of prolonged and repeated trauma," *Journal of Traumatic Stress* 5 (1992): 377–91.

10 American Psychiatric Association, *Diagnostic and Statistical Manual of Mental Disorders* Fourth edition (Washington, DC: American Psychiatric Association, 1994),

11 American Psychiatric Association, *Diagnostic and Statistical Manual of Mental Disorders, DSM-5* Fifth edition (Washington, DC: American Psychiatric Publishing, 2013).

12 Dan Primack, "Exclusive: Theranos 2006 pitch deck." Retrieved from https://axios.com/exclusive-theranos-2006-pitch-deck-1513299967-ad008bbd-b684-4e3f-9301-5d560668d488.html.

13 Philip E. Tetlock *et al.*, "Accountability and ideology: When left looks right and right looks left," *Organizational Behavior and Human Decision Processes* 122 (2013): 22–35.

Chapter One

1   "The Dark Side," *Frontline*, accessed 8/31/2020, https://www.pbs.org/wgbh/pages/frontline/darkside/interviews/.

2   "Full text of Colin Powell's speech: US secretary of state's address to the United Nations security council," *The Guardian*, accessed December 24, 2018, https://www.theguardian.com/world/2003/feb/05/iraq.usa.

3   "The Dark Side," *Frontline*.

4   Ibid.

5   Gareth Millward, "A disability act? The Vaccine Damage Payments Act 1979 and the British government's response to the pertussis vaccine scare," *Social History of Medicine* 30 (2017): 429–47.

6   Seth Mnookin, *The Panic Virus: The True Story Behind the Vaccine-Autism Controversy* (New York: Simon & Schuster, 2011), 66.

7   Donna Hilts, "TV Report on Vaccine Stirs Bitter Controversy," *The Washington Post*: April 28, 1982.

8   Mnookin, *The Panic Virus*, 98.

9   Christopher Gillberg, Suzanne Steffenburg, & Helen Schaumann, "Is autism more common now than ten years ago?" *British Journal of Psychiatry* 158 (1991): 403–09.

10   Mnookin, *The Panic Virus*, 146.

11   Andrew J. Wakefield *et al.*, "Evidence of persistent measles virus infection in Crohn's disease," *Journal of Medical Virology* 39 (1993): 345–53.

12   Mnookin, *The Panic Virus*, 104.

13   Anders Ekbom, Andrew J. Wakefield, M. Zack, & H.O. Adami, "Perinatal measles infection and subsequent Crohn's disease," *The Lancet* 20 (1994): 508–10.

14   Nick P. Thompson, Scott M. Montgomery, Roy E. Pounder, & Andrew J. Wakefield, "Is measles vaccination a risk factor for inflammatory bowel disease?" *The Lancet* 345 (1995): 1071–74.

15   Peter A. Patriarca & Judy A. Beeler, "Measles vaccination and inflammatory bowel disease," *The Lancet* 3435 (1995): 1062–63.

16   Andrew J. Wakefield *et al.*, "Ileal-lymphoid-nodular hyperplasia, non-specific colitis, and pervasive developmental disorder in children," *The Lancet* 351 (1998): 637–41.

17   Mnookin, *The Panic Virus*, 116.

18   Mnookin, *The Panic Virus*, 111.

19   Mnookin, *The Panic Virus*, 116.

20   "Top 10 most highly cited retracted papers," *Retraction Watch*, accessed 2/22/2021, https://retractionwatch.com/the-retraction-watch-leaderboard/top-10-most-highly-cited-retracted-papers/.

21   Mnookin, *The Panic Virus*, 104.

22   Mnookin, *The Panic Virus*, 117.

23   Mnookin, *The Panic Virus*, 116.

24   Mnookin, *The Panic Virus*, 140.

25   Mnookin, *The Panic Virus*, 174.

26   John Carreyrou, *Bad Blood: Secrets and Lies in a Silicon Valley Startup* (New York: Vintage Books, 2018).

27   Dan Primack, "Exclusive: Theranos 2006 pitch deck." retrieved from https://axios.com/exclusive-theranos-2006-pitch-deck-1513299967-ad008bbd-b684-4e3f-9301-5d560668d488.html, accessed.

28   Carreyrou, *Bad Blood*

29   Judith R. Harris, *No Two Alike: Human Nature and Human Individuality* (New York: W. W. Norton & Company, 2006).

30   Harris, *No Two Alike*, 165.

31   Harris, *No Two Alike*, 182.

32   Harris, *No Two Alike*, 183.

33   Harris, *No Two Alike*, 186.

34   Harris, *No Two Alike*, 187.

35   Harris, *No Two Alike*, 209.

36   Harris, *No Two Alike*, 210.

37   "The Dark Side," *Frontline*.

38   "Colin Powell: U.N. Speech 'Was a Great Intelligence Failure,'" *Jason M. Breslow*, accessed https://www.pbs.org/wgbh/frontline/article/colin-powell-u-n-speech-was-a-great-intelligence-failure/.

39   "The Dark Side," *Frontline*.

40   Ibid.

41   Charles J. Hanley, "Half of U.S. Still Believes Iraq Had WMD," *Washington Post* (August 7, 2006).

42   Diana B. Henriques, *The Wizard of Lies: Bernie Madoff and the Death of Trust* (New York: Times Books, 2011).

43   Henriques, *The Wizard of Lies*, 362.

44   Henriques, *The Wizard of Lies*, 363.

45   Henriques, *The Wizard of Lies*, 89.

46   Robert Trivers, *The Folly of Fools: The Logic of Deceit and Self-Deception in Human Life* (New York: Basic Books, 2011).

47   Henriques, *The Wizard of Lies*, 364.

Chapter Two

1   Bessel A. Kolk, *The Body Keeps the Score: Brain, Mind, and Body in the Healing of Trauma* (New York: Penguin Books, 2014).

2   Marvin Zuckerman, *Vulnerability to Psychopathology: A Biosocial Model* (Washington, DC: American Psychological Association, 1999).

3   Jack P. Shonkoff *et al.*, "The lifelong effects of early childhood adversity and toxic stress," *Pediatrics* 129 (2012): e232.

4   Jack P. Shonkoff, William T. Boyce & Bruce S. McEwen, "Neuroscience, molecular biology, and the childhood roots of health disparities: Building a new framework for health promotion and disease prevention," *JAMA* 301 (2009): 2252–59.

5   Andrea Danese, "Commentary: Biological embedding of childhood adversity: Where do we go from here? A reflection on Koss and Gunnar (2018)," *Journal of Child Psychology and Psychiatry* 59 (2018): 347–49.

6   Bruce S. McEwen, "Brain on stress: How the social environment gets under the skin," *PNAS Proceedings of the National Academy of Sciences of the United States of America* 109 (2012): 17180–185.

7   Rachel M. Guthrie & Richard A. Bryant, "Auditory startle response in firefighters before and after trauma exposure," *American Journal of Psychiatry* 162 (2005): 283–90.

8   Michael S. Scheeringa, "Reexamination of diathesis stress and neurotoxic stress theories: A qualitative review of pretrauma neurobiology in relation to posttraumatic stress symptoms," *International Journal of Methods in Psychiatric Research* (2020).

9   Julia A. DiGangi *et al.*, "Pretrauma risk factors for posttraumatic stress disorder: A systematic review of the literature," *Clinical Psychology Review* 33 (2013):728–44.

10   *Cosmos*, 1980, "Encyclopaedia Galactica. Season 1. Episode 12." Directed by Carl E. Sagan. Aired December 14, 1980 on PBS.

11   "Reducing Toxic Stress in Childhood," *Substance Abuse and Mental Health Services Administration*.

12   "SAMHSA's Concept of Trauma and Guidance for a Trauma-Informed Approach," *Substance Abuse and Mental Health Services Administration*, Report No. HHS Publication No. (SMA) 14-4884, (July 2014).

13   "SAMHSA's National Center for Trauma-Informed Care (NCTIC)," *Substance Abuse and Mental Health Services Administration*, (March 2012).

14   Jennifer S. Middlebrooks & Natalie C. Audage, "The Effects of Childhood Stress on Health Across the Lifespan," *Centers for Disease Control and Prevention: National Center for Injury Prevention and Control*, (2008).

15   "5 Things You Should Know About Stress," *National Institute of Mental Health*, accessed September 26, 2020, https://www.nimh.nih.gov/health/publications/stress/index.shtml.

16   "PA-07-314. Mental Health Consequences of Violence and Trauma (R21)," retrieved from https://grants.nih.gov/grants/guide/pa-files/pa-07-314.html, accessed September 28, 2020.

17   "Violence Prevention," *youth.gov*, accessed October 4, 2020, www.youth.gov/youth-topics/violence-prevention.

18   Erica Lurie-Hurvitz, "Early Experiences Matter: Making the Case for a Comprehensive Infant and Toddler Policy Agenda," *Zero to Three*, (February 2009).

19   "ACEs and Toxic Stress," *American Academy of Pediatrics*, accessed September 26, 2020, https://www.aap.org/en-us/advocacy-and-policy/aap-health-initiatives/resilience/Pages/ACEs-and-Toxic-Stress.aspx.

20   "What is toxic stress?," *American Academy of Child & Adolescent Psychiatry*, accessed September 26, 2020, https://www.aacap.org/aacap/families_and_youth/resource_centers/Child_Abuse_Resource_Center/FAQ.aspx.

21   International Society for Traumatic Stress Studies: Trauma and Public Health Task Force, "A Public Health Approach to Trauma: Implications for Science, Practice, Policy, and the Role of ISTSS," *International Society for Traumatic Stress Studies*, 7 (2015).

22   Lisa Amaya-Jackson & Steven Berkowitz, "Making Sense of ACEs: The Adverse Childhood Experiences Study & Beyond," retrieved from www.istss.org/education-research/online-learning/recordings?pid=WEB1215, accessed September 27, 2020.

23   "About Child Trauma," *National Child Traumatic Stress Network*, accessed January 25, 2019, https://www.nctsn.org/what-is-child-trauma/about-child-trauma.

24   Lisa Amaya-Jackson & Sara Johnson, "Understanding the Impact of Childhood Trauma, Adversity & Toxic Stress on the Body & Mind: The Role of Integrated Healthcare," retrieved from www.nctsn.org/resources/understanding-impact-childhood-trauma-adversity-and-toxic-stress-body-and-mind-role, accessed September 27, 2020.

25   Brittney Schaeffer, "What You Should Know About Toxic Stress," retrieved from https://www.nami.org/Blogs/NAMI-Blog/August-2017/What-You-Should-Know-About-Toxic-Stress#:~:text=Toxic%20stress%2C%20or%20trauma%2C%20is,to%20fully%20deal%20with%20it, accessed October 3, 2020.

26   Andrea K. Blanch, David L. Shern & Sarah M. Steverman, "Toxic Stress, Behavioral Health, and the Next Major Era in Public Health," *Mental Health America*, (September 17, 2014).

27   Blanch *et al.*, "Toxic Stress," 4.

28   Jan Fawcett, "What happened to the American dream?," *Psychiatric Annals* 35 (2005): 372.

29   David Finkelhor *et al.*, "Violence, Crime, and Abuse Exposure in a National Sample of Children and Youth: An Update," *JAMA Pediatrics* 167 (2013):614–21.

30   National Research Council and Institute of Medicine, "From Neurons to Neighborhoods: The Science of Early Childhood Development," *National Academy Press*, (2000).

31   National Research Council, "From Neurons to Neighborhoods," 3.

32   Center on the Developing Child at Harvard University, "A Decade of Science Informing Policy: The Story of the National Scientific Council on the Developing Child," (2014).

33   Vincent J. Felitti *et al.*, "Relationship of childhood abuse and household dysfunction to many of the leading causes of death in adults. The Adverse Childhood Experiences (ACE) Study," *American Journal of Preventive Medicine* 14 (1998): 245–58.

34   National Scientific Council on the Developing Child, "Excessive Stress Disrupts the Architecture of the Developing Brain: Working Paper 3," (2005).

35   Center on the Developing Child, "A Decade of Science."

36   Jack P. Shonkoff, "Mobilizing science to revitalize early childhood policy," *Issues in Science and Technology* 26 (2009): 1–12.

37   Jack P. Shonkoff, "Neuroscience, molecular biology, and the childhood roots of health disparities," *Journal of the American Medical Association*, (2009): 2257.

38   Steven Sloman & Philip Fernbach, *The Knowledge Illusion: Why We Never Think Alone* (New York: Riverhead Books, 2017), 15.

39   Ibid.

40   "SAMHSA's National Center for Trauma-Informed Care (NCTIC)," *Substance Abuse and Mental Health Services Administration*, (March 2012).

41   Rinad S. Beidas *et al.*, "Lessons learned while building a trauma-informed public behavioral health system in the City of Philadelphia," *Evaluation and Program Planning* 59 (2016): 21–32.

42   *The Philadelphia ACE Project*, accessed February 26, 2021, https://www.philadelphiaaces.org/.

43   "Working Toward a Trauma-Informed City: Challenges and Opportunities in Philadelphia.," accessed September 26, 2020, https://www.youtube.com/watch?v=nXv65ITR89I.

44   Senate Joint Resolution 59, Wisconsin State Senate, (2013–2014).

45   "Peace4Tarpon: Trauma Informed Building Resiliency," *Peace4Tarpon*, accessed October 4, 2020, www.peace4tarpon.org.

46   Ibid.

47   Ibid.

48   Van der Kolk, *The Body Keeps the Score*, 2–3

49   Van der Kolk, *The Body Keeps the Score*, 21.

50   Ibid

51   Van der Kolk, *The Body Keeps the Score*, 350.

52   Van der Kolk, *The Body Keeps the Score*, 153.

53   Leana S. Wen *et al.*, "Public Health in the Unrest: Baltimore's Preparedness and Response After Freddie Gray's Death," *American Journal of Public Health* 105 (2015): 1957–59.

54   "Trauma and Mental Health Resources," *Baltimore City Health Department*, accessed September 28, 2020, https://health.baltimorecity.gov/trauma-mental-health-resources.

55   Leana S. Wen, "Attachment: Council Bill 15-0235R - Resolution - Trauma Counseling for Children Affected by Violence," *Baltimore City Council* (July 10, 2015).

56   Trauma Counseling for Children Affected By Violence, Council Bill 15-0235R, Baltimore City Council, (July 20, 2015).

57   B'More for Youth! Collaborative, "Baltimore City's Plan to Prevent Violence Affecting Youth," *Baltimore City Health Department*, (2015).

58   B'More for Youth, "Baltimore City's Plan," 6.

59   B'More for Youth, "Baltimore City's Plan," 19.

60   House Resolution 443, United States 115th Congress, (2018).

61 Recognizing the Importance and Effectiveness of Trauma-Informed Care, Senate Resolution 346, United States 115th Congress, (2018).

62 "Trauma and Child Development," *Florida Courts*, accessed October 16, 2020, https://www.flcourts.org/Resources-Services/Court-Improvement/Family-Courts/Trauma-and-Child-Development.

63 Ed Finkel, "Trauma-informed judges take gentler approach, administer problem-solving justice to stop cycle of ACEs," retrieved from https://acestoohigh.com/2014/09/24/trauma-informed-judges-take-gentler-approach-administer-problem-solving-justice-to-stop-cycle-of-aces/, accessed October 16, 2020.

64 Richard A. Webster & Jonathan Bullington, "The Children of Central City," the *Times-Picayune*, June 13, 2018.

65 Ibid.

66 Resolution No. R-18-344, New Orleans City Council, (2018).

67 Child and Youth Planning Board Childhood Trauma Task Force, "Called to Care: Promoting Compassionate Healing for Our Children," (2019).

68 Webster, "The Children of Central City."

69 Altha J. Stewart, "Testimony of Altha J. Stewart, MD On Behalf of the American Psychiatric Association Before the U.S. House of Representatives Labor, Health and Human Services, Education and Related Agencies Subcommittee of House Appropriations Committee: Reviewing the Administration's Unaccompanied Children Program: State-Sanctioned Child Abuse," *American Psychiatric Association*, (2019).

70 Karen Dineen Wagner, "President's Statement on Separating Children from Families," *American Academy of Child & Adolescent Psychiatry*, (2018).

71 "Separating children from their families: Toxic stress and adverse childhood experiences," *Douglas K. Novins*, accessed September 27, 2020, https://www.jaacap.org/toxicstress.

72   Eva H. Telzer, Michelle E. Miernicki, & Karen D. Rudolph, "Chronic peer victimization heightens neural sensitivity to risk taking," *Development and Psychopathology* 30 (2018): 13–26.

73   Alexandria Meyer *et al.*, "A genetic variant brain-derived neurotrophic factor (BDNF) polymorphism interacts with hostile parenting to predict error-related brain activity and thereby risk for internalizing disorders in children," *Development and Psychopathology* 30 (2018): 125–41.

74   Kandauda A.S. Wickrama, Tae K. Lee, & Catherine W. O'Neal, "Genetic moderation of multiple pathways linking early cumulative socioeconomic adversity and young adults' cardiometabolic disease risk," *Development and Psychopathology* 30 (2018): 165–77.

75   Brianna C. Delker, Rosemary E. Bernstein & Heidemarie K. Laurent, "Out of harm's way: Secure versus insecure-disorganized attachment predicts less adolescent risk taking related to childhood poverty," *Development and Psychopathology* 30 (2018): 283–96.

76   Aaron Levin, "Early life trauma changes biology of brain," *Psychiatric News* July 19, 2019 (2019): 17.

77   Merrill Hoge, *Brainwashed: The Bad Science Behind CTE and the Plot to Destroy Football* (Herndon, VA: Mascot Books, 2018).

78   Kieran J. O'Donnell & Michael J. Meaney, "Fetal origins of mental health: The developmental origins of health and disease hypothesis," *American Journal of Psychiatry* 174 (2017): 319–28.

79   O'Donnell, "Fetal origins," 322.

80   Scheeringa, "Reexamination of diathesis stress."

81   Kenneth J. Rothman & Sander Greenland, "Case-control studies," in *Modern Epidemiology,* eds. Kenneth J. Rothman & Sander Greenland (Philadelphia: Lippincott Williams & Wilkins, 1998): 93–114.

82   Doris K. Nilsson, Per E. Gustafsson, & Carl G. Svedin, "Polytraumatization and trauma symptoms in adolescent boys and girls: interpersonal and noninterpersonal events and moderating effects of adverse family circumstances," *Journal of Interpersonal Violence* 27 (2012): 2645–664.

83   Michael S. Scheeringa, "Untangling psychiatric comorbidity in young children who experienced single, repeated, or Hurricane Katrina traumatic events," *Child and Youth Care Forum* 44 (2015): 475–92.

84   Andrea Danese *et al.*, "The origins of cognitive deficits in victimized children: Implications for neuroscientists and clinicians," *American Journal of Psychiatry* 174 (2017): 349–61.

85   Less Ross & Richard E. Nisbett, *The Person and the Situation: Perspectives of Social Psychology* (Philadelphia: Temple University Press, 1991).

86   Stephan Lewandowsky *et al.*, "Memory for fact, fiction, and misinformation: The Iraq War 2003," *Psychological Science* 16 (2005): 190–95.

87   Philip E. Tetlock & Gregory Mitchell, "Why so few conservatives and should we care?," *Society* 52 (2015): 28–34.

88   Albert L. Furbay, "The influence of scattered versus compact seating on audience response," *Speech Monographs* 32 (1965):144–48.

89   Tetlock & Mitchell, "Why so few conservatives."

Chapter Three

1   Herman, "Complex PTSD."

2   Herman, "Complex PTSD," 388.

3   Herman, "Complex PTSD," 379.

4   Herman, "Complex PTSD," 385.

5   John Carreyrou, *Bad Blood: Secrets and Lies in a Silicon Valley Startup* (New York: Vintage Books, 2018), 207.

6   Ibid

7   Herman, "Complex PTSD," 377.

8   Judith L. Herman, *Trauma and Recovery: The Aftermath of Violence— From Domestic Violence to Political Terror* (New York: Basic Books, 1992).

9   Allen C. Steere *et al.*, "Lyme arthritis: An epidemic of oligoarticular arthritis in children and adults in three Connecticut communities," *Arthritis and Rheumatism* 20 (1977): 7–17.

10   Andreas Maercker *et al.*, "Diagnosis and classification of disorders specifically associated with stress: proposals for ICD-11," *World Psychiatry* 12 (2013): 198–206.

11   Paul Cairney, *The Politics of Evidence-Based Policy Making* (London: Palgrave Macmillan, 2016).

12   Cairney, *The Politics of Evidence-Based Policy Making*, 35.

13   Cairney, *The Politics of Evidence-Based Policy Making*, 26.

14   Cairney, *The Politics of Evidence-Based Policy Making*, 62.

15   Cairney, *The Politics of Evidence-Based Policy Making*, 42.

16   Cairney, *The Politics of Evidence-Based Policy Making*, 60.

17   Cairney, *The Politics of Evidence-Based Policy Making*, 92.

18   Daniel Kahneman, *Thinking, Fast and Slow* (New York: Farrar, Straus, and Giroux, 2011).

19   Kahneman, *Thinking, Fast and Slow*, 417

20   Thomas Gilovich & Dale Griffin, "Introduction—heuristics and biases: then and now," in *Heuristics and Biases: The Psychology of Intuitive Judgment*, eds. Thomas Gilovich, Dale Griffin, & Daniel Kahneman (New York: Cambridge University Press, 2002): 1–17.

21   Jonathan Haidt, *The Righteous Mind: Why Good People Are Divided by Politics and Religion* (New York: Pantheon Books, 2012), 47.

22   Jonathan Haidt, "The emotional dog and its rational tail: A social intuitionist approach to moral judgment," *Psychological Review* 108 (2001): 814–34.

23   Haidt, *The Righteous Mind*, 86.

24   Haidt, *The Righteous Mind*, 87.

25   Haidt, *The Righteous Mind*, 88.

26   Haidt, *The Righteous Mind*, 91.

27   Haidt, *The Righteous Mind*, 91–92.

28   Trivers, *The Folly of Fools*, 4.

29   Michelle Baddeley, *Copycats & Contrarians: Whe We Follow Others . . . and When We Don't* (New Haven, CT: Yale University Press, 2018), 134.

30   Richard Dawkins, *The Selfish Gene* (Oxford, UK:Oxford University Press, 1989).

31   Randolph M. Nesse, "Why a lot of people with selfish genes are pretty nice except for their hatred of *The Selfish Gene*," in *Richard Dawkins: How a Scientist Changed the Way We Think*, eds. Alan Grafen & Mark Ridley (Oxford, UK: Oxford University Press, 2006).

32   Herman, "Complex PTSD," 388.

33   Bessel A. van der Kolk, "Developmental trauma disorder," *Psychiatric Annals* 35 (2005): 401–08.

34   Judith L. Herman, J. Christopher Perry, & Bessel A. van der Kolk, "Childhood trauma in borderline personality disorder," *American Journal of Psychiatry* 146 (1989): 490–95; Bessel A. van der Kolk, J. Christopher Perry, & Judith L. Herman, "Childhood origins of self-destructive behavior," *American Journal of Psychiatry* 148 (1991):1665–71.

35   Van der Kolk, "Developmental Trauma Disorder."

36   Van der Kolk, "Developmental Trauma Disorder," 401.

37   Van der Kolk, "Developmental Trauma Disorder," 402.

38   Wendy D'Andrea *et al.*, "Understanding interpersonal trauma in children: why we need a developmentally appropriate trauma diagnosis," *American Journal of Orthopsychiatry* 82 (2012): 187–200.

39   Lisa C. Barry, Julian D. Ford, & Robert L. Trestman, "Comorbid mental illness and poor physical function among newly admitted inmates in Connecticut's jails," *Journal of Correctional Healthcare* 20 (2014): 135–44.

40   Liesl A. Nydegger *et al.*, "Polytraumatization, mental health, and delinquency among adolescent gang members," *Journal of Traumatic Stress* 32 (2019): 890–98.

41   Kirsi Peltonen *et al.*, "Trauma and violent offending among adolescents: a birth cohort study," *Journal of Epidemiology and Community Health* 0 (2020): 1–6.

42   Nexhmedin Morina & Julian D. Ford, "Complex sequelae of trauma exposure among Kosovar civilian war victims," *International Journal of Social Psychiatry* 54 (2008): 425–36; Gadi Zerach *et al.*, "Complex posttraumatic stress disorder (CPTSD) following captivity: A 24-year longitudinal study," *European Journal of Psychotraumatology* 10 (2019); Julian D. Ford *et al.*, "Randomized clinical trial comparing affect regulation and supportive group therapies for victimization-related PTSD with incarcerated women," *Behavior Therapy* 44 (2013): 262–76.

43   Christine A. Courtois, *It's Not You, It's What Happened to You: Complex Trauma and Treatment* (Dublin, OH: Telemachus Press, LLC, 2014).

44   Herman, "Complex PTSD," 387.

45   Julian D. Ford & Phyllis Kidd, "Early childhood trauma and disorders of extreme stress as predictors of treatment outcome with chronic PTSD," *Journal of Traumatic Stress* 11 (1998): 743–61.

46   Bessel A. van der Kolk & Christine A. Courtois, "Editorial comments: complex developmental trauma," *Journal of Traumatic Stress* 18 (2005): 385–88.

47   Patricia A. Resick *et al.*, "A critical evaluation of the complex PTSD literature: implications for *DSM-5*," *Journal of Traumatic Stress* 25 (2012): 241–51.

48   Judith L. Herman, "CPTSD is a distinct entity: comment on Resick et al. (2012)," *Journal of Traumatic Stress* 25 (2012): 256–57.

49   Van der Kolk & Courtois, "Editorial Comments."

50   Julian D. Ford *et al.*, "Disorders of Extreme Stress (DESNOS) symptoms are associated with interpersonal trauma exposure in a sample of healthy young women," *Journal of Interpersonal Violence* 21 (2006): 1399–416.

51 Julian D. Ford, Tobias Wasser, & Daniel Connor, "Identifying and determining the symptom severity associated with polyvictimization among psychiatrically impaired children in the outpatient setting," *Child Maltreatment* 16 (2011): 216–26.

52 Julian D. Ford, *et al.*, "Poly-victimization among juvenile justice-involved youths," *Child Abuse and Neglect* 37 (2013): 788–800.

53 Liz Kowalczyk, *The Boston Globe* Vol. March 7, 2018 (Boston, 2018). Liz Kowalczyk, *The Boston Globe* Vol. March 8, 2018 (Boston, 2018).

54 Bessel A. van der Kolk, "The Body Keeps the Score: Brain, Mind, and Body in the Healing of Trauma," retrieved from https://www.youtube.com/watch?v=53RX2ESIqsM, accessed January 25, 2021.

55 Bessel A. van der Kolk, "Developmental Trauma Panel," retrieved from https://www.youtube.com/watch?v=-pCbbOWKB2I, accessed January 25, 2021.

56 Ibid

57 Van der Kolk, "The Body Keeps the Score," retrieved from www.youtube.com.

58 Ibid.

59 Marylene Cloitre, Karestan C. Koenen, Lisa R. Cohen, & Hyemee Han, "Skills training in affective and interpersonal regulation followed by exposure: A phase-based treatment for PTSD related to childhood abuse," *Journal of Consulting and Clinical Psychology* 70 (2002): 1067–074.

60 Marylene Cloitre, Lisa R. Cohen, & Karestan C. Koenan, *Treating Survivors of Childhood Abuse: Psychotherapy for the Interrupted Life* (New York: Guilford Press, 2006).

61 Linda K. Frisman, *et al.*, "Outcomes of trauma treatment using the TARGET model," *Journal of Groups in Addiction and Recovery* 3 (2008): 285–303.

62 Christine A. Courtois & Julian D. Ford (eds.), *Treating Complex Traumatic Stress Disorders: An Evidence-Based Guide* (New York: Guilford Press, 2009).

63   Marylène Cloitre *et al.*, "Evidence for proposed ICD-11 PTSD and complex PTSD: A latent profile analysis," *European Journal of Psychotraumatology* 4 (2013):20706.

64   Zerach *et al.*, "Complex posttraumatic stress disorder"; Philip Hyland *et al.*, "An assessment of the construct validity of the ICD-11 proposal for complex posttraumatic stress disorder," *Psychological Trauma: Theory, Research, Practice and Policy* 9 (2017): 1–9; Thanos Karatzias *et al.*, "Evidence of distinct profiles of Posttraumatic Stress Disorder (PTSD) and Complex Posttraumatic Stress Disorder (CPTSD) based on the new ICD-11 Trauma Questionnaire (ICD-TQ)," *Journal of Affective Disorders* 207 (2017): 181–87; Evaldas Kazlauskas *et al.*, "The structure of ICD-11 PTSD and complex PTSD in Lithuanian mental health services," *European Journal of Psychotraumatology* 9 (2018): 1414559; Philip Hyland *et al.*, "Examining the discriminant validity of Complex Posttraumatic Stress Disorder and Borderline Personality Disorder symptoms: Results from a United Kingdom population sample," *Journal of Traumatic Stress* 32 (2019): 855–63; Ida Haahr-Pedersen *et al.*, "Females have more complex patterns of childhood adversity: Implications for mental, social, and emotional outcomes in adulthood," *European Journal of Psychotraumatology* 11 (2020); Evaldas Kazlauskas *et al.*, "The structure of ICD-11 PTSD and Complex PTSD in adolescents exposed to potentially traumatic experiences," *Journal of Affective Disorders* 265 (2020): 169–74.

65   Van der Kolk, "Developmental trauma disorder," 407.

66   Marylene Cloitre, Donn W. Garvert, Brandon Weiss, Eve B. Carlson, & Richard A. Bryant, "Distinguishing PTSD, complex PTSD, and borderline personality disorder: A latent class analysis," *European Journal of Psychotraumatology* 5 (2014).

67   Julian D. Ford & Christine A. Courtois, "Complex PTSD, affect dysregulation, and borderline personality disorder," *Borderline Personality Disorder and Emotion Regulation* 1 (2014).

68   Ford & Courtois, "Complex PTSD," 12

69   Todd Grande, "What is the difference between borderline personality disorder and complex PTSD (C-PTSD)?" retrieved from https://www.youtube.com/watch?v=aUv-_3aiNTc, accessed January 21, 2021.

70 "Complex PTSD," *National Center for PTSD*, accessed 11/29/2020, https://www.ptsd.va.gov/professional/treat/essentials/complex_ptsd. asp.

71 American Psychological Association, "Complex Posttraumatic Stress Disorder."

72 American Psychological Association, "Clinical Practice Guideline for the Treatment of PTSD."

73 American Academy of Child & Adolescent Psychiatry, "Practice parameter for the assessment and treatment of children and adolescents with posttraumatic stress disorder," *Journal of the American Academy of Child and Adolescent Psychiatry* 49 (2010): 414–30.

74 American Academy of Pediatrics, "Helping Foster and Adoptive Families Cope With Trauma," *American Academy of Pediatrics* (2016).

75 "Complex PTSD," *National Child Traumatic Stress Network.*

76 National Child Traumatic Stress Network, "Developmental Trauma Disorder: Identifying Critical Moments and Healing Complex Trauma." retrieved from https://learn.nctsn.org/course/index. php?categoryid=78, accessed November 29, 2020.

77 "SM-16-008 Individual Grant Awards," *Substance Abuse and Mental Health Services Administration.*

78 Jonathan I. Bisson *et al.*, "The International Society for Traumatic Stress Studies New Guidelines for the Prevention and Treatment of Posttraumatic Stress Disorder: Methodology and Development Process," *Journal of Traumatic Stress* 32 (2019): 475–83.

79 ISTSS Guidelines Committee, "ISTSS Guidelines Position Paper on Complex PTSD in Children and Adolescents," *International Society for Traumatic Stress Studies*, (2019).

80 Shawn P. Cahill *et al.*, "Sequential treatment for child abuse-related posttraumatic stress disorder: Methodological comment on Cloitre, Koenen, Cohen, and Han (2002)," *Journal of Consulting and Clinical Psychology* 72 (2004): 543–48.

81   Dean G. Kilpatrick, "A special section on complex trauma and a few thoughts about the need for more rigorous research on treatment efficacy, effectiveness, and safety," *Journal of Traumatic Stress* 18 (2005): 379–84, p. 383.

82   Ibid.

83   Resick, "A Critical Evaluation."

84   Ramón J. L. Lindauer, "Child Maltreatment—Clinical PTSD Diagnosis Not Enough?!: Comment on Resick et al. (2012)," *Journal of Traumatic Stress* 25 (2012): 258–59, p. 258.

85   Lindauer, "Child Maltreatment," 259.

86   Ad De Jongh *et al.*, "Critical analysis of the current treatment guidelines for complex PTSD in adults," *Depression and Anxiety* 33 (2016): 359–69.

87   Marylene Cloitre, "Commentary on De Jongh et al. (2016) critique of ISTSS complex PTSD guidelines: Finding the way forward," *Depression and Anxiety* 33 (2016): 355–56.

88   Brent Scowcroft, in the *Wall Street Journal* (2002).

89   Todd S. Purdum & Patrick E. Tyler, in the *New York Times* (2002).

90   Haidt, *The Righteous Mind*, 131.

91   Haidt, *The Righteous Mind*, 104.

92   Donald Rumsfeld, *Known and Unknown: A Memoir* (New York: Sentinel, 2011).

93   Deirdre Barrett, *Supernormal Stimuli: How Primal Urges Overran Their Evolutionary Purpose* (New York: W.W. Norton & Company, Inc, 2010).

94   Less Ross & Richard E. Nisbett, *The Person and the Situation: Perspectives of Social Psychology* (Philadelphia, PA: Temple University Press, 1991).

95   Hoge, *Brainwashed*.

96   Solomon E. Asch, "Opinions and social pressure," *Scientific American* 193 (1955): 31–35.

97   Serge Moscovici, E. Lage, & M. Naffrechoux, "Influence of a consistent minority on the responses of a majority in a color perception task," *Sociometry* 32 (1969): 365–80.

98   Timothy D. Wilson & Elizabeth W. Dunn, "Self-knowledge: Its limits, value, and potential for improvement," *Annual Review of Psychology* 55 (2004): 493–518.

99   Emily Pronin, Carolyn Puccio, & Lee Ross, "Understanding Misunderstanding: Social Psychological Perspectives," in *Heuristics and Biases: The Psychology of Intuitive Judgment*, eds. Thomas Gilovich, Dale Griffin, & Daniel Kahneman (New York: Cambridge University Press, 2002): 636–64, p. 646.

100   Mary S. Wylie, "The long shadow of trauma," *Psychotherapy Networker* (2010): 20–54, p.23.

101   Wylie, "The long shadow of trauma," 51.

Chapter Four

1   Michael S. Scheeringa & Charles H. Zeanah, "A relational perspective on PTSD in early childhood," *Journal of Traumatic Stress* 14 (2001): 799–815.

2   John Bowlby, *Charles Darwin: A New Life* (New York: W.W. Norton & Company, 1992), 60.

3   Jenessa L. Malin *et al.*, "A family systems approach to examining young children's social development," in *Child Psychology: A Handbook of Contemporary Issues*, eds. Lawrence Balter & Catherine S. Tamis-LeMonda (New York: Routledge, 2016): 355–78.

4   Judith R. Harris, "Where is the child's environment? A group socialization theory of development," *Psychological Review* 102 (1995): 458–89.

5   Judith R. Harris, *The Nurture Assumption: Why Children Turn Out the Way They Do.* (New York: Free Press, 1998).

6   Sharon Begley, "The Parent Trap," retrieved from https://www.washingtonpost.com/wp-srv/newsweek/parent090798a.htm, accessed February 11, 2013.

7   Melissa Healy, "Debate rises on parents' influence over children," *Los Angeles Times*, July 4, 1999.

8   Christopher Shea, "The temperamentalist," retrieved from http://archive.boston.com/news/globe/ideas/articles/2004/08/29/the_temperamentalist?pg=full, accessed.

9   Begley, "The Parent Trap."

10   Healy, "Debate rises."

11   Arlene Skolnick, "The limits of childhood: Conceptions of child development and social context," *Law and Contemporary Problems* 39 (1975): 38–77, p. 40.

12   Harris, *No Two Alike*, 252.

13   Christopher Boehm, *Moral Origins: The Evolution of Virtue, Altruism, and Shame* (New York: Basic Books, 2012), 44.

14   Boehm, *Moral Origins*, 165.

15   Haidt, *The Righteous Mind*.

16   Haidt, *The Righteous Mind*, 124.

17   MoralFoundations.org, accessed January 20, 2021, https://moralfoundations.org/.

18   Harris, *No Two Alike*, 252.

19   Harris, *No Two Alike*.

20   David Hume, "The Natural History of Religion," (1757).

21   Montserrat Guibernau, *Belonging: Solidarity and Division in Modern Societies* (Cambridge, UK: Polity Press, 2013), 180.

22   Haidt, *The Righteous Mind*, 202.

23   Harry Markopolos, *No One Would Listen: A True Financial Thriller* (Hoboken, NJ: John Wiley & Sons, Inc., 2010).

24   Markopolos, *No One Would Listen*, 2.

25   Ibid.

26   Ibid.

27 Henriques, *The Wizard of Lies*, 36–37.

28 Henriques, *The Wizard of Lies*, 57–58.

29 Henriques, *The Wizard of Lies*, 89.

30 Henriques, *The Wizard of Lies*, 114.

31 Henriques, *The Wizard of Lies*, 91.

32 Henriques, *The Wizard of Lies*, 350.

33 Henriques, *The Wizard of Lies*, 94–103.

34 Markopolos, *No One Would Listen*, 27.

35 Henriques, *The Wizard of Lies*, 271.

36 Markopolos, *No One Would Listen*, 45.

37 Markopolos, *No One Would Listen*, 53.

38 Henriques, *The Wizard of Lies*, 89.

39 Henriques, *The Wizard of Lies*, 116–17.

40 Mitzi M. Waltz, "Mothers and autism: The evolution of a discourse of blame," AMA *Journal of Ethics* 17 (2015): 353–58.

41 Leo Kanner, "Autistic disturbances of affective contact," *Nervous Child* 2 (1943): 217–50.

42 Leo Kanner, "Problems of nosology and psychodynamics in early childhood autism," *American Journal of Orthopsychiatry* 19 (1949): 416–26.

43 James Harris & Joseph Piven, "Correcting the record: Leo Kanner and the broad autism phenotype," retrieved from https://www.spectrumnews.org/opinion/viewpoint/correcting-the-record-leo-kanner-and-the-broad-autism-phenotype/, accessed February 27, 2021.

44 Bruno Bettelheim, *The Empty Fortress: Infantile autism and the birth of the self* (Free Press of Glencoe, 1967).

45 Ron Grossman, "Genius or Fraud? Bettelheim's Biographer Can't Seem to Decide," *Chicago Tribune*, January 23, 1997.

46   Anne C. Roark, "Bettelheim plagiarized book ideas, scholar says: Authors: The late child psychologist is accused of "wholesale borrowing' for study of fairy tales," *Los Angeles Times*, February 7, 1991.

47   Ron Grossman, "The puzzle that was Bruno Bettelheim," *Chicago Tribune*, November 11, 1990.

48   Theodore Lidz, "Schizophrenia and the family," *Psychiatry: Journal for the Study of Interpersonal Processes* 21 (1958): 21–27.

49   Felicity Callard et al., "Holding blame at bay? 'Gene talk' in family members' accounts of schizophrenia aetiology," *BioSocieties* 7 (2012): 273–93.

50   Paula J. Caplan & Ian Hall-McCorquodale, "Mother-blaming in major clinical journals," *American Journal of Orthopsychiatry* 55 (1985): 345–53.

51   Anna Bokszczanin, "Parental support, family conflict, and overprotectiveness: Predicting PTSD symptom levels of adolescents 28 months after a natural disaster," *Anxiety, Stress, & Coping* 21 (2008): 325–35.

52   Abdel A. Thabet et al., "Parenting support and PTSD in children of a war zone," *International Journal of Social Psychiatry* 55 (2009): 226–37.

53   Kristin Valentino, Steven Berkowitz, & Carla S. Stover, "Parenting behaviors and posttraumatic symptoms in relation to children's symptomatology following a traumatic event," *Journal of Traumatic Stress* 23 (2010): 403–07.

54   Claude M. Chemtob et al., "Impact of maternal posttraumatic stress disorder and depression following exposure to the September 11 attacks on preschool children's behavior," *Child Development* 81 (2010): 1129–141.

55   Bessel A. van der Kolk, "Developmental trauma disorder," *Psychiatric Annals* 35 (2005): 401–08.

56   Rachel M. Hiller et al., "Post-trauma coping in the context of significant adversity: A qualitative study of young people living in an urban township in South Africa," *BMJ Open* 6 (2017): e016560.

57   Betty Pfefferbaum *et al.*, "Children's disaster reactions: The influence of family and social factors," *Current Psychiatry Reports* 17 (2015): 57.

58   Michael S. Scheeringa, *They'll Never Be The Same: A Parent's Guide to PTSD in Youth* (Las Vegas, NV: Central Recovery Press, 2018).

59   Michael S. Scheeringa *et al.*, "Maternal factors as moderators or mediators of PTSD symptoms in preschool children: A two-year prospective study," *Journal of Family Violence* 30 (2015): 633–42.

60   Rachel M. Hiller *et al.*, "A longitudinal investigation of the role of parental responses in predicting children's post-traumatic distress," *Journal of Child Psychology and Psychiatry* 59 (2018): 781–89.

61   Victoria Williamson *et al.*, "The role of parenting behaviors in childhood post-traumatic stress disorder: A meta-analytic review," *Clinical Psychology Review* 53 (2017): 1–13.

62   Roy F. Baumeister & M.R. Leary, "The need to belong: Desire for interpersonal attachments as a fundamental human motivation," Psychological Bulletin 117 (1995): 497–529.

63   Gladwell, *The Tipping Point*, 152.

64   Guibernau, *Belonging*, 172.

Epilogue

1   Arthur C. Clarke, *2001: A Space Odyssey* (New York: New American Library, 1968).

2   Haidt, *The Righteous Mind*; Robert Wright, *The Moral Animal: The New Science of Evolutionary Psychology* (New York: Pantheon Books, 1994).

3   Wilson & Dunn, "Self-knowledge."

4   Henriques, *The Wizard of Lies*, 354–55.

5   Henriques, *The Wizard of Lies*, 356.

6   Henriques, *The Wizard of Lies*, 360.

7   Henriques, *The Wizard of Lies*, 361

8   Henriques, *The Wizard of Lies*, 362.

9   David F. Prindle, *Stephen Jay Gould and the Politics of Evolution* (Buffalo, NY: Prometheus Books, 2009).

10   Prindle, *Stephen Jay Gould*, 71.

11   Kevin Simler & Robin Hanson, *The Elephant in the Brain: Hidden Motives in Everyday Life* (Oxford, UK: Oxford University Press, 2018), 4–5.

12   Carol Tavris & Elliot Aronson, *Mistakes Were Made (but Not by Me): Why We Justify Foolish Beliefs, Bad Decisions, and Hurtful Acts* Third edition (Boston: Houghton Mifflin Harcourt, 2020), 2.

13   Tavris & Aronson, *Mistakes Were Made*, 106–07.

14   Veronica Roth, *Divergent* (New York: Harper Collins Publishers, 2011).

15   Hugo Mercier & Dan Sperber, *The Enigma of Reason* (Cambridge, MA: Harvard University Press, 2017), 1.

16   Henriques, *The Wizard of Lies*, 363.

CPSIA information can be obtained
at www.ICGtesting.com
Printed in the USA
JSHW020023240122
22211JS00005B/7